PLANT HUNTING
ON THE EDGE OF THE WORLD

NUNG WOMAN OF THE NAM TAMAI, BURMA FRONTIER.

Plant Hunting
on the Edge of the World

TRAVELS OF A NATURALIST
IN ASSAM AND
UPPER BURMA

F. Kingdon Ward

MINERVA
1974

ISBN 85636 006 6

First published 1930: this edition
© F. Kingdon Ward and
The Minerva Press Ltd 1974

Printed and bound in Great Britain
by W & J Mackay Limited Chatham
for The Minerva Press Limited
27 Southampton Street London WC2

Dedication

My dear Buttercup,

Travel books must be dedicated; and to whom could I dedicate this one more aptly than to you, who shared the privations, disappointments, and (dare I say?) triumphs of the Assam journey? So you find yourself, for better or worse, godfather to a bantling of sorts.

Yours ever,

K. W.

Preface

THIS travel book, with its strong botanical flavour, is the outcome of two journeys, and two years' work, the second journey being the lineal descendant of the first. Both took me to the 'edge of the world.' For, to the Tibetan, the mighty snow ranges which ring his dry and lofty plateau *must* be the edge of the world! He has but to climb the low passes on *his* side, and peer over the edge of the huge escarpment, to see lying far below the green and fertile plains of Ind, so different from the barren khaki-coloured rocks of his own stubborn land. So he gazes down into the smoking cauldron, which descends for 15,000 feet, whence the rain mist rises like a miasma; and crouching behind his barrier, under the turquoise sky, he draws back from the edge of that frightful abyss and is thankful that he lives on the roof of the world, where the clean air blows freshly.

My journey of 1926 took me to the remotest frontier of northern Burma, hundreds of miles from the railway, whence by devious routes I descended to the Lohit river, and finally made my way through the Mishmi Hills, to Assam and the plains.

In 1928, accompanied by Mr H. M. Clutterbuck, who had been on two voyages to the Arctic, I returned to Assam, retraced the last few marches of my previous journey, and, taking the first turning on the left, reached the edge of the world by another route; and it is a remarkable fact that, though the two main collecting areas were within 75 miles of each other, as the crow flies when sober, each locality revealed a good proportion of peculiar plants.

Having spent ten years of my life in the heart of S-E Asia, learning the business of plant hunting, it will be enough to say that I made these two latest journeys with a three-fold object:

(i) To collect seeds of beautiful hardy flowering plants for English gardens. That is my profession.

(ii) To collect dried specimens of interesting plants for study. That also is part of my profession.

(iii) To explore unknown mountain ranges, and find out something about their past history, the distribution of their plants, and any other secrets they are willing to reveal. That is my hobby.

The ensuing chapters record the journeys undertaken, the routine of the professional plant-hunter, and some of the results. Most of the plants described are now growing in English gardens—and some of them in other parts of the world as well. A list of plants in cultivation will be found in the Appendix.

These expeditions could not have been undertaken but for the interest aroused and the support received. A syndicate of enthusiastic and famous private gardeners under the chairmanship of Mr Lionel de Rothschild—who presented seeds to Kew and Edinburgh—supplied the main financial backing; and generous support was also received from the Government Grant Committee of the Royal Society and from the Trustees of the Percy Sladen Memorial Fund. As the last-named body contributed the largest individual sum, I have called the whole undertaking—for the two journeys complement one another—the Percy Sladen Expedition to Burma–Assam. The herbarium specimens were presented to Kew: minor collections of insects, mammals, and birds to the Natural History Museum.

F.K.W.

MAIDENHEAD 1930.

Contents

List of Plates

Maps

I   The Back Door to India

GEOLOGISTS who read and interpret the face of the earth tell us that India was built in three pieces. First, Peninsular India south of the great plains. If one draws a line across Hindustan from a little north of Bombay to a little south of Calcutta, then the oldest part of what journalists call the sub-continent lies to the south of that line, the newest part to the north. In fact the southern part, which forms a rough equilateral triangle is probably as old as the world, since the world solidified into anything like its present shape.

Not so the great plains of Indus and Ganges to the north, where nightly the Panjab mail roars through the rice-fields on its 3,000-mile journey from Calcutta to Peshawar. This wide strip is the very latest addition to India. When the southern triangle was already infinitely old, when the Himalaya, away up on the northern boundary, were young, and perhaps not quite so high as they are now, the plains were under the sea, or rather they did not yet exist. Peninsular India was, therefore, still a continental island, possibly more closely linked to East Africa than to the mainland of Asia. A broad arm of the Indian Ocean washed its northern coast, and lapped along the foot of the Himalayan ranges which loomed up through the clouds far away across the straits. It was the rubble and silt washed down from the newly risen Himalaya by torrential rains which, during still later ages, filled up the deep strait, and formed the plains as we know them. Thus were joined together in unholy matrimony the rugged old land mass to the south, and the virgin snows to the north, cemented by the plains between. And thus was born Hindustan.

It is comparatively easy to grasp this geological trinity of Hindustan because it corresponds not only with the average schoolboy's idea of India, but with the experience of the average traveller in India. Mountains in the north, plateaux in the south, the plains between; and the scenery, which of course largely depends on the materials used in building the world, corresponds in a general way with this simple analysis.

For its size, Great Britain presents us with as rich a variety of scenery as any country in the world. How distinct are the Fens, the Lake District, the Downs, the Cornish coast! A little reflection will convince anyone that these sharp contrasts in scenery are primarily due to differences in the composition of the rocks and to the way in which they are laid down and heaved up. Britain, in fact, discloses an epitome of the geological record from

Pre-Cambrian to Post-Glacial which any country might envy, and this record is reflected in the scenery.

Not so Hindustan. Its foundations are similar over immense areas; whole chunks of the geological record are missing. Probably no part of it the size of Britain—if we exclude the Himalaya—displays such a feast of variety. But although Hindustan may not, like Britain, contain much in little, it is big enough to contain much; its three plies are in violent contrast, and each is several times larger than Britain. Size and position tell. Great Britain spreads over ten degrees of latitude, and that in the north temperate zone. Hindustan spreads over twenty degrees of latitude, reaching almost from the Equator to the extra-tropical belt; most of it lies within the monsoon region, where the forces of nature are dynamic. Hence there enters upon the scene a factor which, almost negligible in Britain, exercises a powerful control over Hindustan. That factor is climate.

The variations of climate throughout Britain are sufficiently marked to affect the vegetation. but in degree rather than in kind. The keen gardener notices a difference between the climates of Wessex and of East Anglia, for example, especially as they affect alien plants; but Britain, left to itself, would be almost entirely covered with forest, and was so once. It is otherwise with Hindustan. Plains, plateaux, and mountains inevitably conform to their own type of scenery, especially where the rocks are of the same age; but when the plains reach from Bengal to the Panjab, when the mountains stretch in an unbroken line from the Indus to the Brahmaputra, and the plateaux spread through fifteen degrees of latitude, sharp differences of climate, accompanied by drastic changes in the covering of vegetation, disturb the even tenor of the scenery, whatever the underlying rock.

Thus the conception of Hindustan as built in three parts, though true enough in geological time, is only a broad generalisation in common time, for the parts themselves are complex. Anyone who has ever travelled by the Great Indian Peninsular Railway from Bombay to Calcutta in the hot weather must have remarked the contrast between the moist green coastal shelf, at the foot of the western Ghats, and the dry khaki-coloured plateau at the top of the escarpment; or, travelling by the South Indian Railway, between the arid sandy acacia-covered dunes of the south-east coast and the tall green forest of Madras. Keeping to the plains, one may travel in three days from the rice-fields of Bengal to the wheat-fields of the Panjab, or to the Scind Desert. Such is the infinite variety of Hindustan, from stark desert on the edge of the north-west plains to the reeking swamp jungle of the Sunderbunds; from the hot lava tablelands of the Deccan to the rolling downs of Ootacamund; and so over the edge of the escarpment and down to the fœtid jungles of the Coramandel coast. Add to these lowlands the mightiest range of mountains in the world, Himalaya, the abode of snow, clothed at the foot with sub-tropical forest, higher up, with temperate forests of broad-leafed trees, such as we meet with in Europe—oak and maple and birch—and finally towards the top with forests of fir and larch; and our picture of Hindustan loses all clear outline and fades gradually into a vague impressionism. And as its foundations and its vegetation are diverse, so are its inhabitants. It would be impossible for anyone to confuse the tall, lithe, sallow, hook-nosed, wheat-fed Panjabi with the short, black, dish-faced, rice-fed Tamil; yet both are 'Indians' inhabiting what the schoolboy calls India and we have called Hindustan, though their homes are as far apart as London is from Moscow. In a word, India is a geographical expression, equivalent to such ill-defined terms as the Far East or the Near East, or Central America; and to say that India is inhabited by Indians is like saying that Europe is inhabited by Europeans.

See, then, Hindustan—the triangular peninsula, whose base is formed by the wall of the Himalaya, and whose apex juts far out into the Indian Ocean, with the island of Ceylon hooked on to it like a pear-drop. This is the trunk of the Indian Empire. What of the limbs, which include Kashmir, Baluchistan, Sikkim, Assam, Burma, and the Federated Shan States? The only outliers which concern us here however are the two backward provinces—as they are contemptuously called by the Barons of Hindustan—Burma (including the Shan States) and Assam.

Burma and Assam have surprisingly little to do with India, either in geological or historical time; and not much to do with it in space. They are the backwaters of the great human migratory streams. Their population, eddying between the cold tablelands of innermost Asia and the fertile plains bordering the Indian Ocean, have drawn into their vortex the flotsam and jetsam of both. They are the overflow of the two huge reservoirs of humanity in Asia—India, and China; yet they, and they alone, have banked up those reservoirs and kept them asunder; have stemmed and diverted the tides of the Celestial Empire as they swept southwards and westwards, and delivered Hindustan from the Dragon Throne.

That these outposts now form a part of the Indian Empire at all is due to a Pecksniffian conspiracy on the part of the Barons of Hindustan. Wiping their eyes, these worthy mandarins proclaim how much they have done for their poor relations, and how little appreciated is their kindness. What ingratitude! But let us suffer in silence. The meek shall inherit the earth. But let us at all costs keep our poor relations poor!

Assam is in contact with Hindustan, as Kashmir is, but it lies to a flank, tucked away in a far corner, under the mighty shadow of the Himalaya. Burma does not even touch Hindustan, save indirectly and remotely through Assam. These two provinces cleave together, as brother and sister; though divided by uninhabited hills and dense forests, yet they share many things in common, and together form the bulwark which protects the North-East Frontier of India.

If Hindustan is mainly inhabited by permutations and combinations of three diverse elements, Aryan, Mongol, and Dravidian, Burma and Assam

3

are hardly less mixed; and, being smaller, and having to bear the brunt of such infiltration as takes place along the frontier, they show a more concentrated mixture. In fact, the fertile plains, inhabited by the peoples who give their names to the provinces, form but a small portion of the lands we call Burma and Assam. Three-quarters of both provinces are mountainous and covered with dense forests, inhabited only by rude tribes. These are wild regions which the tourist who does Burma in three days only dimly hears of, if at all. For six months the passes through the mountains into this warren, away up at the sources of the Irrawaddy, are blocked by snow; for six months the mountains are swathed in impenetrable mists and drenched with rain, the forests are alive with leeches and biting flies, the paths are washed away, the rivers inflamed. Such is the formidable barrier which curves round the North-East Frontier of the Indian Empire between the plains of Hindustan and the plateaux of China and Tibet. It is a desolate region thinly inhabited by numerous tribes caught up in the web of hills, speaking different languages, having different customs and traditions, and bearing as little relation to one another as do the various races of Hindustan. And so the traveller who penetrates into the backblocks of Burma will find himself in contact, not with the Burmese, but with Kachins, Marus, Lisus, Hkamtis, or Khanungs, all utterly different from the Burmese and from one another; or, if his footsteps take him to Assam, with Mishmis, or Abors, or Nagas—a veritable Tower of Babel. But let us lift the veil a little farther yet, for it is into the uttermost ends of Burma and Assam that we shall presently penetrate.

People have been pouring into Hindustan for thousands of years, even before history began, certainly before European history began. Always the strangers, whether Arab, Aryan, or Mongol, came into India from the west or north-west. The land invaders came in by Kashmir and Afghanistan over what is now the North-West Frontier. This is the front-door to India, a door which always stands open. Later came the sea-raiders—Portuguese, Dutch, French, and English. These also came from the west by the sea gateway to India, which is called Bombay.

On its eastern flank, however, Hindustan is secure. Impassable rivers, impenetrable jungles, and impregnable mountains, form a triple line of defence which no large body of men has ever forced. Penetration there has been, not always peaceful; but invasion never. And yet just beyond the barrier was felt the pressure of great populations and heard the tramp of armies. Southwards men swarmed amongst the approaches and fought each other to the death: only to find that they were still cut off from Hindustan by more mountains and by the ocean itself. In the north the barrier always held. Nature herself has hedged the North-East Frontier of India with such defences that nothing is left for man to do. On the far side of the barrier is the bleak wind-swept plateau of Tibet, sloping gradually down to the more fertile plateau of Yunnan; though even here, so lofty is the land and so dry the climate behind the great rain-screen of mountains that the rivers can only score deep ugly gutters across its hard face.

The pastoral folk of the plateau, who grazed their flocks on the thin pasture, must often have looked towards those forbidding mountains, buried under snow, or wrapped in mist, and wondered what lay beyond them. And perhaps they looked *over* them, down to the grey plains, dim in the distance; for the passes lie on the very rim of the escarpment. Yet even those who wished to exchange the free pastoral life of the plateau for the more intensive agricultural life of the plains must have been daunted when they dropped over the edge of their high world and found themselves in the grip of the jungle. If snow and blizzard held no terrors for them, the rank heat of the jungle did. Not the high wind-swept passes, but the leech-infested jungles below, and the frozen marches which reach out to the north, league on league, bar the way to India. North of the Himalaya, stretching east and west for a thousand miles, lies the comparatively fertile valley of the Tsangpo. Beyond that—nothing; nothing for thirty-five hundred miles but the grim desert, salt, and sand, and bitter tundra, as far as the icy wilderness of the Arctic itself. It is *that*, the dead heart of Asia, which protects the northern frontier of Hindustan.

On their side, the plainsmen lifting up their eyes to the mighty snows of the Himalaya, were awed. Nothing would induce them to leave their snug houses on the plains, to dare the cold and silence of that terrific obstacle. For them the Himalaya was Ultima Thule!

But the Himalaya end abruptly, sawn off at the great bluff which overlooks the plain of Assam, where Namcha Barwa towers, a frozen steeple above the thunder of the Tsangpo. Or so it seems. Is there not a way round them, instead of over them? Let us try to reach Hindustan from the east.

But here at the outset we find an unexpected difficulty; the strike of the country has completely changed. The east-west barrier has indeed gone, only to be replaced by one not less formidable. A series of mountain ranges, thin but high, and keen as tempered steel, confront us, running due south from Yunnan through Burma to Farther India; thus they reach the tropic sea. For several hundred miles they are reinforced by great rivers compressed between sharp blades of rock, whose edges are cold with rime; and lest a gap should remain, mountains and rivers, harnessed together, curve round from the north-west to merge into the frozen wastes of high Asia. Thus the defences cover the whole North-East Frontier.

In the top right-hand corner of the Indian Empire—that is to say in Burma–Assam—the two defensive mountain systems meet; there the bulkhead which separates plain from plateau has been shaved down till it is a mere hundred miles deep. Here, if anywhere, is the joint in the armour. Here, if anywhere, is the weak link in the chain of mountains, through

Map I

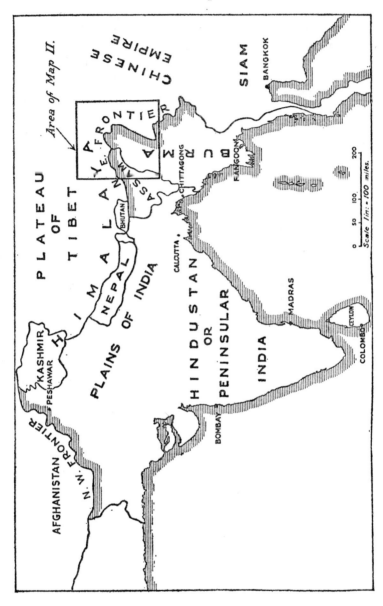

Hindustan and the Himalaya

which might prowl the hosts of Midian. But the hosts of Midian never came, never saw, never conquered; or, having come, and seen, they retired. Rather than face what lay before them, they turned, and crossed a thousand miles of desert till they reached the other side of India, by Kashmir, and the gateway through Afghanistan.

Thus has the strike of the country on the eastern flank of the Indian Empire determined the flow of the peoples, as it has that of the rivers. It has shepherded them into the one narrow corridor—the Mekong—where they must pass in single file, quietly and without haste. On to this breach men have converged from half Asia; through it they have filtered. Pressing steadily southwards, along the deep and narrow grooves between the blade-like ranges, they walked past Hindustan under cover of the mountain walls which overshadowed them. And so, as the long thin mountain ranges flared, dimpling, down to the plains, radiating like the fingers of an outspread hand, they came to Indo-China, to Burma, Siam, and Cambodia; and Hindustan lay back in the setting sun, with all the Bay of Bengal between, and knew not the southern Mongols. It was an afterthought which presently carried a backwash westwards into Assam.

And yet there *is* a way, hazardous though it be, into Hindustan through the North-East Frontier. The direct overland route from China to India is long and arduous, difficult at the best of times and under the most favourable circumstances, but not impossible to small parties of men, and not incapable of improvement. Just as Bombay is the sea gateway to India, so Assam is the back-door. As regards distance, it is the shortest cut; yet it is the longest way. Men undoubtedly came into India by this route, just as others came to Burma. Others again, driven back by the plainsmen, became entangled in the jungles, thus further strengthening the defences; for, once in possession, the tribesmen have always disputed the passage of the mountains by strangers from either side. They prefer to worship their *nats*—the spirits which rule the world of the jungle—in their own way, and brook no interference. They have little traffic with each other; though of necessity those on the outer fringe trade with the more robust people of the plateau and those on the inner fringe with the more cultured people of the plains.

And here we may lightly touch upon a matter which goes far to show how the tribes of the hill jungle are held in thrall; and how, while helping to keep asunder the people of the plains and the people of the plateaux, they are themselves bound to both.

There is one commodity which all men, of whatever colour, crave. It influences their lives. No hardship is too great to be borne, if only the need be thereby satisfied. This commodity is not bread, nor opium either, but common salt; common, that is, almost anywhere but in the jungle. Now common salt is supplied to the world from two sources; from the sea and from continental salt lakes, brine-wells, or deposits of rock-salt. In Europe it is impossible to withdraw oneself more than about 600 miles from the sea; excluding Russia, and ignoring the Caspian the limit is reached at 300 miles. There are besides great salt deposits. Thus in Europe the salt traffic has no special significance, and all wants are easily supplied. In Asia one may be 2,000 miles from the nearest sea, though, on the other hand, salt lakes abound in the heart of the continent. But in South-Eastern Asia the belt of jungle betwixt plateau and plains appears to lack salt. This belt is separated from the sea-coast by all the width of the plains; from the salt deposits of the plateau by a high and broken escarpment. Access to either source is gained with difficulty; the inland salt belt, consisting of strata in which brine occurs and chains of salt lakes, runs far to the north in Tibet and eastwards, in China, along the Mekong corridor. Thus the tribes of the Burma–Assam frontier have fallen between two stools. Salt they must have; to get it they must either go down to the plains or up to the plateau.

The tribes who inhabit the foot-hills on the fringe of the plains naturally seek salt from the people of the plains. They do not need to go far for it; and they are permitted to come and go as they please, so long as they keep the peace. But robbery under arms is tempting to wolves who find themselves amongst sheep; and many were the raids for commodities other than salt, before the jungle wolves discovered that, since the British lion took over the shepherding of the flock, the game was not worth the candle. The sheep have since found out the same thing too, at shearing-time; but that is another story.

The tribes who inhabit the jungle on the edge of the escarpment, however, have a hard time. Almost naked as they are, they must face the snow-bound passes and the bitter cold of the plateau in order to reach the salt belt. What advantage is there in bright sunshine beneath the turquoise dome of Tibetan heaven, when the wind flays you alive? And this journey they make every year, though many leave their poor cold bones to bleach on the wind-swept braes.

We who waste salt every day of our lives, who buy it cheaply enough everywhere and never miss it from the table, hardly realise how necessary it is to our welfare, or how the lack of it may rule men's lives and cause their deaths. Our indifference is shown by the very name, common salt. And indeed we have no occasion to get excited; salt *is* common, and therefore cheap. But in the jungle it has more purchasing-power than silver!

Above 6,000 feet, jungle cultivation ceases. On the other hand, very rarely do the Tibetans descend below 10,000 feet[1]. Between the last tribal villages in the jungle and the first Tibetan villages on the plateau lies a belt of hill country, perhaps fifty miles in depth, rising gradually, though with

---

[1] There are, of course, exceptions, particularly on the Assam frontier. In Zayul province there are many Tibetan villages below 10,000 feet, some as low as 5,000 feet. A few Tibetans have crossed over into the headwaters of the Irrawaddy and established themselves at 7,000 feet.

many ups and downs, as range succeeds range, to the alpine pastures. This country, heaved up on edge, smashed and bent beyond recognition, and the whole glorious ruin submerged under forest, is totally uninhabited, and of great extent. What a country for game! Here are food, water, shelter in abundance. And yet there is little game, certainly very little big game. The reason is—lack of salt. One further confirmation. The jungle is full of blood-sucking creatures—leeches, horse-flies, sand-flies, blister-flies, mosquitoes, ticks, and other minor horrors. There is an orgy of blood-thirst. Blood contains salt: and it has occurred to the writer, when itching all over from innumerable punctures, and deprived of sleep, that the course of evolution has tended towards the development of a blood-sucking proletariat in the jungle; not primarily at the expense of man, but of all warm-blooded life. This belief has been reinforced by watching the behaviour of butterflies, scavengers such as flies, and especially bees. Any of these insects will settle on you and greedily suck up sweat, when you are hot and bothered. Sit down in the forest on a fine day, and the bees come round in battalions. Insects quickly discover a jungle camp and buzz round the cookhouse all day in the hope of picking up salt.

It is, then, owing to the necessity for going outside the jungle in search of salt that the tribesmen are forced to mix with those above and below them in space. They certainly do not relish mixing with their neighbours, any more than they welcome strangers to their own dismal jungles. They are afraid of the Tibetans, above them, and despise the plainsmen below them. Also they are suspicious of each other. Thus common salt, which keeps these dour people moving, has a civilising influence, in so far as it compels them to meet their neighbours, who otherwise would be loath to visit *them*! Wedged between the plateaux and the plains, they are likely to retain their independence for some time yet.

They are useful, these jungle tribes. Though uncouth, they are not savages. They form a buffer which will delay the inevitable clash between the people of the plateaux and the people of the plains. Meanwhile they are the filter through which the plateau men pass gradually down the escarpment to the plains.

Thus Kachins, Lisus, Khanungs, Mishmis, Abors, and the rest, many of whom we shall come to know better in the course of our travels, extend in a continuous belt round the North-East Frontier. They are the custodians of the back-door to India.

Who these people really are, whence they came here, or how, or why—these are questions which cannot be fully answered. Some are undoubtedly stragglers, who lagged behind during the slow passage from the plateau to the plains; others are no less certainly a backwash from the plains, flotsam stranded by conflicting tides of migration. The jungle filters out those of coarser fibre, and stamps them with the mark of the wild. But it is unlikely that we shall ever know all their history. They are too rude to have left any records; even had they done so, the all-devouring jungle would have defaced and swallowed them ere now.

Since, then, Burma and Assam form the apex of the North-East Frontier of India, which is to be the scene of adventure, it will be convenient to clear the ground a little further yet by saying something more definite about each of these great provinces.

Burma, it is to be noted, is not only the country inhabited by the Burmese, but the much larger territory which formerly owed allegiance to the Kings of Burma. When the British took Mandalay and brought the dynasty of Alaungpaya to an end, they took over all the commitments of the deposed Government; and although no doubt many of the feudatory states had fallen into arrears with their tribute, nevertheless the territory which once had been, and theoretically still was, under the Burmese yoke was extensive. The British had only to revive a custom which had fallen into abeyance (i.e. the payment of tribute—or rent, as it became), and to insist on its being honoured in the observance, to weld the Burmese Empire together again. Easier said than done; but done it was.

Therefore, when garrulous tourists who have spent a week in Rangoon tell you that they have 'seen Burma', you are justified in being sceptical. Modern Rangoon, in fact, is anything but a Burmese town; and that for plain reasons. Before the days of quick sea transport, and under Oriental conditions of land warfare, the centre of gravity of Burma lay in the Mandalay district, where for fifty miles the Irrawaddy flows from east to west. Here, in the very centre of the country is a large fertile plain. Here a succession of Burmese capitals was established, which controlled the middle Irrawaddy, the Chindwin, and the exits from Burma to the East. Here then on the central plain was the Burma of the Burmese, surrounding the court of Ava—subsequently moved to Mandalay, the new capital, close by. In those days Lower Burma, as we know it to-day, was the home, not of the Burmese, but of the Talaings or Peguans, a people as different from the Burmese as the English are from the French. These Talaings had once ruled over both Upper and Lower Burma, but were finally overthrown by Alaungpaya, who descended the Irrawaddy and defeated the Talaings. Alaungpaya then, naturally, returned to Ava; and for some years the dynasty founded by him ruled over a united Upper and Lower Burma. In those days only he who held Ava could hold Burma. But with the coming of the sea-raiders the centre of gravity shifted from the central plain to the coast, and with it, the capital. Burma was threatened, not from the eastern hills to which the long-since discomfited Shans had retired, nor from the direction of China, but once more from the south, and under entirely novel conditions—by white people from overseas. It was *they* who, having established themselves on the coast, built Rangoon, made themselves strong, and then, like the Talaings, invaded Upper Burma. Under the invaders, Rangoon grew up a cosmopolitan seaport, more 'Indian' than Burmese; though it happens also to be the home of the peerless Shwe Dagon pagoda, which is visited annually by thousands of devout Burmese pilgrims. Thus the Burma of the Burmese has always been on the central plain; and the transference of the 'capital' to Rangoon has not altered the fact.

To see something of the real Burma, then, one must at least visit Mandalay or Moulmein; and though the Burmese of Moulmein are mostly Talaings, that is nowadays to all outward appearance, perhaps, a finer distinction than need here be stressed.

West of the Irrawaddy valley lies the Shan plateau, inhabited not only by Shans, but by many hill tribes, who, like the Shans, have no connection with the firm next door. In the eastern hills are more tribes. The whole upper part of the province, for two hundred miles north of the railhead at Myitkyina, away to the sources of the Irrawaddy, is a mesh of mountains, covered with dense forests, and sparsely inhabited by primitive peoples. Some of them, such as the Kachins and Marus, are related to the Burmese; others to the Shans; others, again, to the Chinese or to the Tibetans. Thus Burma, like India, though on a smaller scale—for Burma is only about twice the size of Great Britain—is a convenient geographical expression, not the home of a race, or even of a nation, It is, however, necessarily bounded by well-defined obstacles.

Hence it is not really possible to do Burma while the boat waits, and the popular idea that it is a land of temple-bells and languorous maidens smoking cheroots, of pagan gods with ruby eyes and strong silent Englishmen struggling with dacoits—which, by the way, are armed robbers, not snakes —is an exaggeration. The man who is home from Burma may have just come from Rangoon, where he has enjoyed most of the comforts, social and moral, and all the pastimes of England, with the thermometer standing at 90° F.; or he may have recently left the solitude of Fort Hertz or Loimwe, and spent three weeks on the road in Burma before embarking at Rangoon.

Assam lies to the north-west of Burma. It should not be confused with Siam or with Annam. Just as Burma is mainly the valley of the Irrawaddy, so Assam is mainly the valley of the Brahmaputra. Just as Burma is inhabited by a variety of races and tribes, who paid tribute to the ruling Power, so Assam has its own assortment, who however did not long pay tribute to the Assamese. Nor do they all pay tribute to the present dominant race, that is to say, the British. From this it may be inferred that Assam is even more remote and backward than Burma.

The Assam valley lies almost east and west. North of the Brahmaputra the ground begins to slope up to the foot-hills of the eastern Himalaya, where dwell the Daphla, Miri, and other tribes. South of the river are the Garo, Khasi, and Naga Hills, with Manipur beyond, all peopled by tribes, some of whom, like the Kachari, are the remnants of once powerful races.

At the head of the valley the converging mountains close up and rise in serried ranges to the escarpment of the Tibetan plateau; and here in the tangled valleys live the most dangerous of all the tribes—the Abor, Chulikata, Digaru Mishmi, and head-hunting Nagas.

By the geographer and the naturalist, however, Assam and Burma may be regarded as one—a single wedge thrust up between Hindustan and China, blocking the way to Tibet: a wedge which serves, not to unite India and China, but for ever to keep them apart. From the apex of this wedge a range of hills runs southwards, dividing Assam from Burma and thrusting the Lohit river westwards to one side, the Irrawaddy southwards to the other; and from the very earliest times the peoples who filtered through this back-door from the plateau to the plains were likewise cut into two streams, ever diverging.

If, then, there is an apparent breach in the mountain system between the Eastern Himalaya and the plateau of Western China, we can now see how difficult it is to storm. Whether the line of attack is by Assam or Burma, it is a matter, not of days, but of weeks to reach the snows. Every obstacle lies across one's path. Here whole mountain ranges have been in conflict. Dense jungle, and all the discomfort that entails, impassable rivers, snowbound passes, incredible rain, above all lack of roads, of transport, of food, or shelter in an almost uninhabited region, are the difficulties which must be faced by anyone who wishes to reach the Alps by this direct route. Add to this, that the tribes who inhabit the North-East Frontier are some of them hostile, and most of them unfriendly, and it will be realised what the traveller has to expect.

Having gone at some length into the question where, I must now answer the question, what. Then, with so much clear, I can embark on the problem, how—and that will be best answered as we go along, by starting on our travels and doing the work in hand.

2 A Plant-Hunter's Paradise

OUR objective, then, is the North-East Frontier, the eastern gateway to India; our object, plant hunting.

Now plant hunting may be of two kinds, though in practice these are usually combined. There is first of all botanical collecting, whose high priests have no ulterior object in view other than the advancement of learning and the satisfaction of curiosity. New species, that is to say species hitherto unknown to organised knowledge, old species in new places, or additional material of rare and imperfectly known species are equally welcome to the keen botanist. Their appearance is a matter of complete indifference to him; he upholds the socialist doctrine that all plants—or at least all flowering plants—are equal, and greets Comrade Thistle as genially as he hails Comrade Rose. With the cynical eye of science he rates the most trivial Groundsel as the equal of the noblest Pine. And this colossal hypocrisy he almost persuades himself to believe, and really tries hard to live up to. Actually, however, being a human being first and a botanist last, he has likes and dislikes just as other human beings who are not botanists have. He may indeed confess to a secret passion for Buttercups and Daisies so absorbing as to make him look askance at Palms and Blue Gums; but it is at least equally likely that his first choice lies amongst spiny Cacti, or giant Redwoods, or juicy Aloes.

Secondly, there is horticultural collecting, which is quite another matter. Appearance now becomes a first consideration in one's appraisement of a plant. Novelty, combined with a good appearance if possible, is at a premium. Above all, hardy? or half-hardy?—*that* is the question!

The field botanist is mainly concerned with the distribution and classification of plants, and the company they keep; and for this purpose a string of names and a pile of mummies to work on are as good as anything else. He works in secret places; uses a language of his own, incomprehensible to the layman; and reaches conclusions which the layman never hears of, and would not understand if he did. But the plant-collector is only concerned with good-looking plants, new or rare, and with introducing them alive into Britain with such directions as to their welfare as will keep them alive. He wants as many people as possible to enjoy the fruits of his labours, to see plants which otherwise they never would see. Let us peep a little more closely into his work.

13

Anyone looking round the parks and gardens, the plantations and estates, the hothouses and conservatories, and even the flower-shops of Britain might well feel that the plant-collector's task was a forlorn hope. For what new thing can he expect to find in this age, which will add one jot or tittle to the massed beauty of English gardens? Search where he may, what chance had he of finding anything a tithe as good as what had been found in the past? Precious little, you say! He is a hundred years too late! On every hand he sees the magnificent Conifers introduced from North America by Douglas; in private gardens the fiery-flowered trees of the Southern Andes, introduced by Lobb; the Bamboos and flowering shrubs introduced from Japan by Maries; the Japanese Conifers introduced by John Gould Veitch; and the roses and shrubs from China introduced by Fortune. He sees in our conservatories all that wealth of tropical foliage plants, ferns and orchids, discovered and introduced by Pearce, Burbridge, Curtis, Burke, and a dozen others. It would seem that the whole world had been combed, and combed again, to satisfy the English lust for flowers!

Nor are these all. There are many flowers which have been with us so long, which are so familiar to us, that we often forget their origin. It would be as difficult to imagine England without lilac and laburnum, crocuses and chrysanthemums, dahlias, begonias, asters, calceolarias, wallflowers, and lilies as it would be to imagine London without its sparrows and pigeons. Yet these plants have all been imported: you do not see them growing in the hedgerow.

Not only, therefore, is the standard a high one; not only might we despair of finding anything to rival our most familiar trees and flowers; but we may well wonder whether there can be any new plant left to be introduced, so great is the variety we possess, and so far afield have collectors searched. What new lands are there which would repay exploration?

One must confess this much at least: that to find anything new, worthy to rank with the best plants introduced in the past, the collector must search far and critically. But he need not despair. The world is a big place. True, it is unlikely that any modern introduction, fifty or a hundred years hence, will attain to the privileged position enjoyed by the horse-chestnut or the Atlas cedar to-day. True, also, that nothing short of a cataclysm will oust the established favourites. But that there are new countries and new plants I shall endeavour to prove, at least we shall come across many new plants in the course of these travels!

The plant-collector still aims at introducing new plants into Britain. There is room for a few more, and vacancies are always occurring. Many plants known to science are not, and never have been, in cultivation. Others, once in cultivation, have been lost through one cause or another. Nor can any of us resist the appeal of novelty, however much we may condemn it as a cult. Science is never satisfied; and we cannot rest so long as we have reason to believe that there are plants unknown to science. It is the same with beauty: if there are ways different from the old ways of expressing it, we must cultivate them.

What, then, are the desirable qualities which the collector seeks in a new plant?

In order to answer this question satisfactorily, let us take a country walk in December anywhere in England, avoiding as far as possible private estates. We observe that some of the land is wooded: in the pastures trees are scattered, and between the fields are hedges. But, for all the variety of form, everywhere we notice a sad lack of colour. The trees are leafless and forlorn; the sky is lowering; there are no flowers. Beauty there is of a type, just as there is a harsh beauty in the desert; the rugged strength of the oak is best revealed when it is stripped; the tresses of the birch dragged out by the wind, the massive bare arms of the beech, the gaunt elms, are all beautiful. But it is a rather grisly beauty. Here and there are holly-trees covered with scarlet berries, or bunches of mistletoe clotted with pearls which gleam coolly amongst sea-green blades; but the surrounding gloom only serves to throw these into stronger relief.

If, however, instead of walking in the country we confine our exploration to a great city such as London and walk through the parks and squares, we at once notice a difference in the vegetation.

To begin with, there are many evergreen trees and shrubs; others are gay with coloured berries: scarlet, orange, pink, blue, white; and there are few weeks in the year when the beds are not bright with flowers. So much for the Winter. In Spring and Summer the display of colour is overwhelming. Beginning with crocus, daffodils, grape-hyacinths, chionodoxas, and anemones, we come to lilac and laburnum, horse-chestnut, rhododendron, magnolia, roses, fuchsia, tropæolum, chrysanthemums, dahlias, and many more, familiar to every Londoner at least. So familiar in fact that many people are surprised to hear that the horse-chestnut and the plane, which are amongst the commonest London trees—the rhododendron, chrysanthemum, and Lombardy poplar, so abundant in the suburbs—are not indigenous to Britain at all; though a moment's reflection would satisfy anyone that he had never seen one of these growing really wild. These two pictures of England bring home to us what the introduction of plants from abroad has done. Colour in a plant, whether in flower, foliage, or fruit, has first claim on our notice. What is colourful in Summer may be admirable, but what is colourful in Winter is invaluable. Colour in Britain, as our country walk taught us, is rare enough to be precious, at least in Winter—and Winter lasts for five months of the year. Indeed, it is instructive to imagine what England must have looked like in Winter little more than a century ago, before most of our evergreens were introduced. How bleak was the outlook on a raw Spring day! How drab the landscape! Little wonder that the English—who had ample opportunity—turned their attention to flowers from overseas. Our gardens, parks, and markets testify to this floral invasion of Britain; although we must not confuse the huge mass of imported cut flowers, so familiar to town-dwellers in early Spring, with naturalised aliens grown on the premises.

We may assume, then, that there is still room for new plants in these islands, so long as they provide colour, particularly in Winter or Autumn; also for evergreen trees and shrubs of comely form.

But there is one field of exploration which the modern collector has made his own. A glance at any of our great flower shows, such as those held by the Royal Horticultural Society in that Holy City of Flowers which men call London, will convince anyone that the great majority of our newer plants are small fry. Here are to be seen in wonderful variety dwarf rhododendrons, hollies, barberries, and honeysuckles; blue poppies, rock, meadow, and woodland primulas, saxifrages, gentians, irises, larkspurs, and many more. Now the rock garden was a feature almost unknown to the great collectors of the nineteenth century. It is the child of the twentieth century, and was developed not only as a home for rock-plants, but also for the purpose of introducing an element of surprise. It contrasts bluntly with the terraces and parterres of the formal garden—a gaunt wildling to mock the stately paddock. By a trick we can mass colour in reserve and launch it in one devastating explosion. You walk across a billiard-cloth of lawn, descend steps, pass by a pool on which float water-lilies, turn a corner, and before you have time to draw breath a flash of colour explodes in your face. It is the rock-garden, masked behind the trees. When your eyes have recovered from the shock, its beauties begin to reveal themselves; a frill of flower-foam creeping along the ledge; a wave of colour swamping a rock; moons bobbing on a choppy sea; a dappled surf blazing warmly in the sunshine, and comets trailing luminous tails in the wind. These figures are plainer than pictures in the starry sky: but at a little distance the rock-garden is a sheer colour bomb.

Modern collectors may also claim to a share in the rhododendron. They did not, of course, introduce the first rhododendrons into this country; the rhododendron revolution dates from Hooker's discoveries in Sikkim eighty years ago. But as a result of following up those discoveries, they have raised the rhododendron almost to the position of the first flowering shrub in Britain and given it an importance never dreamed of even thirty years ago.

It is evident that plants have been introduced into Britain from the earliest times. Probably the Vikings brought some with them. Certainly the Romans did. Nevertheless it is chiefly to Englishmen that we are indebted for the sight of so many foreign plants; and we can rest assured that a great many more will be introduced yet. Every generation is inclined to think that it has completed its task and left nothing for its successors to accomplish. Explorers are peculiarly prone to this complaint, and are never tired of telling the younger generation that there are no more worlds to conquer. There never was a greater fallacy; and there never were more explorers than there are to-day. As far as botanical exploration goes, the collector can do as useful work to-day as in the past, particularly in his chosen field. Imagine a ten years' floral truce, during which not a single new plant was to be introduced into England! In that time, it is no exaggeration to say, we might easily lose fifteen or twenty per cent. of the rock-plants at present in cultivation. How many of the dozens of new hardy plants we are now experimenting with have come to stay? Probably only a very small fraction.

This invasion of Britain by alien plants was inevitable—as inevitable as its invasion by man. Let the patriotic folk who deplore the naturalisation of so may foreign plants to the discomfiture of our native flora consider that and take heart. Britain is a foggy island in the Atlantic Ocean, lying off the Eurasian continent—the greatest land mass in the world. She has been in the past both the unlawful prey of the seafaring people from the adjacent coast, and the last refuge of people driven westwards by the pressure of the East. She has been at once a prize and a sanctuary. Gradually her people, with their backs to the sea, learned their lesson; from the beginning they grew up a nation of sea-rovers and travellers.

Successive waves of invaders and refugees brought with them the plants of the continent; just as the Englishman who lives abroad takes his favourite plants with him. The hill-stations of India are gay with roses and honeysuckle. This was the first phase of plant introduction into Britain.

The second phase came later and resulted in vastly greater importations. The English had in the meantime become a great maritime nation. Wherever they went—and they went everywhere—they brought back treasure: the treasure of mother earth; gold, and precious stones, and—plants. Anything which struck them as strange, or wonderful, or beautiful they brought home. It is surely significant that Captain Cook was so struck with the beauty and strangeness of the vegetation in New South Wales, that he named Sydney Harbour, Botany Bay.

After this it was only a question of time before the professional plant-collector appeared on the scene and began to explore the botanical world systematically. It has been urged against further plant introductions—I am not here concerned with plants of economic value—that the newcomers are too much like the old—that nothing of startling originality is ever found. But this complaint might with equal justice have been made long ago. After all, the number of unique plants is limited: and they are mostly more grotesque than beautiful. At least the alien newcomers depart more from their predecessors than do the annual hosts of nursery novelties amongst such flowers as roses, chrysanthemums, and daffodils. I have no word to say against these last; indeed I greatly admire them. But live and let live! Is it really any easier to distinguish between say, Rose 'Hon. Mention' and Rose 'Miss Anne Thrope' than between *Primula sikkimensis* and *P. Florindæ*?

Nor could we stop the search for new plants if we would. For why should we stop at any arbitrary point? If there are more beautiful flowers in the world hiding their light under a bush, by all means let us expose them. A healthy curiosity alone, the prying eye of science, demands this: and the horticulturist is not behindhand.

For the reasons given, then, the writer believes that the work of botanical exploration should proceed; until we are convinced that there are no more beautiful, or curious, or striking, or useful plants to be discovered on the face of the earth, we cannot rest. Are we so convinced yet? By no means. It is true that several favourite and favourable regions are almost worked out. We can hardly hope to obtain strictly new plants from the Alps or the Pyrenees or the Balkans, or even from Japan or New Zealand or North America. But that botanical paradise, Western China, doubtless contains many a good pocket yet, despite its immense yield in the past. He would be a rash man who proclaimed that the Himalaya was bankrupt of floral treasure. Even the Andes, where plant hunting seems to be rather a pleasant picnic, continue to produce good plants.

But the real treasure-house of the world, the last stronghold of the collector in Asia, is the North-East Frontier of India; and although many known species are bound to recur there, inasmuch as collectors have sapped towards the heart of that region from east and west and south, it will be obvious from what follows that new species continue to be found.

To say that it is becoming harder every year to find new plants is to utter something perilously like a truism; and when the field is narrowed down to *hardy* plants, and to those hardy plants which have the qualities of excellence, it is difficult indeed!

Moreover, I mean harder in a particular sense. No mere intensive search over ground which has been well covered before will avail to-day; it is on new mountain ranges that one must seek new alpine plants. The difficulties which face the modern plant-hunter are of an entirely new order. There are, of course, the ordinary difficulties and hardships of travel in the jungle; lack of food, of transport, of communications; the hostility of the natives; the unfriendly climate. But added to these there is the political difficulty. Fifty years ago Governments were not so concerned about the fate of their nationals as they are to-day. The world was less known and more tranquil; the unknown was assumed to be harmless. Explorers did not queue up as they do now, and they required less police control. Nowadays Governments are too wise. The field between the administrative frontiers of the Eastern empires is narrowed: the tribes, pressed from all sides, are more restless. China and Tibet have become 'civilised', with the result that China is distracted by civil war, while Tibet applies the Aliens Restriction Act. Not so many years ago one might enter Tibet and travel there safely. In these hard times, to cross the Tibetan frontier uninvited is to provoke questions in Parliament and rude letters from harassed Government officials. It is no part of the plant-collector's business to score a spectacular success by crossing some forbidden frontier. He wants to collect plants, and to do that he must have a free hand, not sneak along in disguise, afraid to show his face.

And so it is the quest for new plants which brings us to the Edge of the World; the North-East Frontier of India, more especially that corner of it where Assam, Burma, and Tibet interlock.

It forms the escarpment between the pastoral plateaux in the interior, which are anything from 6,000 to 16,000 feet above sea level, and the agricultural plains of the coastal belt, less than 1,000 feet above sea level. Here the earth's crust has been heaved up on edge, bent, sharpened and smashed, and the whole glorious ruin submerged beneath the enduring forest. Great rivers, rising on the plateau, have drilled their way through to the plains and to the sea, tearing deep rents in the escarpment, without making the passage through the barricade from the plains to the plateau any easier. And it is here, in the midst of the most formidable tanglement in the world, amidst roaring rivers and snowy peaks, in the sheer heart of the forest region, that we seek the plants we desire. Not on the plains at the foot of the escarpment, where the climate is sub-tropical—nor on the high plateau, on the roof of the world, where the climate is sub-arctic—are hardy plants to be found; but between the two, at altitudes varying between 7,000 and 13,000 feet.

Having enquired somewhat into the questions where and why, I now turn to the more important matter of—how!

3   Through Darkest Burma

THE province of Burma stretches northwards some 200 miles beyond Myitkyina, which is the northern terminus of the Burma Railway, and the starting-point for the mule caravans going to China, to the jade mines, and to the outposts of Empire. Beyond Myitkyina one thinks of distance not in miles, but in marches. There are no railways, or motor-roads. Even the Irrawaddy is unnavigable, and you travel afoot. In the dry season (December–March), the river drowses forty feet below the top of the bank, but already it was beginning to mutter in its sleep. On three sides the blue mountains hem in the plain, curving down like horns, which point southwards; on the China frontier, forty miles to the east, they rise to a considerable height, but to north and west they are lower. The northern territory of Burma, which is the valley of the upper Irrawaddy and its tributaries, is mountainous, and the whole country is covered with dense evergreen forest. This territory is inhabited mainly by tribes of Tibeto–Burman origin, namely Kachin or Chingpaw, Maru, Marip, and Nung; but they are ruder than Burman or Tibetan.

Thirty miles above Myitkyina, the Irrawaddy, almost a thousand miles from the sea, splits into two great branches, an eastern (the main branch) and a western. The road to Fort Hertz lies up the western branch or Mali Kha, which flows through a comparatively flat valley. It is a good road too, at least in the dry season, and it winds over the hills and far way to the Shan plain called Hkamti Long, where Fort Hertz is reached at mile 214. The traveller who for the past fortnight has been crossing hills over 2,000 feet high may feel a little surprised to find that his net gain in altitude as compared with Myitkyina is just 800 feet, Fort Hertz being only 1,400 feet above sea level. But he has no cause to grumble. The road is easy, with well-appointed bungalows at each stage—a stage averages ten to twelve miles—with good fishing (no licence required), and romantic scenery. The innumerable rivers which have to be crossed are spanned by bridges, and the gradients are everywhere easy; he can ride his pony the whole way. In fact it is a first-class mule-road.

However, should the traveller, scorning comfort, wish to sample wilder country, he can if he likes follow the eastern branch of the river, called the Nmai Kha, northwards under the shadow of the China frontier. Here the mountains are far higher, and so too are the passes. The rivers stampede wildly down from snow-clad alps, and the forests in Spring blaze with

Map 2

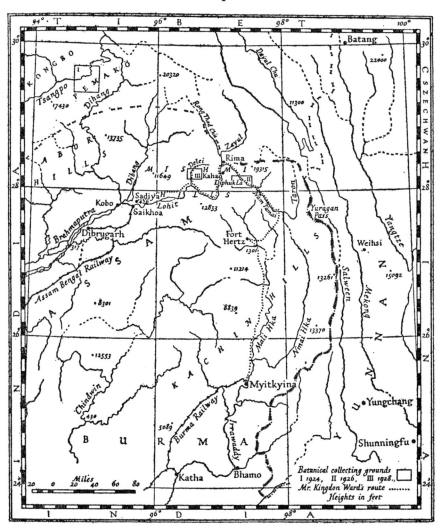

Assam and Upper Burma

Rhododendrons. But the traveller cannot expect to take his mules far in this direction. Even mules have feelings. Government built a mule-road for several stages up the Nmai Kha, to link up with some of the easier passes into China; but this road presently ends in the air, and henceforth the traveller must go on Shanks' mare, with coolies to carry his loads. Before long he finds himself enlisting hands as well as feet; and it will take him three times as long to reach Fort Hertz by this route as by the easier one: and as we are ultimately bound for an even wilder country than any to be found along the China frontier, we need waste no more time over it now.

About half-way to Fort Hertz by the western valley, the traveller will notice to his right a high hill; the direct road passes within ten miles of it. This is Sumpra Bum, the new district headquarters, recently transplanted from Fort Hertz, which is considered unhealthy. The Burma Government is now constructing a dirt motor-road from Myitkyina to Sumpra Bum, and this will eventually no doubt be carried as far as Fort Hertz. That is the only logical thing to do. Incidentally, it would be easy to construct an aerodrome at Fort Hertz; and a 'plane could fly from Myitkyina to Fort Hertz in under two hours at cruising speed. There are no high mountains to be crossed, and no difficulties of any sort, except during the rainy season, when communication would probably be interrupted—as it is now. However, at the time of which I write, namely the Spring of 1926, there was neither motor-road nor airway; and I covered the distance by the old-fashioned, decorous, and placid method, using Chinese mules hired in Myitkyina. The journey took eighteen days. For the first thirty miles, to the confluence, the road keeps close to the river. One can drive a car, or ride a bicycle, over this section, which is what in Burma is called a cart-road; that is, any sufficiently wide road on which the gradients are not too steep for a bullock-cart to negotiate. At the confluence the road enters the hills, but continues a cart-road as far as Nsop Zup, forty miles from Myitkyina. Beyond Nsop, the gradients are too steep for carts.

At Nsop the botanist gets his first thrill. Here the long ribs of slate rock, which in March are exposed in the river-bed, are covered with wild Roses (*R. bracteata*) and crimson Azalea (*Rhododendron indicum*). The combination of the two seems to suggest the near presence of a temperate flora; but this is quite illusory!

Now the road leaves the river, and plunges more deeply into the hills. The jungle is very fine, the country sparsely inhabited. But forest means rain, and jungle means heat, and the climate even at 3,000 feet is never salubrious. There are three seasons; the rainy season, comprising Summer and Autumn, the hot weather (Spring), and the cold weather (Winter). Even in Winter, which is not of course really cold, the jungle after sunset is steeped in such a clammy mist that by dawn water is dripping from the trees like rain; often the mist does not disperse till the sun is high in the heavens. During the hot weather the atmosphere is drier, but in the valleys

KACHINS GINNING COTTON.

BRIDGE OF CREEPERS, SEINGHKU VALLEY, BURMA FRONTIER. 6,000 FEET.

the heat can be very trying; also there is a haze which limits visibility, until the next thunderstorm sponges it out.

A hundred and twenty miles north of Myitkyina we begin to see the low rolling country away to the west, and the hill range which divides the Mali valley from the Hukawng valley and Assam: there is still snow on it in April. The Hukawng valley, which is the source of the Chindwin river, has been in the limelight of late years; first as the best route for the proposed Burma–Assam railway connection; secondly, heralded by a publicity campaign of unusual severity, as the playground of the New Abolitionists, who suddenly awoke to the fact that slavery was rife in the unadministered territory, and released the alleged slaves wholesale. 'Burma's gift to the Empire,' the sycophant Press ecstatically called it.

Our daily routine on the march is quite simple. Up at daybreak, a quick cup of tea and a biscuit, and by eight o'clock we are on the road. Before the heat becomes oppressive, we reach the next bungalow, and halt; about one o'clock we have breakfast. During the afternoon heat-wave, we rest, and in the cool of the evening we can go down to the nearest river and fish, or stroll in the jungle and collect specimens, as the fancy takes us. Everything is provided. The bungalows are furnished, not only with bedsteads, chairs, and tables, but with all household requisites. Each bungalow is looked after by a *chowkidar* or caretaker, who is usually either an ex-Military Police Gurkha, or a tame Kachin. He keeps the place clean, and also provides water and firewood at a nominal charge fixed by Government. Often he supplies milk, eggs, and fowls, as a side-line. At two or three points along the road there are Chinese stores, where one can buy tinned milk, kerosene, and such-like; but the charge for these is phenomenal rather than nominal.

Beyond Myitkyina the mountains are covered with evergreen rain forest, which stretches well beyond the actual Tropic of Cancer, until stopped by the high mountains of the north. Such tropical, or, at any rate, subtropical, hill jungle covers most of the upper Irrawaddy basin and its tributaries.

From Machega, mile 123, the highest point on the road, one gets a first glimpse of the snow-clad mountains to the north, over 12,000 feet high, where the Mali Kha rises.

At last the low hills are left behind and the road winds down towards the plain. Here we reach the river again and cross to the left bank by a suspension bridge, thrown across the entrance to the gorge. A few miles up-stream, where the river broadens out, we re-cross by a bamboo trestle bridge, or, in the rainy season, when the trestle bridge is swept away, by boat; and here on the bank stands the last bungalow before Fort Hertz is reached. The reason for this double crossing of the Mali Kha is to avoid the more treacherous crossing of the Nam Yak, a big tributary which flows in from the south on the right bank.

From the last bungalow at Naung Hkai to Fort Hertz is fourteen miles

23

in a dead straight line across the Hkamti plain. The southern end of the plain has apparently never been cultivated and is covered with high grass and scattered bushes. The land is too low-lying and swampy to support forest. Low bush-clad ridges indicate former banks abandoned by the river as it changed its course, and there are several *nallas* filled with jungle. Except for these welcome breaks, the whole plain consists of grass-land.

Fort Hertz occupies the apex of a tongue-shaped terrace about fifty feet high, which juts out into the cultivated plain and is truncated just above the Shan-Chinese village of Putao. The surrounding plain is under Rice, with considerable grazing areas along the banks of the rivers for large herds of buffalo and cattle. Scattered about are Shan villages screened amongst clumps of Bamboo and fruit-trees.

The plain is entirely surrounded by hills, those to the north and west being covered with snow throughout the Winter. Before the road to the south was built, it was as difficult to quit the plain in this direction as in any other; for the country was then just as wild and inhospitable southwards as it is to the north, east, and west to-day. Consequently the small Shan colony who inhabit the plain was completely cut off from contact with the outside world. They preyed upon their weaker neighbours, the Nungs, who inhabit the jungles to the north-east, and were in turn preyed upon by the stronger Kachins, who live on the hill-tops to the south. Since the British people assumed the liabilities of the late King Thibaw, however, our policy towards all the frontier tribes has been one of live and let live.

The plain of Hkamti Long is certainly an ancient lake-bed. Rivers poured into this lake from the surrounding hills, even from the south, as the Nam Yak does to this day. No doubt the floor of the lake has been much scoured since the water found an outlet, and it is impossible to say at present how high the lake-level stood; obviously it stood higher than the highest river terrace. Nor do we know for certain when this diluvial period was, except that it was probably contemporaneous with the last glacial epoch, or some portion of it. During the same period the plain of Manipur to the west, so like the Hkamti plain in appearance, was also a lake. The Hukawng valley was either a lake, or else a much larger river than the Chindwin then occupied it.

Meanwhile, the high mountains to the north-east sent large glaciers down their valleys—we shall see their remains presently. The Mali Kha of course did not exist; when it came into being it drained the Hkamti Lake. In those days the Nam Tisang, which to-day occupies a valley much too big for it, may have been the western branch of the Irrawaddy. The eastern branch, or Nmai Kha, probably followed its present course; but the Irrawaddy below the confluence had not yet carved for itself the first defile. It flowed instead several miles to the east, in a wider channel. The difficulty of course is to correlate dates so as to picture the whole country as it was at any given time. The lake basins of Western China were, according to Gregory, probably formed during the Pliocene[1]. Many, but not all of these have subsequently been drained; the Manipur, Hkamti, and other lakes may have been formed at the same time.

The mountains due north of Fort Hertz, where the Mali Kha rises, are not very high. But the range extends in a north-easterly direction forming the divide between the Irrawaddy system and the Lohit river. Farther north, where the sources of the eastern Irrawaddy are born, some of the peaks attain over 19,000 feet; and it was there that I was going. Here was a range of mountains, connected on the one hand with the Himalaya, on the other with the alps of Yunnan, but only indirectly through the plateau of Tibet. A long time must have elapsed since the rivers on each side carved this block into virtual isolation; it might well therefore contain many plants hitherto undiscovered.

There is one pass over this range giving direct access to the province of Zayul, in the south-east corner of Tibet. The Diphuk La, as it is called, 14,320 feet, lies at the head of the Seinghku valley, one of the minor sources of the eastern Irrawaddy; and though little frequented, it is regularly used[2].

The Seinghku valley, however, is very remote. It is seventeen stiff marches from Fort Hertz to the last village up the Seinghku, with every sort of obstacle between me and my goal. Still I had much to be thankful for. The territory through which I had to pass is administered, the Nung tribes are friendly, even meek, and there is a good path for the first fifteen marches, with a rest hut at each stage. It was too late in the season to engage mules; they all leave Burma and return to China in the middle of May, and I did not reach Fort Hertz till the middle of April. But it is doubtful if I should have got any Panthay muleteers to go with me even had I arrived earlier; they have a deep dislike to going beyond Fort Hertz at any season.

It was, therefore, necessary to engage coolies, to carry the baggage; but as this had all been arranged for me by the Superintendent, Fort Hertz, I had no trouble on that score. All food, both for myself and servants, had to be transported to the Seinghku, since we could not rely on getting anything in the jungle. Moreover, there had been famine in the hill country for the last two years. I took stores for six months, these comprising jam, milk, butter, tea, coffee, biscuits, sardines, Quaker oats, potted meat, and chocolate; the whole weighing about 250 lbs. Also a case of rum. Besides these, I took four months' rations, consisting of rice, flour, and *ghyi* (clarified butter used for cooking). These weighed 800 lbs.; further supplies were to be sent out to me later. Thus over fifty coolies were required to carry the loads, which included besides the above, tents, bedding, clothes, books, camp furniture, photographic apparatus, oil for lamps, and collecting

[1] *Phil. Soph. Transactions*, Royal Society of London, January, 1925.
[2] Due north of Fort Hertz is another pass, the Kumjawng or Kronjawng Pass, 9,632 feet, leading down to the Lohit river and Assam. It is used only by a few Mishmis in the Winter.

material, chiefly botanical presses and quantities of thick paper. My servants comprised a Burmese cook, engaged in Fort Hertz—rather a scallywag, a Kachin 'boy' from Myitkyina, and a Nung child of fifteen, also from Fort Hertz, who had attached himself to me. He was known as Chokara.

Our road lay eastwards across the plain to the Mali Kha, and down that river a short distance to the Shan village at the foot of the hills. In the rainy season the whole journey can be done by boat, but there was not enough water in the small streams for that yet, so we walked to the bank of the Mali Kha, and embarked in a canoe which was waiting for us. Next day we left the plain, and ascending the first ridge, entered the jungle.

Between the Mali Kha and the Nam Tamai are two high ranges of hills, with the Nam Tisang—a tributary of the former—flowing between them. Each hill range is further divided by a smaller river. It is four marches from the Mali to the Tisang, and four from the Tisang to the Tamai; so that in eight days one crosses four hill ranges and four rivers, the journey being a constant succession of ups and downs.

Arrived at the Nam Tisang, five days out from Fort Hertz, my coolies set down their loads and went back to their homes. They had done their share. We now set about collecting a fresh relay. But fifty Nungs are not to be had by a stamp of the foot in this wilderness, and it took two days to collect them from up and down the valley. However, they were very docile, and went off in batches to the Nam Tamai with loads as fast as we could discover them.

After crossing another hill range, and another river, we approach the last and highest range of all, which is the divide between the western and eastern branches of the Irrawaddy. That night a terrific thunderstorm, accompanied by torrents of rain, swept the hills. The cold glare of the lightning, reflected from the curtain of rain, showed only tossing trees, flapping leaves, and white spray hissing over the rocks as the rain rods rebounded. From below, during a lull, one heard the voice of the torrent in the valley rise sharply. Trees came crashing down, and the explosions of thunder were deafening. But the storm passed almost as suddenly as it had broken, and the terrified jungle sank to rest under a calm glittering sky; even the steady drip from the trees ceased at last.

We made an early start next day as we had a climb of over 2,500 feet to the top of the divide. The storm had blown down several trees, and the rain had scored the path. Gradually the jungle was succeeded by temperate rain forest, where we saw various Rhododendrons. *R. stenaulum*, a sinuous tree with a smooth copper-red trunk, was enveloped in blossom, although the previous night's wind had strewn the path with its pale rose corollas, mingled here and there with the larger milk-white corollas of *R. dendricola*.

A stiff ascent brought us to the ridge, 6,725 feet, where the path wound about through the gloomy moss-bound forest, as though seeking a convenient spur for its plunge of nearly 4,000 feet in two miles to the Nam

Tamai. Away to the north we caught a glimpse of the Alps along the Tibetan border, white with snow. The descent to the river is rough and steep, and it grows rapidly hotter as the mountains close round us once more. The forests of Rhododendron, Birch, Michelia, Oak, Maple, and other temperate trees are left behind. Half-way down I noticed a Fagræa in bloom.

A sagging and wobbly cane suspension bridge spans the river, on the opposite bank of which stands the rest hut. There is some cultivation, and scattered up the slope are the long, low huts of the Nungs.

The Nam Tamai, one of the two big streams which make up the Nmai Kha, is here 3,000 feet above sea level. It is a swift river of considerable size, frequently broken by rapids and cascades. I was interested to find that the water temperature was no less than 11° F. colder than the Mali Kha, proving beyond any doubt that it comes from the high alps. Thus we had only to follow it up far enough in order to be quite certain of finding ourselves amongst snowy peaks; yet after following it for six days we had added only a thousand feet to our height!

Arrived at the Nam Tamai, our coolies returned to their homes. A fresh lot, ordered by the Superintendent, were waiting for me, and we pushed on next day (April 30).

One cannot but be struck by the almost complete lack of flowers in the jungle. The explanation is simple. Flowers need above all else *light*, and in general, the brighter the light, the more brilliant the flower colours. Without sufficient light, flowers do not develop, even on plants which normally produce conspicuous flowers. One notices this with certain rock Primulas, *P. Dubernardiana* and *P. pulvinata* for example. In the darker and damper crevices of the cliffs these form magnificent cushions of fresh green foliage, but without a flower; while at the same time wizened-looking plants with stunted leaves on the sunny cliff-face are a mass of bloom. Certain exotic plants cultivated in Britain have continued to grow beautifully for years, but have never flowered; and this may well be because they have never received sufficient light stimulus.

In the jungle are a few flowers, such as species of Arisaema (Arum-like plants), Orobanche, Tacca and several Orchids, often saprophytic. These nearly all have dull-coloured flowers, brown or yellow, occasionally black. But by far the greater part of the jungle undergrowth consists of flowerless plants such as Mosses and Ferns. To find plants with conspicuous flowers, one must search the trees themselves, high up, where many Orchids which crave the light will be found.

The importance of light too is proved by the great number of flowers met with along the banks of the road. Here are found Begonias, Violets, Orchids, Chirita, Lysimachia, Impatiens, and many other herbaceous plants. No matter how rare these may be in the jungle, they grew like weeds here. On the open banks, besides flowers, thousands of seedlings are germinating. Light retards growth, but it promotes the germination of seeds, and flowering. One must conceive the jungle, with its tall strong trees, as evolving from plants stimulated to rapid growth by darkness, but having to compete in a height contest in order to reach the light necessary for flower production.

There is ample cultivation in the valley of the Nam Tamai, considering the steepness of its flanks. Yet we saw few huts, these being usually well screened. The Nungs are timid, gentle creatures, neither truculent like the Mishmi, nor swaggering like the Chingpaw, with moderate physique and great staying power. The children always look dreadfully undernourished. No doubt they actually were now, since there had been a famine the previous year. Many of the Bamboos had flowered, and the extra food supplied by their seeds had caused a great increase in the number of rats. The rats had overflowed into the fields, and eaten the crops; and the next harvest was three months hence. Nor was the present outlook promising. The Nungs have only one method of cultivation, and are at the mercy of the weather. A slope is selected and the forest cut down, only the biggest trees being left standing, for want of tools to fell them. After lying in the sun for two or three weeks the tangle of dead creepers and trees is set on fire, and finally the charred branches are carried away, the ground is raked over, and the crops are sown. This must be done before the rains set in properly, in June. Therefore, the forest must be burnt not later than the beginning of May, and what is wanted is fine weather in April or March. If April is wet—as indeed it was in 1926—the jungle of course cannot be burnt. When one considers under what appalling difficulties the Nungs labour, the marvel is that they do not all die of starvation. A hill clearing can only be used once. After the reaping of the crop it becomes smothered with weeds, which are gradually replaced by a dense growth of secondary jungle. This secondary growth is far thicker than the original forest; if left alone long enough, it would no doubt revert to jungle, but meanwhile it is much more difficult to cut down than the forest, and six or eight years must elapse before the impoverished soil is fit for cultivation a second time. Sometimes Bamboo takes the place of forest, just as Grass does in temperate latitudes; and then when the Bamboos flower, the rats increase out of all reason. And so it goes on. Then again it is necessary to select slopes which are not too steep or rocky; and they must be below the 6,000-feet contour, otherwise the crops will not ripen. Of these, Maize is by far the most important, forming perhaps, in a normal year, 75 per cent of the people's food. Secondary crops are Eleusine, Mountain Rice, Buckwheat, and Job's Tears, with such vegetables as Cucumbers, Pumpkins, Beans, and Sweet Potatoes.

The extent of suitable land below 6,000 feet is not infinite; and if we suppose that any area of land must lie fallow for eight years, a simple calculation shows that if x acres are sufficient to feed a family for a year, that family requires altogether $8x$ acres to keep it going. This fact alone limits

28

the population of a given valley. The only possible way in which the same amount of land can support a larger number of persons, is by increasing the yield per acre. This would doubtless be practicable, the yield at present being meagre; but innovations are less readily adopted by tribes in this state of fixed civilisation than by more advanced tribes which have crystallised into nations.

At the end of the third day's march up the river we halted to change coolies again. Here we saw the visible effects of the famine, in a graveyard; the graves were obviously recent, for in this climate they hardly last a season. Mock birds perched on tall poles represented the souls of the departed flying away; it seemed natural to see so pretty a thought amongst so simple and child-like a people. On the graves, as though loth to let the dead depart altogether from their homes, and perhaps to lure them back, the living had placed their daily needs—so few and plain; a pipe, a hat, a cooking-pot, or basket.

Many of the Nung girls of the Nam Tamai tattoo their faces, drawing a few lines which curve round the chin from the angles of the mouth; and a round dot is added on the tip of the flattened nose.

But the population even of the Nam Tamai is scanty; that of the whole vast jungle country negligible. From the last Shan village on the edge of the Hkamti plain to the Nam Tisang, four days' journey away, not a single hut is seen; and for three days' journey from the lip of the Nam Tisang valley, till you drop down into the trough where the Nam Tamai flows, the country is equally uninhabited. Except in the larger valleys, there is no acre of God's earth which even the hillman can cultivate. Everywhere the jungle is triumphant. It is the absence of man which the traveller finds so depressing, and even sinister. He feels himself in the presence of a nameless power, slow in action, but inevitable and overwhelming in its results; a power against which he sees man, adapted though he is to his surroundings, strive in vain, advancing here, retreating there, but never more than barely holding his own. It is the power of the jungle.

But if man is right in the background, there is plenty of animal life. Birds, though shy, are plentiful. They are most numerous in Spring and Autumn, when, besides the regular inhabitants of the jungle, the migrating species are halting on their way to and from the Alps. Many of them have brilliant plumage, though the dull-coloured ones are often the most interesting and instructive to watch. Although some, such as the Coppersmith, have the most monotonous and maddening cries, it is a mistake to believe that this is true of all, or to draw the conclusion that in return for their gaudy colours God decided that the jungle birds should only cackle, and cluck, leaving the gift of song to the plainer birds of the north! A curious bargain! But it is not true. In the bright April dawn, when the night's rain is sparkling on the leaves, I have heard the voices of birds singing sweetly in the Irrawaddy jungle.

For six days we marched north-westwards up the valley of the Nam Tamai, the country growing ever wilder, the spurs steeper, the mountains higher. On the fourth day we noticed tall Pine-trees (*P. excelsa*) on a rocky ridge not 2,000 feet above us, and presently I was thrilled to see a great snow-covered pyramid filling the valley ahead. At last we were approaching the alps. On the sixth day we heard a terrific tumult of water, which grew gradually louder; it was the confluence between the Seinghku Wang and the Adung Wang.

4 The Burmese Oberland

THE nameless mountains at the sources of the Irrawaddy which I have called, derisively perhaps, the Burmese Oberland, trend almost north and south, the headwater streams of the Irrawaddy rising successively from the eastern flank of the main range and taking a general southerly course. From the western flank of the same range rise streams which flow to the Lohit-Brahmaputra, so that this range is here the Irrawaddy–Lohit divide. A little farther north, beyond the sources of the Irrawaddy, it becomes the Salween–Lohit divide. It is to the southern portion of this immense mountain range, with its chief satellite ranges and main spurs, that the name Burmese Oberland is applied.

The Tamai river is the second headwater stream of the eastern Irrawaddy, the main stream (and therefore the real source of the Irrawaddy) being the Taron, which flows close up against the China frontier. Pressed between the Tamai and the Taron are two smaller rivers, which rise amongst the lower spurs of the Irrawaddy–Lohit divide, all four flowing southwards for some distance before combining to form the Nmai Kha, or eastern Irrawaddy. On an ordinary atlas map of Burma, neither of the two middle streams will be marked, so small are they; but it may give some idea of the scale of the country if I say that the Dablu, which is the smaller river, is about forty, the Tazu about fifty, miles long. On May 9, then, we reached the Seinghku-Adung confluence, these two rivers combining to form the Tamai. There is a rickety, swinging cane bridge across the Seinghku, just above the confluence. The Seinghku is the most westerly headwater of the eastern Irrawaddy, and is about twenty-five miles long. It rises near the Diphuk La, in lat. 28° 10′ N., long. 97° 20′ E., a high pass leading precariously into the province of Zayul, in the extreme south-east corner of Tibet.

May had come, and I was eager to reach the alps as soon as possible. The shortest way was up the Seinghku valley, though I could not hope to reach the highest peaks by this route; to do that I must continue up the main (Adung) valley. But, being delayed again, owing to lack of transport, I decided to branch off north-westwards up the Seinghku valley; the peaks at its head, though they do not reach the snow line, are over 17,000 feet, and are therefore quite high enough to support a rich alpine flora!

Our first night at the confluence was a memorable one. When I went to bed, the wedge of sky to the south, framed between the dark cliffs of the

Nam Tamai, was beautifully inlaid with stars, the red tail light of the Scorpion glowing in the very centre. A few hours later I awoke, dreaming that someone had called up the fire brigade; a stream of water was playing on my head, and a syncopated sound of dripping told of more streams directed elsewhere. Presently I realised that the hut was not really on fire, but that the roof was in need of repair, and it was raining sharply outside. Next day repairs were effected, the dense jungle which surged right up to the door of the hut was cut back, and the coolies dismissed to their homes and fields.

By May 11 fifteen fresh coolies had assembled and went off with loads a day's journey up the Seinghku, returning for more as quickly as possible. In this way we gradually moved the baggage up the valley. Anxious as I was to get on, however, so interesting was the hill jungle that I did not grudge the six days spent here.

The altitude of the confluence is 4,000 feet, and high up on the south face of the cliff which frowned down on my camp were numerous blue Pine-trees—probably *P. excelsa*, though I could not reach them. *Rhododendron notatum* was in flower all round me, usually perched in the highest trees; and a small Elæocarpus-tree in full bloom was humming with bees. Wonderful Ferns grew everywhere, and I collected some thirty different kinds here.

On May 15 I started with the last batch of coolies up the Seinghku valley. There is no track worth mentioning. In places we had to scale the cliffs by crazy bamboo ladders, holding on by roots and creepers; elsewhere we pushed through the thick jungle which came down to the water's edge, or scrambled over the boulders. In the afternoon we reached a grassy alp where stood three miserable huts; the river was spanned by a hammock bridge made of cane and creepers, and on the opposite bank was a fourth hut. From the tangle of trees and shrubs on either side trailed festoons of white flowered *Rhododendron notatum*.

Pitching my tent in the meadow, close beside a Tibetan family who were tending a herd of goats, I settled down to await the arrival of fresh transport; for the Tibetans had promised to conduct me to their village, another day's march up the valley. Meanwhile they were building me a log house.

The valley was still lined with sub-tropical jungle, but by this time there was a hint of temperate forest in it too; snow lay on the tops of the hills across the river. There were Peach-trees and patches of Opium Poppy round the huts, and fields of golden corn. *Decaisnea insignis* was in flower, with a yellow-flowered Schizandra, and I could see Conifers higher up. On the heavily wooded rocky ridge, a thousand feet above my camp, grew masses of *Berneuxia tibetica*, which has glossy leaves and white flowers like a Shortia. Amongst several Rhododendrons was the pretty little yellow-flowered *R. insculptum*, which grew like mistletoe in the trees; but *R. stenaulum* was over.

At last, on May 22, the Tibetan contingent arrived, a rough-looking lot of rascals, very tall compared with the little Nungs, ugly, and good-humoured. There were only ten of them, so most of the baggage had to be left behind; but at all costs I must push on, and next day we started for my base camp.

The first few miles were uninteresting, but presently we came to a clearing where stood an abandoned village. A beautiful Illicium (*I. Griffithii*) was in flower, and there were Birch-trees. Then we left the river and, ascending a steep ridge, entered a forest of Rhododendrons. By far the most abundant was a small tree with hard, glabrous leaves having a horny margin, probably *Rhododendron tanastylum*; but none of them were in flower. This species is very common also in the Mishmi Hills, between 7,000 and 9,000 feet altitude. Unlike the scarlet-flowered Burmese 'Irroratums' found scattered in the hill jungle, *R. tanastylum* grows socially, and is the first Rhododendron we met with to do so. The flowers of the Assam plant are a dark amethyst purple, heavily printed with dusky commas; whereas the true *R. tanastylum* has scarlet flowers. It is hardly hardy.

Another tree, or rather shrub, which grew on the Rhododendron ridge was *Acer sikkimense*, a brilliant object in fruit. There were several Orchids in flower on the rocks and trees; but whereas on the plains the great majority of Orchids flower in the hot weather, just before the rains, in the hills some flower in the Spring, others in the Summer (these are mostly alpine species), and some at the beginning of the fine weather, just after the rains. The only species in flower now were an epiphytic white-flowered Vanda, and an Otochilus with little spidery flowers.

The two most interesting trees on this ridge, however, were *Eriobotrya Wardii* and a big-leafed 'Irroratum' Rhododendron, of which I shall have more to say later. *Eriobotrya Wardii* was leafless, and its fruits I mistook at first for flower-buds, so that I was easily deceived into thinking that it was a Magnolia; nor was I more enlightened as to its true affinity when later I found a small tree with leaves, but no fruits. It was not till October, when the leaves had fallen and all the branches were breaking out in a lovely lather of Meadowsweet flowers, scenting the forest, that I realised the tree belonged to the Rose family, and was in fact a Loquat.

Arrived at the top of the ridge we traversed through thick forest for a mile, and presently emerged on to a wide terrace, where stood half a dozen Tibetan log cabins. Part of the terrace was cultivated, and part of it abandoned to Bracken and meadow. We did not, however, halt here, but descended several hundreds of feet to the river again, and soon reached another meadow, similar to the last, but smaller. A wooden cantilever bridge spanned the river, which had now become a large torrent; on the opposite bank a cluster of fluttering prayer flags indicated the headman's house, and the village of Haita. On the near side, close beside the river, a square log hut, ten feet by ten, roofed with Bamboo and tiled with the huge leaves of *Schefflera Wardii*, had been constructed; it was my new Summer residence.

Now I took stock of our surroundings. There was no flat ground. The mountains sloped steeply up for 3,000 feet from the torrent, and were heavily wooded to the summit. Looking up the valley, I could see nothing but mountains, also covered with forest, though snow was visible here and there. Only the lowest slopes were cultivated, and on the strip of pasture which lined the torrent, a few log huts were threaded; beyond the last hut the forest closed in again, the trees almost meeting over the rushing river. Flocks of sheep and goats grazed in the pasture, which was permanent. The altitude was between 6,000 and 7,000 feet. It is unusual to find Tibetans living as low down as this. But in the course of the last hundred years or so, there has been a tendency for people of Tibetan stock to cross the passes south of the plateau and to settle at the heads of the valleys which lead down to the plains. Thus they have crossed over to the headwaters of the Irra-waddy, and into the valleys of the Dihang and Dibang, and have descended the Lohit valley to below Rima, the altitude of which is but 4,000 feet. So long as they can keep cattle and sheep and goats they are content; and the inhabitants of the Seinghku valley spend most of the Summer in the high alps.

The present is a guide to the past. One sees in this slow migration exactly what must have been going on for ages, often more rapidly, no doubt; the gradual movement of the plateau peoples southwards down the dry valleys, through the jungle belt, to the shining wet plains; and their gradual trans-formation from a pastoral to an agricultural basis. One can trace the Tibetan stock right through Burma at least; and the only reason why one cannot trace it through the Assam opening seems to be that the people who emerged from the jungle into the head of the Assam valley immediately found them-selves in conflict with powerful kingdoms already established in Upper Assam. One must conclude that the movement into Burma took place long prior to that into Assam. In Burma the people of Tibetan stock eventually prevailed; in Assam they did not. Had the Tai (Shan) race, or the Peguans (Mon-Khmer), finally conquered the Burmese, we should see a very dif-ferent state of things in Burma to-day. Had people of Tibetan stock entered Assam earlier, the course of history there likewise would have been entirely different.

The temperate forest round my base camp in the Seinghku valley was full of interesting trees, such as *Schefflera Wardii*, and Schima, both in bloom. In the meadows were thickets and hedges of Buddleia, Euonymus, Viburnum, Rosa, and Berberis. Other plants collected were Aristolochia, *Clematis napaulensis*, and *C. urophylla*. But it was evident that I had not yet reached the Alps. This might do for my lowest camp, though during the Summer the meadow was quick with leeches, as was also the forest for at least another thousand feet; but it would never do as a main collecting centre. I therefore decided to establish an alpine camp some miles farther up the valley: and this was easily arranged, because the Tibetans were just

34

now preparing to take their flocks up to the high pastures, where they had camps of their own. A hut was built for me at 11,000 feet, a day and a half's march for coolies carrying loads; and I prepared for a six weeks' botanical campaign. Eight days passed, however, before I could leave my base camp, and I fretted and fumed, believing it was already well past the time when I should be in the alps; but all to no purpose, for the Tibetans were still busy in their fields, and could only spare a few old women, so that I had to send messengers down the valley to hunt up the indispensable Nung. He comes obediently enough when summoned, but it takes time to dig him out of his jungle; and I raged inwardly. Little did I realise the immense quantity of snow which lodges in the upper Seinghku valley, and the time it takes to melt! As it turned out, it would have been very little use my being even in Snowy Camp (9,000 feet) before the first week in June: although there is no denying that many of the scarlet alpine Rhododendrons were even now blazing furiously in the snow!

Meanwhile there was plenty to do here, and having observed a limestone ridge overlooking my camp, I set out one day with two natives, to climb it. We soon reached the top of the cultivated slope, where Maize was planted, and plunged at once into the forest. Not much cutting was needed here, except to mark the route, and we made good progress, as far as the belt of tree Rhododendrons and Magnolias—*R. sino-grande* and *M. rostrata*, with Michelia, *Bucklandia populnea* and other trees casting such a dense shade that the undergrowth could make no headway. Immediately afterwards however a change came over the scene. The slopes which hitherto had been steep and steady were now broken up by huge rocks piled distractedly on top of each other and swamped under a dense tanglewood of stunted trees and gnarled shrubs. Moss clothed everything. It formed a soft carpet over the rocks, and dripped from the trees. It would have been difficult to climb up so awkward a ruin had it been bare; in face of this barricade it was impossible. For an hour the men worked, hacking a narrow path through the tanglewood, while I collected such plants as I could reach. *Rhododendron vesiculiferum*, with pinkish purple flowers, grew here, so too did a far more beautiful plant, *R. megacalyx*. In a frame of narrow silver-frosted leaves the globes of *R. sidereum* shone like yellow suns, and a hard glitter as of hammered gold radiated from *R. aureum*. These were the only Rhododendrons in flower. Another very interesting plant in the tanglewood was *Ilex nothofagifolia*, a small tree with flat branches and tiny rounded thin leaves.

At last we succeeded in cutting our way through the tanglewood. A short climb amongst the rocks, where the ground was more open, and we found ourselves on the limestone ridge, which was well wooded. Broken and battered Tsuga trees grew here, amongst a wild wilderness of shrubs and bushes, including many Rhododendrons. Higher up were Junipers, gnarled stumpy trees of *R. siderium*, bushes of *R. tephropeplum*, *R. aureum*, *R. Martinianum*, and *R. crassum*. These formed impenetrable thickets on the more sheltered slope; but we had little difficulty in getting along the sharp crest of the ridge itself. And it was here that I found the most beautiful shrub of all—the Silver Barberry. There are dozens of Barberries in cultivation; every eastern tide throws up new ones, though it is often a matter of nice discrimination to tell Tweedledum from Tweedledee. Apart, however, from the incomparable Chilian species *Berberis Darwinii*, and its even finer hybrid *B. stenophylla*, a few Oriental Barberries really are distinct, and *B. hypokerina* can join this noble band with a good conscience, and, it is to be hoped, a good constitution. The first plants I saw had neither flowers nor fruit, so there seemed no reason why it should not be a Holly—or, rather, Holly, as understood in England; that was what it most nearly resembled, judged by its leaves alone. But one must picture these Holly leaves rather long and narrow, set jauntily on sealing-wax red stems without thorns, the upper surface not polished but of a translucent malachite green, with a delicate network of jade veins traced on it, and the under surface softly whitened as though a flocculent film of silver had been freshly precipitated on it. The flowers, as I saw later, of a cheerful but not distinguished yellow, borne in firm clusters, are followed by little plum-purple pear-shaped fruits. The old leaves then turn scarlet, and the plant is as lovely in Winter as in Spring.

The Silver Barberry was not common. It grew scattered all up the ridge, a short stiff shrub crouching down against the ruptured limestone; though few of the plants bore flowers and fruit. Mature plants have half a dozen spreading little branched stems, not exceeding eighteen inches in height, but leafy from base to apex. I never met with this plant again, and it deliberately avoided growing in thickets with the common herd of Rhododendrons. It is growing in England now, but it is not common there either—at most a few dozen plants. Its nearest relation is *B. insignis* from Sikkim, a plant which, lacking the silver deposit on the leaves, has much less charm.

On the rockwork of the ridge there was found also a peculiar variety of *Cotoneaster horizontalis* which belied its name; it certainly was not horizontal, but poked out many long shoots, which gave it a lean and hungry look. In October its angular legginess was hidden under a wealth of scarlet berries. One other interesting shrub grew here, a species of Enkianthus. It bore globular cherry-red flowers, singly or in pairs, in the leaf axils. The pedicels, though rather long, are rigid, and the plump flowers, when ravished by sunlight, looked just like red Chinese lanterns hanging by bent wires from a tree. At a little distance however, a good flowering specimen looks more like a cherry bush in full fruit. In autumn the leaves turn scarlet, and the wiry pedicels, by a sharp upward thrust, reverse the ripe capsules. This Enkianthus also grows in the Mishmi Hills.

So much time had been spent cutting through the tanglewood defences, that we could not follow the ridge up as far as I should have liked, but on subsequent visits I found several interesting plants here, including *Acer*

Wardii, species of Lonicera, Hypericum, Deutzia, Hydrangea, Vaccinium, Smilax, Prunus, and a new species of Clematis (*C. biternifolia*) not seen in flower. Subsequently I discovered that this ridge was part of a thin belt of limestone which ran diagonally up the valley, that is in a direction almost due north and south, culminating near the pass in peaks 16,000 and 17,000 feet high. The rock is a closely bedded crystalline limestone, which is squeezed between schists and slates, making up the bulk of the mountains. The only shrubs I found on the limestone, and nowhere else, were the Silver Barberry and *Rhododendron Martinianum*; but in the alpine region the limestone peaks had a flora of their own.

The next few days were spent trying new routes up the heavily forested flanks of the mountains which enclosed the valley, but without much success; in the end the limestone ridge was considered the limited objective of this particular camp, and we improved the path.

One great advantage of living with the Tibetans was that I got fresh milk and butter every day. Wild Raspberries were plentiful; and at this time I was able to have fresh Raspberries and milk frequently. About this time the yak, goats, and sheep were being driven up to the lower pastures, but the path through the forest was too steep and narrow for the yak to carry loads. At last, my alpine cabin being now completed, I persuaded the Tibetans to supply ten coolies, and with a few Nungs who had come up from the Tamai, we started on June 1. The Tibetans were reaping their Spring crop of Barley—if that can be called reaping which consists in plucking every head separately and throwing it into a basket.

As I intended to stay in the alps at least six weeks, and there were four mouths to feed, we required a good deal of rice, flour, and other basic supplies, besides our bedding, tents, abundant drying paper, and the usual collecting, photographic, and camp equipment. What we actually took with us that day consisted of tent, bedding, drying paper, and food for a week: the remainder was to follow us up as soon as we could get coolies, and the spare parts were stored in the headman's house.

What a day that was, the glorious first of June! My hopes ran high, and my heart beat joyfully, as we cleared the pastures and plunged ankle deep into the black mud of the rain forest! A day to remember when much else has gone into the limbo of forgotten things! Not only did it see the fulfilment of a long-cherished ambition, the ambition to set foot on that remote and mysterious mountain range, the Irrawaddy–Brahmaputra divide; but that fulfilment beggared my wildest dreams!

Yet there was nothing in those first few miles by the ravening torrent to whet the appetite, or even to hint at what lay beyond. When we entered the primeval forest, I was struck by the immense bulk of the big trees, all swaddled in moss. The exotic-looking leaves of *Schefflera Wardii*, the creepers and Ferns and epiphytes, and exuberant growth along the banks of the torrent, suggested an almost tropical luxuriance; but this was deceptive, because we were, really, in the temperate rain forest. As we ascended by an execrable path—it was wonderful how the clumsy yak had ever climbed it —the forest underwent a rapid change. Enormous Oaks and Cinnamon-trees, Michelias, *Magnolia Campbellii*, already in leaf with a few lingering flowers— always white—Rhododendrons, and Ilex-trees, supported a host of epiphytes, but few climbing plants. Nevertheless, amongst the latter was *Aristolochia Griffithii*, with blatantly ugly flowers, dour in colour, fœtid, shaped like a goblin pipe, but undeniably efficient. Amidst so much sentimental beauty, the hideous, calculating, mechanical efficiency of this plant was almost a relief! I cut off several flowers and hung them up outside my tent and noticed how bluebottles and other flies were attracted by the horrid stink!

It was now late in the afternoon. A fine drizzle filled the air, which was noticeably colder. Although we had been climbing for some time we were still in the rain forest. Quite suddenly we emerged from the heavy dripping gloom of the forest into a blaze of light. A wilderness of tall herbs and bushes hid the steep track, and the icy breath of the alps smote us. Even the red glow of Rhododendrons was cold and comfortless as the Winter sun; for here was snow, not in wads and fraying patches, but in enormous mounds which looked as though they would never melt! The river rushed headlong down the V-shaped valley, whose flanks rose at an angle of 40°; out of the higher slopes tall cliffs thrust themselves threateningly. Two huge snow fans, one on either side of the valley, had united to throw a safe bridge, many feet thick, across the frantic river; and on a grassy alp, amidst a tangle of shrubs and rocks, where temperate forest and Fir forest met, I pitched my tent beside a decrepit bothy. As soon as the men had lit a fire, I clamoured for tea, feeling both cold and hungry; I *must* make a first dash amongst the alpine flowers before dark! With half an hour's daylight to go—for the cloud rack swaddled the hills, and the twilight in these latitudes is of short duration—I ran across the snow bridge and up the steep cone towards a high bank of earth, which sloped up to the cliffs; but I had scarcely reached the bank when I stopped suddenly in amazement. Was I dreaming! I rubbed my eyes, and looked again. No! Just above the edge of the snow, a vivid blush pink flower stood out of the cold grey earth. It was as big as a Rose, and of that fresh clear pink seen in Madame Butterfly. Of course it could not really be a Rose, and I was glad of that; it would too easily account for the superb colour! Tea roses do not grow just like that, in spite of all the wonderful things that do happen in this Aladdin's treasure-house. But what could it be? Yet so fascinating was it to stand there and gaze on this marvel in an aching pain of wonder that I felt no desire to step forward and break the spell. Indeed, for a minute I was paralysed with an emotion which perhaps only those who have come across some beloved alpine prize in Switzerland can faintly appreciate. I can recall several flowers which at first sight have knocked the breath out of me, but only two or three which have taken me by storm as did this one. The sudden vision is like a physical

Meconopsis betonicifolia pratensis (THE TURQUOISE POPPY).
BURMA FRONTIER, 11,000–12,000 FEET. JUNE-JULY.

GLACIER LAKE BELOW THE DIPHUK LA, 13,000 FEET.
BURMA FRONTIER.

blow, a blow in the pit of the stomach; one can only gasp and stare. In the face of such unsurpassed loveliness, one is afraid to move, as with bated breath one mutters the single word 'God!'—a prayer rather than an exclamation. And when at last with fluttering heart one does venture to step forward, it is on tiptoe, and hat in hand, to wonder and to worship.

And so it was now. I just stood there transfixed on the snow-cone, in a honeymoon of bliss, feasting my eyes on a masterpiece. The vulgar thought —is it new ?—did not at this moment occur to me, if only for the reason that I had not the faintest, foggiest notion to what genus, or even to what family, it belonged! It was enough for me that I had never set eyes on its like. However, as long as I stood there, overcome by emotion, I could state no fact about the plant, apart from its sheer colour and brilliance. Yet it was with a certain reluctance that I now approached it more nearly, breaking the fragile spell I had woven about the Tea Rose Primula—for a Primula I perceived it to be as soon as I realised that the flower was a head of flowers. And *what* a Primula! The rosy globe resolved itself into a tight head of flowers, eight in number, borne on a short but sturdy stem. Each flower measured an inch across. Later the saw-edged ribbon-like wash-leathery leaves grew up, the stem lengthened until it stood four inches high, and behold *Primula Agleniana* var. *thearosa*, the Tea Rose Primula! In the autumn the leaves wither and the spherical capsules, filled to the brim with coffee-brown seeds, crumble like scorched paper. There remains only the hard pointed leaf-bud to pass the winter beneath the snow.

The Tea Rose Primula is an alpine which grows normally on steep rubble slopes amongst the gneiss cliffs, at an altitude of about 10,000 feet. The coarse soil lies at such an angle that it must obviously be well drained, though at the same time water is certainly flowing steadily through it all the Summer; it is a rather hungry soil, not containing any large quantity of humus, and the plant sends its long roots far down into this poor material to extract what nourishment it needs. It grows, not singly, but in colonies thinly scattered up the stony gulch, which is lined with dense thickets of *Rhododendron sanguineum* and *R. tephropeplum*; and again more thickly along the base of the cliff, flowering before the end of May and ripening its seed in September. It is buried under the snow for at least six months in the year.

It might at first sight be thought helpful to growers if one were to record what alpine plants are found growing together. In actual fact, though interesting enough, such records have no practical value, and for this reason, that in the alps, plants seem much more susceptible to slight alterations of soil and aspect than in more crowded areas, and such alterations take place very abruptly. Two plants, separated by only a few yards, may be living under quite different conditions; on the other hand, in many an alpine meadow conditions must be practically the same for all, which may be why so many alpines grow in considerable numbers. This is true of Primulas and other alpine and bog plants, as well as of Rhododendrons. Such meadow plants, for instance, as *Primula involucrata Wardii*, *P. microdonta alpicola*, *P. Florindœ*, *P. silaensis*, *P. melanodonta*, *P. Beesiana*, and many more, grow in vast drifts: it would be difficult to name a meadow plant which does not! Dwarf Rhododendrons like *R. riparium*, *R. fragariflorum*, *R. lysolepis*, and many others, do the same.

The Tea Rose Primula though local was common just here between 9,000 and 10,500 feet, associated with *Omphalogramma Souliei*, *Pinguicula alpina* and *Cassiope selaginoides*. It also grew beneath bushes of *Rhododendron sanguineum*. On the other hand, the presence of all or any of these was no proof that the Tea Rose Primula grew there!

The original *Primula Agleniana* is a fine plant, taller than the Tea Rose variety, with ivory white, faintly yellow, or flushed flowers. It, too, grows in the Burmese Oberland, but farther east along the China frontier. In the Mishmi Hills, still farther west, is found the Gamboge Primula, a lovely golden-flowered plant. Both varieties are as sharply marked off from one another as each is from *P. Agleniana*, and their brilliant colouring ranks them as superior to the type, whose pale flowers are rather of the ready-to-wear order.

These three Primulas, together with one other, the Daffodil Primula from Tibet (*P. falcifolia*), form a natural group within the large Asiatic section 'Nivales,' which contains many handsome plants. These, however, are scarcely known in Britain, being unaccountably difficult to grow, and of the thirty or more species which have been tried, none perhaps is more stubborn than *P. Agleniana* and its near allies. All four, though they have the typical flowers and foliage of the 'Nivales' section, differ remarkably in their fruits, which are globular structures almost enclosed by the calyx, and filled with seeds; these are sluiced out by rain as the capsule crumbles. The typical 'Nivales' capsule, on the other hand, is a long sausage-shaped tube, projecting far beyond the calyx, with a few seeds at the base which are shaken out by the wind; moreover, it is persistent.

At the moment *P. Agleniana* is in cultivation, but one fears that in a very few years it will be as extinct (in England) as the dodo.

Back in camp as darkness fell, I sat down to gloat over the day's finds, and attend to the more prosaic routine of preserving and cataloguing them. The Irrawaddy–Lohit divide had begun well; and I went to bed that night supremely happy.

When morning came I decided to spend a few more days in this camp. Not only was there an enormous quantity of snow up the valley, but there were lots of alpine flowers here. In the course of the next week I ascended both the snow-cones, and discovered many fine plants.

Above my camp, forest occurred only in patches, both in the valley and on the slopes. It consisted mostly of Silver Fir, Spruce, Juniper, and Larch, with *Rhododendron arizelum*; but a few broad-leafed deciduous trees were also scattered about, including several species of Acer and a Pyrus with very big leaves—a fine foliage plant. Where there was no forest, the slopes were covered with a dense scrub growth, mostly Rhododendron, including the two crimson-flowered species *R. chœtomallum*, with furry red leaves, and *R. sanguineum*, with silvery leaves. Broken faces were covered with a dense tanglewood consisting of *Magnolia globosa*, a large shrub, its leaves covered with long champagne-coloured silken hairs; *Viburnum Wardii*; *Rhododendron euchaites*, flowers yellow rimmed and streaked with brick red, giving a general effect of tawny orange; species of Rose, Barberry, Enkianthus, Cotoneaster, Maple, Pyrus, Prunus, and Rhododendron. The very first day in my new camp I found *Primula eucyclia*, *P. Genestieriana*, and *P. euosma*.

As already remarked, the mountains rose steeply from the torrent, and were covered with dense impenetrable scrub. Water had everywhere gashed the flanks, leaving bare cliffs whose wet brows were bound with scarlet Rhododendron. These gullies, presently to be swept by avalanches of stones, but now clogged with snow, afforded the only possible route through the dense barrage of scrub up to the cliffs. Later they, too, became unscalable, or at any rate desperately dangerous, being filled with huge rocks wrenched from the cliffs above, which overbalanced at a touch, and set the very fabric of the mountain shaking and sliding. They were safe now, however, for the packed snow cemented the rocks, and I could climb up and up till the splintered cliffs lay far below, and the rock became firmer as I approached the crest. But it was quite low down under the splash of a cascade that, in darkness and saturation, I found mossy beds of *P. eucyclia* starred with lilac and violet flowers, the petals fringed, the eye yellow or red as in an allied species, *P. Normaniana*. It is a delicious dwarf, bearing its flowers in pairs, or occasionally in threes, on crimson threads. Coral red runners radiate from the plant, and throw up sprigs of chubby leaves, which take root; thus cuttings strike easily and afford a ready means of propagation. The tiny leaves borne on crimson stalks are deeply cut after the manner of a Geranium. *P. eucyclia* flowered profusely on banks and rocks, beneath the heavy shade of Rhododendrons and *Magnolia globosa*, within splash of the cascade. Rarely did it venture away from the moss beds, weaving a thin carpet over the grit; when it did it flowered with more restraint, but set fruit more freely. It is a forest Primula related to the Himalayan *P. vaginata*, and not occurring above 10,000 feet.

A single Rhododendron bush found standing by itself in one of these gullies, proved to be a magnificent form of the very variable *R. eclecteum*. Though only eight feet high, it bore large flowers of a glowing rose in massive trusses amongst leaves six inches long. But it was rather the vegetation in mass which was so wonderful. Huge beds of glittering snow lined the valley, chilling the air, and the clouds which clung to the mountain-tops sifted out a fine but persistent rain. In cloud and gloom a blaze of scarlet

Rhododendron rolled like a river of fire down the slope, and sent long red tongues leaping and threatening. Up on the cliffs floated puffs of white *R. bullatum*, and the silver, jade, and clear amber of *R. megeratum*, which rejoiced under the cascades. Some of the blood-red Rhododendrons seemed to burn their way through the snow, and set torrents coursing down the furrows. I spent a joyous week in Snowy Camp, collecting new and rare plants every day; and then on June 9 we moved up the snowbound valley to River Camp, where my log hut had been built at an altitude of 11,000 feet.

5 Hanging Gardens of the Forest

THE darkness of the temperate rain forest, due to its heavy roof of foliage, including the big-leafed Rhododendrons, is much increased throughout the summer by the mist and rain which shroud it in perpetual gloom. To this darkness must be attributed in part at least the thinness of the undergrowth and especially the lack of flowers. True, the jungle is as dark; and the jungle appears at first sight to be stuffed with a dense and impenetrable undergrowth. But this is largely an illusion. The jungle is dense because the trees grow close together, and because the space between the trunks is utilised by huge climbers, many of which, having reached the tops of the trees, come tumbling down again in cascades of foliage. The heat too encourages the growth of large foliage plants; and finally there is no cessation of growth, or at most only a slight check, in the Winter. Flowers are just as rare in the jungle as they are in the temperate forest; and there is nothing in the former corresponding to the the blaze of Spring Rhododendrons in the latter.

In the jungle the big trees are usually crowded with plants growing on their branches, on their trunks, and even on their leaves, which may be encrusted with mosses and lichens. The most familiar examples of these perching plants are the Orchids. They have been forced to ascend the trees by the darkness below; many other plants with large showy flowers have been likewise driven upwards to the roof, in search of the necessary light. These perching plants are popularly called parasites; but since they ask neither food nor drink from the trees on which they perch themselves, but only the light and air which their position ensures, they are not really parasites at all, but epiphytes. Epiphytes are almost as common in the temperate rain forest as they are in the jungle, though very few of them are Orchids. Apart from mosses and Ferns, the most conspicuous, if not the most numerous, are the Rhododendrons and their allies.

The perching Rhododendrons generally have scaly leaves and thin seeds which are long in proportion to their breadth, with a conspicuous wing at each end. Nearly all of them belong to the series 'Maddeni,' 'Boothii,' and 'Vaccinioides'; a few like R. *bullatum* and its close relatives have furry leaves; but beneath a thick coat of fur, the leaves are also scaly. 'Maddeni' Rhododendrons are first met with in the hill jungle, where R. *notatum* descends to 4,000 feet. It is a bushy shrub with white delicately scented flowers, which never exceed four in a truss. Often the corolla is marked on the outside with broad bands of purple, which at a short distance give a pink flush to the whole flower. At the base of the corolla is a yellow spot, like a pale candle-flame. In the hill jungle one first becomes aware of the presence of *R. notatum* by seeing its corollas strewn on the ground; the plant itself is usually invisible, perched fifty feet up in a tree, and completely hidden from below by the dense foliage. It will, however, be quite certain to poke its head out in the daylight above, and could one only look down on to the tree one would see a spout of white foam in the maelstrom of green. Sooner or later an accessible plant will be found, perhaps on a boulder in the bed of a mountain stream, perhaps on the crest of a ridge. Although found as low down as 4,000 feet, *R. notatum* is commoner 1,500 or 2,000 feet higher, where it is equally at home on tree or rock. Many Orchids will grow as readily on rock in the open as on trees; they seek the light, and if this is to be had for the asking on a bare cliff, they would as lief grow there as in the treetops. An epiphytic Rhododendron can be grown in the rock garden like any other small Rhododendron—what is an alpine Rhododendron but one which has climbed up and up out of the pit into the light of day! But the forest epiphyte retains the characteristics of the rain forest plants, and is not likely to be very hardy.

R. notatum is a Winter-flowering species. I have seen it in bloom as early as November, and as late as May—not the same plants, of course. The most beautiful specimen I ever saw was by the Nam Tamai, where that river comes zooming out of the densely forested gorges above the Seinghku confluence. The water was ice clear, gleaming like jade where the sun smote on a deep pool, crested with frosty foam where it slammed against the boulders, and all the time singing, singing. An Alder-tree leaned out of the forest on one side and stretched half-way across the river; from the opposite wall another tree lurched over to meet it till the two mingled their branches high overhead. Immediately above and below, the river gurgled over the rocks, which bared their teeth in a defiant grin; but beneath the arch it slid by in a smooth trough. From either tree-trunk spouted a fountain of Rhododendron blossom, the one pearl white, the other blush, turning the arch into a natural pergola; and from time to time a pink or white corolla fluttered down like a hurt butterfly, and swam away on the current. Such was *R. notatum*. It may however be remarked that *R. notatum* is so like *R. dendricola*, another Burmese epiphyte, as to be hardly worth distinguishing.

In the lower temperate rain forest, at 5,000 to 6,000 feet, epiphytic Rhododendrons become common. *R. vaccinioides*, a quaint little bush of rather straggling habit, with small glossy Box-like leaves and minute white or pinkish flowers, may be found as low as this; but it is more commonly met with rather higher up. Its close relatives, however, *R. insculptum* and *R. asperulum*, occur here. *R. insculptum* has orange flowers supporting a ring of brick-red anthers; the spoon-shaped leaves are comparatively large and fat, with the veins deeply engraved. It is not a common plant, neither is the somewhat similar *R. asperulum* which has pink flowers opening a month later. Not one of them is a garden plant, nor are any of them likely to be hardy. At first sight *R. asperulum* might easily be mistaken for *R. vaccinioides* itself, but when both have been seen in flower, no confusion between them is possible. To begin with, *R. asperulum* is not found above 6,000 feet, whereas *R. vaccinioides* is not found below 6,000 feet. *R. asperulum* blooms six weeks earlier than *R. vaccinioides* and its flowers are twice as big, though otherwise the two plants are much alike. The three species mentioned are all found in the Seinghku valley, and the two latter have been found nowhere else; but the group illustrates once more the link between the Sikkim and Yunnan floras. Other related species are found as far away as Japan, and the group is evidently an ancient one which has survived in these forests.

All the 'Vaccinioides' Rhododendrons depart widely from the familiar in most respects, but in nothing is this so obvious as in their fruits. The capsule is an inch long, but not much thicker than a knitting-needle, about six times as long as it is wide, and of a bright crimson tint. Nor are the seeds less extraordinary. When ripe, the capsule opens to its full extent, the five splinter-like valves curling right back, and leaving the central axis with a tress of fluffy golden hair sticking to it. The tiny smooth rounded seeds have a number of fine golden yellow threads attached to each end, and it is these, lying lengthwise in the capsule, which, becoming dishevelled, give an appearance of floss silk.

It has frequently been said that epiphytic Orchids are peculiarly adapted to their mode of life. Their thick leathery or flesh leaves, often much reduced or deciduous, enable them to withstand drought; their sensitive roots, which continue to grow till they touch something and then stick, avoiding light, are freely produced; their bloated stems, often swollen out into pseudobulbs, which store up water; and their minute dust-like seeds, easily carried by the faintest zephyr, all help to fit them for an arboreal life. If that is so, then Rhododendrons also are well adapted to that mode of life. Though few of them are deciduous, yet their leathery leaves, usually covered below with a thick fur, or with an intricately woven pelt, or with wax, or even with a coat of mail, are both cold and drought-resisting; that is to say, they prevent excessive loss of water by evaporation. Further, these leaves also have the power of lowering themselves on their stalks, till they lie almost parallel to the stem, and of curling their edges inwards, and finally of rolling themselves into a complete tube: all of which are devices to reduce surface and hence to lessen evaporation.

Rhododendrons root easily, and the roots, keeping close to the surface, are able to absorb the film of moisture left on the spongy soil by every passing cloud. Their small seeds, though not so minute as those of Orchids, are nearly always winged for flight; only the high alpine species have wingless seeds, and they are so small and light that, when dry, a puff of wind scatters them. True, the Rhododendrons have no special water reservoirs such as the Orchids have; but being woody plants they are able to retain water more easily in their tissues without such aid. Both Orchids and Rhododendrons produce vast numbers of seeds; and this also is a necessary precaution for success in the epiphytic world. One might then expect most Rhododendrons to be epiphytic, since they seem well adapted to an arboreal life. Yet they certainly are not. The truth is that woody plants do not usually need to adopt an epiphytic mode of existence. They can meet their most powerful competitors on level terms, and fight for a place in the sun with weapons as good as, or even better than, theirs. In the mountains they have found conditions which suit them, and have varied widely, to meet all possible emergencies, thus greatly strengthening their position. They have outstripped their rivals everywhere; and nowhere more than in the alpine region. The intense cold of the high alps, the gloom of the rain forest, the steamy heat of the jungle, have no terrors for them; and it would be strange if with all their audacity they had not experimented with epiphytism. A few have permanently adopted this risky life, mostly with reservations; and the temperate rain forest is their home. But neither the mass production of seeds nor extreme lightness can be regarded as a direct adaptation to epiphytism. For the majority of Orchids are earthbound and yet produce seeds of this type, and the majority of Rhododendrons which are also earthbound have seeds like their epiphytic relations.

Rhododendron vaccinioides and its allies are the most highly adapted of all; they are fitted for an epiphytic life and for no other. Their small size— they are confined to a region where most of the Rhododendrons are trees —their tiny crowded leathery leaves and above all their tailed seeds, enabling them not only to be borne on the lightest breeze, but also to entangle themselves in the bark of the nearest tree, are proof of this. They are quite unlike any other Rhododendron; indeed no layman, seeing *R. vaccinioides* for the first time, in or out of flower, would ever guess that it is a Rhododendron at all. He might derisively ask *why* it should be called one; and although the structure of the flower does recall that of a typical Rhododendron, the plant has so many peculiarities that the botanist would find it difficult to supply convincing arguments in support of his contention. The truth is that no botanist has seen fit to question Hooker's decision that *R. vaccinioides*, which he first found in the Sikkim Himalaya eighty years ago, is a true Rhododendron. It is widely distributed in the temperate rain forest between 7,000 and 8,000 feet, from Sikkim to the Burmese Oberland. Specimens from Burma were originally described as a new species, *R. sino-vaccinioides*—not a very happy name; but there can be no doubt of their identity with the Sikkim plant. Its flowers open in July, that is during the rainy season, and are the smallest known in the genus, not exceeding a third of an inch in diameter, and of a watery pink or almost white colour.

In the upper temperate forest, epiphytic Rhododendrons are so plentiful as to form a conspicuous feature of the vegetation, at least while they are in flower. One species in particular is outstanding both for its abundance and for its heartiness under the most dismal conditions. This is *R. bullatum*, which bears large fragrant white flowers, in pairs, or sometimes in threes, never more. First met with at 7,000 feet where it flowers in May, it is last seen at 10,000 feet where it is still in flower in the middle of June. It is a brave sight at the beginning of the rainy season to see across the green billows of jostling tree-tops a cloud of *R. bullatum* floating on its couch of moss on some dismantled and derelict Larch-tree. Peeping out through the feathered jade of young foliage, the chains of flowers look like hot-house Orchids. Later, the driving rain begins to knock the flowers from their hold, and they come tumbling down; though flights of large moonstone blossoms cling aloft, further reduced each day until by the end of the month the last one has been blown down.

Its hard leaves are deeply grooved by the veins above, and beneath are covered with a thick cinnamon red fur, very different from that of any other epiphytic Rhododendron. Moreover, under the fur are scales. Not less remarkable is the large leafy red calyx which, though overshadowed by the widely distended corolla, eventually almost envelops the globe-like capsule.

This is not the only woolly-leafed epiphyte. More strange, though less beautiful, is *R. seinghkuense*. This species is often found growing on derelict Fir-trees which have been crippled by the lash of the wind, and had their wounds dressed with moss to hide the disfigurement, though presently it becomes their shroud. It is not a tidy plant. Its thin scraggy stems bear few leaves, though these are covered below with wool of an even more fiercely foxy red than those of *R. bullatum*; and again beneath the fur, scales are hidden. The flowers are small and few, but of a good douce yellow; and with a more trim growth, with a less precarious hold on life, *R. seinghkuense* might grow into an attractive plant. For Nature hardly gives it a fair chance. It grows commonly on the open ridge at 9,000 feet, and is frequently torn from its hold by the sloughing away of immense cancerous growths of moss and bark. Under the protection of the forest, where it is occasionally met with, it is neater.

Other interesting Rhododendrons which grow on trees for choice, hang down in long festoons. Such are *R. pendulum*, the 'climbing Edgeworthii' (K.W. 5440) and an unnamed species from the Tsangpo gorge (K.W. 6250). They nearly all have beautiful foliage, woolly and inlaid with glittering scales beneath, and their long branches trail, like comets' tails beset with shining stars, from the boughs of the trees in the heart of the forest. There is also a tiny plant with very narrow scaly leaves, and immense capsules, nearly two inches long and half an inch across. I only found it in fruit, but as it flowers when quite young, and less than a foot high, it ought to display itself in England this year (K.W. 6310). It looks to be closely allied to *R. Lindleyi*, a beautiful but rather tender species.

One of the best epiphytic species is *R. mishmiense*, a plant closely allied to the rare *R. Boothii* from Bhutan, but distinguished at sight by the thick beard of bright gamboge bristles on the pedicels. As in all the species of this alliance, the flowers are comparatively small: but those of *R. mishmiense* are larger than usual and more numerous, there being commonly six in a neat truss, of a vivid chrome yellow, with mahogany red anthers. It is a leggy stripling, as plants which back out of the struggle and mope alone on the granite cliffs are sure to be; but it will probably respond to kind treatment in England. More common in the tree-tops than on the rocks, I often picked up its flowers in the forest without ever catching sight of it.

R. monanthum, also in the 'Boothii' *galère*, is a horse of another colour. The flowers, though of a clear quince yellow, with a mouthful of red anthers, are wee and solitary, and the whole plant scraggy and fustian. It is a Winter flowering species, remarkable for nothing; even its distribution from the Tsangpo gorge to the Mekong is normal.

Although the virginal *R. leucaspis*, also from the gorge of the Tsangpo, was actually collected in fruit, growing on a cliff, there seems no reasonable doubt that this white flowered 'Boothii' is also truly epiphytic. It has always been a matter of regret to me that I went through the gorge of the Tsangpo in the Winter instead of in early Spring, when the Rhododendrons bloom. Here is temperate rain forest *de luxe*, and there are many interesting and doubtless beautiful epiphytic Rhododendrons. At the upper entrance to the 200-mile gorge the cliffs are covered chiefly with a thin coat of *Pinus Armandi* and Rhododendron: then come more varied forests with Larch, Maple, Birch, and thickets of Bamboo, with Rhododendrons in greater variety, including the first epiphytes. In the very bowels of the Himalaya, where the gorge is 10,000 feet deep and the frenzied river sometimes only 50 feet wide, the temperate forest includes magnificent trees of *Pinus excelsa* and *Magnolia rostrata*, with a wealth of Rhododendrons, from big trees to small perching plants. One can picture the violent scene in early Spring. The galloping river, jammed between cliffs, under the lid of the world, all the forest of the Himalaya in one sweep from subtropical jungle to the last straggling Fir-trees, and in the middle the Rhododendron forest tumbling over the cliffs in cascades of red-hot lava, from the eternal snow to the earth-shaking river.

I collected about twenty-five species of Rhododendron in the gorge of the Tsangpo. Several have flowered in England already, and have turned out to be beautiful—most of them new species. As they were all out of flower when I collected them, the cynical will say I was lucky! But then it is much harder to see a Rhododendron, especially a small one, in the gloomy forest, when it is out of flower!

As already remarked, many of the scale-leaved Rhododendrons of the lower forest flower during the Winter, when the weather is fine. *R. notatum*, for example, and *R. chrysolepis*, flower before Christmas. About February, *R. arboreum*, *R. Lindleyi*, and the white-flowered *R. leucaspis* open their buds; in April, *R. Nuttallii* follows. Not so often do Rhododendrons flower in the Autumn, before the rains are over. Yet this is what a small epiphyte did in the Mishmi Hills. *R. concinnoides* is a scraggy little plant, with small bronzed leaves and tiny purplish-pink tubular flowers; it is abundant on big Fir-trees between 9,000 and 11,000 feet. We had watched it anxiously right through the Summer, till in September at the lag end of the rains, it flowered. It had been a dreary month with mist and rain day after day, and scarcely ever a gleam of sunshine. I had gone up the ridge as usual from our camp one day, when the tearful leaves were shivering and chattering in the cold mist, and the valley lay smoking below. I climbed slowly, the better to observe the forest—I never went up that ridge without seeing something new to me—when my eye was caught by a number of small pale pink corollas scattered on the ground. For once there was no question of searching for the source. I knew to what they belonged, having marked down a dozen plants within easy reach a month before; also the capsules, now nearly a year old, were presently collected for seed. *R. concinnoides* has small oval, rather thick leaves, bronzed below with close set golden scales, and an almost tubular corolla, pale purplish-pink above, fading to white at the base. This was one of the commonest as well as one of the loftiest epiphytic Rhododendrons in the rain forest. It occurred abundantly on the trunks and branches of old Fir-trees, usually quite low down, especially if the tree itself grew on the ridge. It came into flower in late September, a month before the end of the rains, and continued far into October. Plants found in June bore fat capsules, which must have been quite six months old; for it is hardly likely that a plant which grows as high as 10,000 feet would be in flower after Christmas, when the temperate forest is under snow! The species is of interest by reason of the colour of its flowers, which are pinkish-purple. Almost every other known epiphytic Rhododendron has either white or yellow flowers. Orange, scarlet, blue, and violet are never found amongst epiphytes (they would be invisible in the tree tops), and even this pinkish colour is a distinct departure from the normal.

Found growing as high as *R. concinnoides* is a curious little epiphyte allied to *R. cerinum*. This has the distinction of being, not merely uninteresting, but positively ugly. The flowers are small to begin with, and are made to look ridiculous by having the corolla lobes reflexed against the tube. Their colour is a jeering yellow, suggestive of a bilious headache, and this groundwork is made still more unpleasant by a rash of greenish-yellow pimples erupting over the interior. Such an unhealthy-looking flower (I thought), even if not actually contagious, is best avoided. Having written this much, and cast it into the nethermost pit, I thought no more about it. But life is full of surprises, and it must be a grim Rhododendron indeed which has not one redeeming feature! One wet and blustering Autum day, while struggling along the 11,000-feet ridge towards Polon, I was surprised to see a scarred Fir-tree, sombre in its rifle green, lit by a bunch of bright scarlet—whether leaves or flowers I could not make out at that distance. But when I came closer, what was my astonishment to observe that the colour was caused by my much despised and quarantined Rhododendron! Leaves and fruits had turned vivid scarlet! I found that if exposed to the weather on the open ridge, they always did this, expecially at the higher levels; but that in the shelter of the forest the leaves hardly change colour at all and probably remain green throughout the Winter!

This Rhododendron has another claim to distinction in its numerous flowers, loosely borne on long wiry pedicels; the flowers, revolting though they may be, number six or eight in a truss, and their slenger stalks are a full inch long. They are followed by thin slightly curved scarlet capsules, something like those of R. vaccinioides, except that the seeds are not tailed. This species, for which, when the flowers had gone, I conceived quite a liking, is abundant, in the Mishmi Hills, between 9,000 and 11,000 feet. It occurs also in the Burmese Oberland, and perhaps in the Tsangpo gorge.

With these two is associated a third species, the lovely R. megeratum, whose bright yellow flowers beaded with mahogany red anthers are borne in pairs amongst bristling electro-plated leaves. Immense bushy bunches of R. megeratum sprout from the blasted Fir-trees along the windy ridge, or cling to the bare granite cliffs, which heave themselves out of the forest. Indeed, that all these epiphytes seek is light and air is proved by their indifference to arboreal support, if raw rock is available. Wherever a cliff stands naked in the forest, there under the rain which drops from its lip hang bunches of R. megeratum. And the barer the cliff, the better R. megeratum, drenched in spray and grilled by the Spring sun, blooms; only when heavily shaded is it shy of flowering. It is one of the prettiest of the smaller Rhododendrons. Its twigginess and compact bushy habit ensure neatness. There are no loose ends. A crop of merry flowers stand lapped by tiny bright green waves of foliage, silvered beneath, with scattered golden scales which glisten like flecks of mica; and over all eddies and drifts a spider web of pale Lichen.

It may be noted that R. megeratum was originally described as having solitary flowers. This, however, is a mistake; at least there is no recognisable difference between the Chinese R. megeratum and the imperial form of it from Burma and the Mishmi Hills, other than the paired or triple flowers of the latter. It flowers in May or June, according to altitude; and it is important to get seeds from as high an altitude as possible for introduction to England as there may be a tendency for the leaf-buds to break later.

Undesirable as the rain forest is as a place of residence, its beauty in Spring is undeniable. The rugged wooden pillars which support the roof, support also a world of flowers. They rise from a thin and shallow sea of Fern brake. Slender wands of Bamboo ringed with stout prickles, fill in the background between the heavy timber. Higher up a clump of snowy Orchid (*Cœlogyne ocellata*) appears from amongst the dark foliage like a flock of tiny white birds; and a purple Pleione pokes a dainty head out of a mossy hassock, in the fork of a battered Fir. This particular Pleione is almost always solitary—a single dainty pouting purple flower speckled and crested with yellow inside. From the next tree hang streamers of woolly Rhododendron. Then from over the knotted limbs, all padded and festooned with luscious moss, and a welter of leaves which chime and ring with harmonious colours, lean down strange faces; the stippled cowls of Arisaema, or the thin hungry flowers of Globba. And as you gaze upwards into the dim roof, the canopy grows ever more opaque; a desperate confusion of interlacing branches, leaves, and jostling plants all clogged with moss. But woe to the big trees which must support this burden—the Larches, and Junipers, and Firs, Oaks, Cinnamons, and many more. Few escape, except those which, like most of the Rhododendrons, are so smooth, that no moss or lichen can lodge on them, or such as the Birch which continually slough great papery sheets of bark, punched with slots like a pianola record. For moisture and darkness have filled the forest with lurking death. The very ground from out of which the tree Rhododendrons grow is permanently mulched, the air is rank with the breath of decay, and between the stems of trees and Bamboos, silently, caressingly, steals the cool wet mist. Nothing is ever dry. Everything is choked and stifled with moss; the deep silence of the rain forest, save for the kettledrum roll of raindrops on the armoured leaves of Rhododendrons, is due to this padding of the interior. And embedded in these cushions are the perching plants. It is almost fantastic to see the limbs of strong trees, bound into shapeless cocoons, by this stealthy scourge. From this spongy bed the epiphytes draw their water. Their soil is the vegetable mould derived from the decay of bark and leaves. The rain is sprayed through the tree-tops by Wind. Up here in the swaying branches are light, air, and space, never drought; and scores of plants have hauled themselves painfully upwards, out of the wet dusk where the sour odour of decay rises from the earth, to enjoy this new freedom. And here out of sight they flower as they could never flower below, often revealed to us only when their spent corollas come tumbling to the ground.

Yet these plants, in the temperate rain forest, do not always grow high up. There is no need for them to do so. If they can clear the thatch of Rhododendron leaves, thirty or forty feet above the ground, that is sufficient; above that there is ample light. On the long hog's back ridges which flare down from the great peaks, where the Fir and Larch-trees are clipped and stunted by the wind, the epiphytes perch themselves only a few feet from the ground. One can pull down great bunches of *Rhododendron megeratum* or of *R. concinnoides* as one marches along the ridge; they are bedded in moss as usual, but at this altitude over them clings a more deadly tangle of Lichen. It seems at first surprising to find so many epiphytes, other than Ferns and moss, as high as 10,000 feet, almost as high as continuous forest extends, in fact. Evidently then cold has no effect on epiphytism as such; if a plant is constructed to withstand the Winter, it can stand it as well up a tree as anywhere else. It is also clear that the one thing which *does* control the epiphytic life is water; a moist atmosphere and a sufficient supply of water to the roots. It is hardly an exaggeration to say that, other things being equal, within the limits of the forest belt, the number and variety of epiphytic plants depend directly on the saturation of the atmosphere at all seasons. In a dry climate epiphytism might conceivably be possible: it could not conceivably be necessary, for the ground vegetation is never sufficiently dense to warrant it. In the park-like open forests of the Shan Plateau or of Annam, where the atmosphere is comparatively dry and hot for several months, epiphytes are quite exceptional. Such as there are, they are mostly Orchids, and especially species of Dendrobium, which drop their leaves in the hot weather, and store water in their stems.

In the temperate rain forest, the belt rich in tree Rhododendrons is by far the most prolific source of epiphytes; that is between 7,000 and 9,000 feet altitude. Four-fifths of the epiphytic Rhododendrons are found here, besides most of the other perching plants. The general order of appearance of the epiphytic Rhododendrons is as follows: Lowest of all at 4,000 to 5,000 feet are found certain of the 'Maddeni' series, *R. notatum* and *R. dendricola*, though both extend higher. Next, at 6,000 to 7,000 feet, the 'Vaccinioides' group, *R. insculptum* and *R. asperulum*, with *R. vaccinioides* itself a little higher. Also the yellow-flowered *R. chrysolepis* and *R. Taggianum*. At 7,000 to 8,000 feet, *R. Lindleyi* and such species as *R. cerinum* and *R. bullatum* find their lower limit. At 8,000 to 9,000 feet these last become plentiful; *R. concinnoides* and *R. megeratum* are beginning to appear, the beautiful yellow-flowered *R. seinghkuense*, and the far more handsome *R. mishmiense*, besides *R. flavantherum*.

Altogether about twenty species are known to grow commonly, if not almost exclusively, as epiphytes. But it must not be imagined that because many epiphytic species occasionally lodge on the cliffs, that all cliff-growing species are capable of growing on trees; clearly the alpine species are not, though the great majority of them are rock-plants. The epiphytic species are necessarily small shrubs. But while the epiphytic Rhododendrons increase in numbers and variety as we ascend the mountain, since all Rhododendrons increase, naturally the epiphytic Orchids decrease.

Seen from outside every tree of the rain forest stands out sharply defined, distinguished either by its colour, its form, or the shape of its leaves. If it is Spring, some trees will be in flower; if it is Autumn, some will be fiery with scarlet and orange. In Summer, the surface of the forest is covered with silver or glaucous fountains when the Rhododendrons are breaking into new leaf.

The jungle looks very different, for the tree-tops are hidden beneath a curtain of creepers. Nearly all have the same rounded dome shape, though some are taller than others; a monstrous tyranny of foliage making a chess-board of black shadows and metallic reflections in the crude tropical light.

It is owing largely to the absence of big climbers from the temperate forest that each tree-top is able to keep its individuality. For woody climbers are comparatively rare. The commonest are species of Schizandra and Clematis. Others are Actinidia, Lonicera, Zanthoxylum, Hydrangea, Rosa, Holboellia, Stauntonia, Akebia, and Vitis. Perhaps it is the speed with which tropical plants grow which keeps their stems so straight. The Rhododen-drons are terribly gnarled, and the reason for this would seem to be that their shoots are ever dodging this way and that after a ray of light. It is as though they were straining themselves to be big trees, whereas they are really small ones; hunchbacks, trying to stand upright. Only the biggest trees are erect.

In the lower strata of the temperate forest are epiphytic species of Agapetes and Pentapterygium. These grow uneasily on the trees, often low down. Their lean, wiry, almost leafless stems, swell up at the base into large tumour-like growths, consisting of water-storing tissue; but their glassy urn-shaped flowers, red or pink, tipped with green teeth, and variously water-marked with zigzag patterns, are pretty. There are few forest trees, especially in the lower forest, which do not support some epiphytes; at least all of them are covered with Ferns and Mosses or, at higher levels, with Lichen. The more Moss a tree can bear, the more epiphytes are likely to cling to it: which no doubt is why damaged trees support so many. Amongst trees conspicuous for their alien vegetation are the Conifers (*Juniperus incurva, Larix Griffithii*, Tsuga, and Abies), Oaks (*Quercus semiserrata, Q. incana*, and others), Cinnamomums, Michelias (*M. Wardii*), and Laurels. In the end the Moss, and the perching plants which anchor themselves in in it, kill many of the trees. Limb by limb they strangle it, till nothing but the trunk remains. Conifers seem to suffer most, also *Ilex nothofagifolia*. The moss spreads and sprawls over their flat branches, choking the leaves. It takes time. Many of the forest giants are very, very old. They have upheld generations of epiphytes. Mutilated, battered, and bruised by storms, they still grow proudly erect, and defy their enemies. The very conditions which allowed them when young, to thrive and to attain their present size and venerable old age, are now their undoing; for the moist temperate climate of the hills, with its short but restful Winter, and its warm rain-drenched Summer, which has promoted unlimited growth, has filled the dark interior of the forest with the deadly canker of moss.

6　A Day on the Edge of the World

I AM sitting by the fire in my log hut in the Seinghku valley. A keen wind is blowing through the chinks and crannies but wrapped in a long woollen *chupa*, by the fire, sipping a nightcap of rum and hot water, I do not feel the cold. From outside comes only the shrill voice of the stream bubbling over the stones, and the occasional clatter of falling rocks high up on the screes; otherwise it is very still. By ten o'clock I am yawning, and having written up my diary, I prepare to turn in. But first I take a look round outside to see that all is well. The fine mist which usually fills the air after dark has disappeared and the sky is riddled with stars. Far down the valley a scimitar moon is being withdrawn slowly from a scabbard of cloud. "To-morrow it will be fine," I say to myself, stamping my feet, for at 11,000 feet altitude it is chilly at night even in July, and there is much snow higher up the valley; "I will go for a big climb"; and with that pleasant thought I crawl between the blankets and snuggle down for the night.

At six o'clock next morning Chokara comes in and lights the fire, above which, on a bamboo rack, paper, clothes, and bundles of specimens are drying in the smoke. Laphai follows with coffee and hot chuppatties. "It is a fine day, *Duar*," says he, and adds that Maung Ba, my cook, is sick with fever. I get out of bed with a shudder, fling on a *chupa*, gulp some scalding coffee, and begin to dress—shorts, a warm flannel shirt, woollen jacket, two pairs of thick socks, and well-nailed climbing-boots. While breakfast is being brought in—porridge and curried chicken to-day—I prepare for the climb.

The botanist need never burden himself with much apparatus in the field. A bag for plants is better than the metal vasculum sold to budding botanists in England; one or two tobacco tins are carried in the pocket for very small specimens, and a biscuit tin may be taken as well for fragile flowers. Field-glasses, a pocket lens for resolving doubtful points quickly with fresh material, a note-book and pencil, a compass, a strong knife, a pair of Rolcut secateurs for cutting prickly shrubs and the tough stems of Rhododendrons, and some string—the sort of miscellania a schoolboy might cram into his pocket—completes the list. A lunch ration consisting of several biscuits, a few raisins or figs, and a slab of chocolate is also taken, more in case of accident than to be eaten at a fixed hour.

I call Chokara and issue final instructions. "Change the plant paper and get my clothes dried. Tell Laphai to take the gun and see if he can shoot a pheasant. Have tea ready for me when I return." Then I go across to the men's hut and have a look at Maung Ba, who is rolled up like a cocoon by the fire. Some medicine is prepared for him and I depart; one advantage of living simply is that if my cook does go sick, anyone else can make curry and rice for me, brew tea or coffee, and fry chuppatties. All the same it *would* be nice to start off one morning on a breakfast of kidneys and bacon and hot buttered toast, or perhaps a fried sole and a mushroom omelette . . . one can have great fun making up imaginary menus!

And now, which way shall we go? Up the main valley, or up the branch valley? The former leads to the Diphuk La; the latter, which recently was filled with mountainous masses of snow, leads to an enclosure, surrounded by high bare cliffs, with snow beds in the topmost valleys. As soon as the snow is softened by warm winds and rain in May blowing up from the jungle, avalanches begin to slip down the steep gullies and pile up vast heaps in the main valley, which in the middle of June is still snowbound, though the flanks are by then stripped clean. But the torrents of icy water which come rushing down the gullies, and the cascades which cleave in a film to the cliffs, prevent direct access to the high peaks; and as for the screes, falling stones are a constant menace.

However, on this occasion, I decided to go up the branch valley, past the highest clump of Fir-trees, and the tall granite cliff over which hung a ribbon of white water. There was a cattle-path above the furious torrent, which led to a cluster of bothies about two miles up the valley; but the yak had not yet eaten their way as high up as this.

I walked fast at the start, both to get warm and because I was anxious to reach a new hunting-ground high up. Anyone set down in this country for the first time would have found a score of flowers to beguile him in the first hundred yards; indeed, no botanist who was a complete stranger to this part of the world would have got half a mile from camp that day, so overwhelmed would he have been with the marvellous wealth of alpine vegetation all round him. Picture the scene! A steep glen is enclosed by mountains rising for 3,000 feet above the foaming torrent. Massive cliffs rise bluntly on one side, stone chutes, wide at the base, but tapering for a thousand feet to where a sword-cut gapes in the brow of the mountain, slope up on the other. Ahead, the domed bulk of a granite mountain on the main watershed dominates the glen; and everywhere there is snow. The furious torrent dashes over the rocks with a roar, and the tinkle of water falling over the edge of the world into the main valley is heard. The narrow path, which frequently twists to avoid enormous blocks of stone, is lined with bushes, mostly species of Rhododendron. A dense scrub clings round the base of the cliff; and on the banks and rocks are Primulas, Poppies, Anemones, the yawning violet mouths of *Omphalogramma Souliei*, purple Morina, clusters of yellow Saxifrage, frail Veronica, pink Nomocharis, and a great many more flowers. But I had been ten days at River Camp already, and most of these flowers I knew well. Many of them I had seen before, in the Himalaya or in China; I was pleasantly aware that beautiful flowers surrounded me on every hand. Was it not enough that I was filled with the quiet joy of living amidst glorious scenery—it was glorious when it was visible—breathing the keen mountain air, and feeling fit to keep going for ten hours, or twenty if necessary, and to climb to any height likely to be reached by plant life!

But I had not gone far when my attention was drawn to a dwarf Iris, whose stemless flowers opened, as it seemed, straight out of the ground. They grew singly or in clumps of two or three, on a turf slope, sodden from melting snow. I dug up several plants and placed them in a tin; next day when I opened the tin, there was a delicious scent as of fresh greengages, but this was too delicate and refined to be noticeable in the open. This bulbous Iris was quite rare, and in fact I saw it nowhere else in the valley. I therefore made special efforts to collect seed of it in October and discovered about a dozen capsules, only just appearing above the surface of the soil (K.W. 7063). Two years later, in the Mishmi Hills, I found the same plant again. Here it was much more abundant, forming large solid clumps, sometimes with a dozen or more flowers in each; though one was lucky to find a single ripening capsule where there had been a dozen flowers!

The same grassy slope which produced the dwarf Iris was speckled with the mop heads of a pigmy Primula, *P. Genestieriana*. This neat little plant draws itself up to its full stature of half an inch on the Rhododendron moorland at 14,000 to 15,000 feet, and bursts into a puff-ball of tiny flowers, which may be pink, purple, or violet. I took endless trouble to collect seed of the minute creature, but it was all wasted energy, for the plant refused to grow in England, and is too small to be of much account if it did!

After that I came to hillsides covered with a mixed heath of dwarf Rhododendron, especially the purplish pink *R. riparium* and the larger *R. saluenense*, with flat Tyrian-purple flowers and glistening bands of silver scales on their backs. Mixed with these was one of the aromatic 'Cephalanthum' Rhododendrons, a taller and more erect plant, doubled over with compressed heads of tiny pink flowers, like blobs of sea-foam.

A large bush Rhododendron which I named Cherry Brandy (*R. cerasinum*) overhung the torrent, and was particularly lovely when wet. It had pendent bells of a bright cherry red, with cream rim, in trusses of five or six; and looked like a fruit salad. The rather rounded leaves are smooth beneath, except for a coating of wax, as seen in *R. Thomsoni*. In Tibet in 1924 I had collected the same plant, the flowers like red garnets, with five jet-black circular pit glands at the base. It grows also in the Mishmi Hills, where it sometimes has carmine flowers; but the cherry and cream variety from the Seinghku is probably the handsomest.

By this time I was clear of the larger scrub, and glancing up the screes,

I was just in time to see a flower twinkle, as a bayonet of sunlight stabbed the clouds. Approaching, I stood in silent wonder before the Ruby Poppy. In Sino-Himalaya, the mountain Poppies are generally blue, sometimes yellow, very rarely red. Therefore a red Poppy here is as exciting as a blue Poppy in England. Also it was exquisite. A sheaf of finely drawn olive green jets shot up in a fountain from amongst the stones, curled over, and ere they reached the ground again, splashed into rubies. Thus one might visualise *Meconopsis rubra*, if one imagines a fountain arrested in mid-career, and frozen. But it was not till later, when on a stormy day I saw whole hillsides dotted with these plants, that I really believed in *M. rubra*. As the wind churned up the clouds, a burning brand was lit, and touching off the flowers one by one, up they went in red flame! That was convincing. "The Ruby Poppy!" I thought, "what a plant for the rock-garden! But then, of course, it won't grow in England!"

And so on up the valley, over beds of snow, across frothing streams, in a wilderness of meadow flowers rioting over a carpet of Rhododendron. There were sky-blue Poppies and yellow Primulas, pink and red Nomocharis, several kinds of Pedicularis, Monkshood, Trollius, the silken white *Anemone Wardii* and—yes! Golden Anemone! In stature and foliage this last is very like *A. Wardii*, and in fruit I could not tell them apart; and yet in flower it has these brazen yellow discs, just as *Meconopsis rubra* is practically *M. impedita* with blood-red flowers. But *M. rubra* grew everywhere, and there was no true blue *M. impedita* in the Seinghku valley; whereas the Golden Anemone grew just here and here only; everywhere else it was replaced by the far more abundant white Anemone.

Reaching the bothies at an altitude of 12,000 to 13,000 feet, I found myself on a hillock, clearly an ancient moraine, through which the torrent broke, to fall over a ledge into the valley below. Beyond this, streams wandered across a wide sandy flat, amongst small bushes of Rhododendron and Willow. All around the screes slanted up steeply for hundreds of feet, and at the head of the basin, a low cliff, its edge bevelled by the scour of ice, blocked the valley. Above that again was a smaller amphitheatre, floored with moraine material and surrounded by straight bare cliffs.

The broom-like Rhododendron which grew in the sand was capped all over with tight heads of flowers of so dusky a purple that in the shadow they looked like royal mourning; in the sunlight, however, they became a daring plum-juice colour which glowed amongst the frosted leaves. It is *R. rupicola*, one of the 'Lapponicum' Rhododendrons, dwarf or brushwood plants, with very small crisp leaves, and flowers which display perhaps a greater variety of colours than any other group in the genus; in fact, almost any colour, except red or orange. Nor are the flowers ever spotted or blotched.

Meanwhile, I had not been idle. A number of plants had been transferred to my bag or into one or other of the tins. I had noticed the type of rock met with, the various plant associations, and the general features of the valley, down which once upon a time a glacier had flowed. I recorded those plants which were rare or local, confined to certain gullies or cliffs, and those which were common everywhere. All this was intensely interesting; I only lacked a companion with whom I could share these delights.

Whither should I go now? Should I continue up the main valley or ascend the scree and try to reach one of the hanging valleys? I chose the latter, because that would bring me out on the open top, where I could wander about more freely, and perhaps enjoy a view. Presently I found myself in a steep gulley, choked with enormous rocks. I had great difficulty in surmounting some of these obstacles, since there was always the danger of pulling the rock down on me as I hauled myself up, if it happened to be insecurely perched.

Now I noticed a very curious thing. As I ascended towards the crest of the main watershed which separates the Irrawaddy from the Lohit the climate became drier. Even the flora showed this. More conclusive was the weather, which I could see for myself improved towards the top of the valley. On several occasions afterwards, both in June and July when climbing above 13,000 feet, in bright sunshine, I looked back, like Lot's wife, and saw a pillar of cloud by day hanging over my camp. But the mist bank stopped short there at 11,000 feet, as though held back by some invisible barrier—really the dry air sweeping over the pass off the plateau. It was this mist bath which prevented the melting of the enormous heaps of snow in the lower valley, and kept the air so cold.

The range then was a climatic barrier of the first importance—was, in fact, itself part of the great rain screen which separates the wet hills of the frontier from the dead heart of Asia. I was already on the edge of the drier region and might reasonably expect to find a different flora on the other side of the pass. What I did find will be described in a later chapter.

The gulley now grew steeper and narrower, and presently ended in a chimney, up which I scrambled, to find myself in a hanging valley, with a small lake at its head. At the foot of an escarpment was a boulder strewn slope which dipped gently down to the lake stream. Beyond the lake, its base hidden by a fold in the ground, was a sugarloaf peak, about 17,000 feet high; and on its flank lay a snow bed.

It was a glorious flower-spangled valley, tucked away here on the crest of the range. Long ago it had clasped a glacier, but all that remained of it were these snow beds, cowering in the topmost hollows, and dwindling year by year. A larger glacier, fed from several of these hanging valleys, had flowed down the big valley up which I had come, past my camp, where it had joined the main ice stream from the Diphuk La; and the combined stream had flowed on down the valley to Snowy Camp, just below which it had ended.

What had brought about this profound change? Climatic revolution? There was no means of knowing. But in those days, when the valleys were filled with ice, there could have been no alpine flowers here. On the other hand, forest may have prevailed at higher levels than it does now; for the climate was probably moister, which would have favoured tree growth. In Tibet, many glaciers in the Tsangpo gorge descend far below the tree line to this day. In the Seinghku valley isolated clumps of trees, Fir and Larch, survive on sheltered slopes and ancient moraines some distance above the general timber-line; and these appear to be outliers of more extensive forests, dating from a moister age, rather than pioneers which have recently established themselves. In this age an alpine climate is in the ascendant, and it is the forest which is being forced back; the great amount of smashed timber, often buried in the gravel and silt washed down the mountain, is good evidence for that. The glaciers are still retreating all over Sino Himalaya—in the Eastern Himalaya, in Tibet, in the Burmese Oberland, in Western China, everywhere; they have been retreating for a long, long time. They may even have retreated farther, and faster, on the inner dry ranges than on the outer wet ranges. No one knows why they are retreating; in fact, hardly anyone knows of the existence of all these glaciers and vanished glaciers! As they retreat, the alpine flora advances, and the forest is cut off, or pushed back. This matter of former glaciation is of particular interest to the botanist, because it helps to throw light on the distribution of plants in Sino-Himalaya.

In the midst of these thoughts, suddenly I noticed that the ground under my feet was soft with the cushions of a Primula, which resembled a large violet-flowered Primrose. Unfortunately, this distinct species, *P. chamœthauma*—Wonder of the Snow—belongs to a group, alien to Europe, which obstinately refuses to grow at sea level, even in Britain; and despite its resemblance to a Primrose (which is more imaginary than real) and a fat packet of seed which I collected, *P. chamœthauma* is not in cultivation. Like the beautiful and elusive *P. sonchifolia*, the seeds germinated, soon to perish miserably; and the only species of the 'Petiolaris' section which remains somewhat precariously in cultivation is *P. Winteri*.

P. chamœthauma is extremely abundant in the high alpine valleys of the Seinghku, above 13,000 feet—though it may be found as low as 12,000 feet. It is gregarious, and I saw more than one turf slope absolutely violet with its cabbage leaves and massive heads. A single plant I noticed had white flowers.

On patches of gravel, carefully avoided by *P. chamœthauma*, the exquisite Claret Cup (*P. silaenis*) grew in scores. It is about an inch high, its stem as fine as thread, and its wine-purple bell-flowers hang singly or in pairs, rarely in threes. The spoon-shaped leaves form a neat rosette on the ground, from which rises the fairy staff, with the red bell swinging by a ligament from its apex. This is one of the most charming of the Amethystina or Jewel Primulas. They are almost entirely unknown in England, except in the anhydrous state.

Several large chunks of rock, broken off the cliff above, had rolled down the slope here, and the alpine flowers had already healed the scars. One was a complete rock-garden in miniature. Against a blood-red film of Scarlet Runner (*Rhododendron repens*), the violet stars of little *Primula bella* twinkled brightly, and soft purple clouds of *P. bryophila* flung pale shadows over the constellations. The thought struck me, why not have a rock-garden of my own, in camp? There were several enormous erratic blocks, which had been carried down the valley by the glacier and dumped close to my log hut; nothing would be easier than to convert one of them into a rock-garden, where I could cultivate any number of high alpines. The advantages of such a scheme were twofold. Small alpines which grow by themselves in isolated gullies and on remote cliffs, however conspicuous in flower, are very easily passed over when out of flower; add to this, that in October they might be under snow and not merely invisible but unapproachable, and the advantage of moving them to a place of safety becomes obvious. In the second place, to have them on the spot in the Autumn, seeding into my hand so to speak, would save much unnecessary climbing. I therefore resolved that in future, whenever I found a tiny alpine of which I required seed, I would dig up a certain number of plants, carry them back to my camp and plant them in my garden as a reserve. In fact, I did this, transporting plants of *Primula rhodochroa*, Claret Cup, and Blue Microbe (*Primula fea*), all of them exquisitely minute. They all set seed, but not one of them is in cultivation now—I do not think any of them even flowered, nor had they done so would anyone but the most enthusiastic rock-gardener, or a botanist, waste a thought on them. They are too minute; one almost requires a pocket-lens to see them at all! It is only when, like Claret Cup, they grew in such countless thousands that you could not set foot on the slope without crushing dozens; or when, like Blue Microbe, they haunted the highest, starkest cliffs, where nothing else could or would grow, that one became aware of them at all. These jewel flowers will not grow under any conditions we have so far been able to devise for them in this country.

I now scaled the cliff and found myself looking over into the next valley. Descending into that, I walked up a slope rich with meadow flowers, all the time keeping a sharp lookout for the rare or unknown plant. *Primula serratifolia* grew here in clumps; also several species of Lloydia, with white or egg-yellow flowers, Bergenia, Saxifrages, Globeflower, Pedicularis, and a Fritillaria. And presently I came on what I sought—a plant quite new to me. From a nest of narrow-toothed softly hairy leaves, sprang a white powdered stem, six inches high, ending in a poker head of powder-blue narrow tubular flowers. It was *Primula Wattii*, one of the 'Soldanellas' Primulas, so called from some resemblance to *Soldanella alpina*, a plant often seen flowering in the snow on the mountains of Europe. This is the first record of *P. Wattii* outside Sikkim, 400 miles to the west; and its unexpected discovery so far east filled me with delight. Another interesting fact was that some days before I had found two white-flowered Primulas on a fresh earth slip, about 2,000 feet below this. I was curious to know what they were, and had hunted high and low for more plants, without success; and now at last I had found them 2,000 feet higher up on the same slope—*Primula Wattii*! Evidently these two plants had sprung from seed which had been carried far down the slope by some casual agency, and had lived to flower; but why were they white, instead of blue? It did them no service, for I marked both plants carefully, and neither set a single seed! *P. Wattii* was not common. The plants were widely scattered over the grassy slope, and in a side glen I found some more; nowhere else did I see a single plant. I worked like a horse—or a chamois—collecting seed of this plant in October, but the plants raised did not prosper.

Above me an overhanging brow of rock cut right across the face of the mountain, and was carved into a series of towers. Beyond this the ridge climbed in lame steps up the escarpment beneath an immensity of scree. On the grey grass cliffs, strung out in flights along the fissures, was Blue Microbe (*P. fea*), an elfin Primula so wee that the threadlike stem will pass through the eye of a needle, while the pagoda bell flower is no larger than a Brownie's cap. This bell is crimson at the base, changing to blue above, and is hung from the stem by the finest silken cord. Two, sometimes three, bells nod on each stem—no more. So much for *P. fea*, another homeless orphan; but the frail beauty of this gem is almost as apparent in the dried specimen as it is in the living plant.

Searching for plants no larger than this is like looking for ore in a rock. They seem to have crystallised out of the grey magma. At a distance of a few yards, they are quite invisible in cracks and crannies where nothing else grows. From the hummocky turfed steps fluttered the green ribbon leaves of *P. bryophila* and a few thorny Barberry bushes crouched between the rocks. The talus tipped from the crags here overflowed the ridge and at a height of about 14,000 feet I found myself walking on a firm snow crust, where ridge and scree rolled hand in hand to the foot of the final precipice. From this point I turned my steps downhill towards camp, thinking mainly of tea and dry clothes. The day was far spent. What did it matter to me that I had in my bag several beautiful plants never seen before by man, besides others, which, if not actually new, were so in effect? Several of these, could I but introduce them into Britain, would elicit a chorus of oh's and ah's at the Chelsea Flower Show. Did not that mean fame? A temporary notoriety perhaps! But did that matter now? No, certainly not. What mattered now was that I was tired, cold, and hungry; I wanted to rest and I wanted some hot tea. But sheer force of habit made me keep a good look-out for plants as I followed the ridge between the two glens, and presently dropped into a gulley.

Meanwhile, I mused on the day's work, and especially on *Primula Wattii*.

As I have said, it was not a new species, but its discovery here was of peculiar interest. How did it get here? It did not suddenly appear in two places 400 miles apart. It must have travelled along the mountain ranges between, though under existing conditions it could not do so. Conditions then must have changed. We have seen, for instance, that the whole of this region was once buried under ice, which has since disappeared. That probably takes us far enough back in time for our purpose. But long before that, there must have been great movements of the earth's crust, since the sedimentary rocks have been bent in all directions, buckled, flung up on edge, and crystallised.

The central core of mountains comprising Sino-Himalaya have a peculiar structure. The high peaks stick up here and there abruptly like rocky islands from an ocean floor; the surrounding alpine slopes are as smooth, undulating, and easy as the surface of a calm sea. Here one can wander without hindrance, anywhere above 14,000 feet. Far below in deep troughs the torrents plunge and roar, and as you descend towards them, you notice the slope steepen more and more sharply until finally it breaks off in a sheer cliff. It is this bulge in the slope which prevents you from seeing the high peaks on either side as you march up the main valley; the peaks lie far back, and what look like the summits of mountains against the sky, are really nothing but a row of stacks marking the shoulder where the slope suddenly eases off on to the ice shelf—all that remains of the ancient plateau.

The simple explanation of this structure is that the whole mountain country was originally a plateau, like the plateau of Tibet, of which it still forms an outlying part. At that time it was under ice, and wide shallow valleys lay between one range and the next; the flanks of those valleys were the rolling slopes across which we have been wandering, where to-day flowers blow.

As the glaciers shrank the streams cut ever deeper into the rock, while the uplands were still preserved beneath a coat of snow, and when the ice finally disappeared water quickly completed the task of cutting deep and narrow grooves in the plateau. The structure of the country is conclusive on this point. It is the same in Tibet, in Western China, in the Himalaya, in Burma, and in Assam. If other evidence were needed, it will be found in the plants themselves. The ancient plateau, that is to say the ice shelf, which is all that remains of the plateau, has a flora quite different from that of the valleys. It is this highly specialised plateau flora which alone invites comparison with the Arctic flora; and it is not too much to say that no plant which grows habitually on the ice shelf will be hardy in Britain. English weather will on the whole satisfy the average alien from a temperate climate, but the specialist plant from the hot desert or the cold desert of the 100 per cent. saturated atmosphere cannot brook it. Even plants like Primula and Meconopsis, which belong to hardy genera, fail completely with us if they come from the plateau. We cannot grow any of the 'Amethystina'

Primulas, and the 'Rotundifolia' are almost as bad. *Primula minor, P. dryadifolia, P. fea, P. rhodochroa, P. bella,* and others have all been tried and found wanting. *Meconopsis speciosa, M. impedita, Wardaster lanuginosus* (the Flannel-leafed Aster of Muli), *Myosotis Hookeri,* and *Campanula calcicola,* all typical plateau plants, have fared no better.

Despite their proximity, even contact, plateau flora and valley flora remain distinct. It is not merely a matter of altitude. These plants, which must have inhabited the plateau ever since it was freed of ice, have a different constitution. Several of them are widely distributed between the Karakorum and Western China, e.g. *Potentilla peduncularis, Anemone polyanthes, Myosotis Hookeri, Braya sinensis, Draba alpina.*

So much for my thoughts as I slid and slithered back to camp.

But during much of the time one is engaged in thinking of less romantic things—food and warmth and sleep, for instance, and the mere routine of carrying on. One must needs be not only self-contained but self-reliant. Should any of the men fall sick, one turns doctor; should they quarrel, or steal, one turns J.P. One may also be called upon to cook, to interpret, to mend apparatus, or in short to do any odd job, besides collecting, examining, and describing specimens. Above all, one's servants have to be fed and looked after in a country where they cannot buy food for themselves.

Most people find it difficult to sleep at altitudes much greater than those to which they are accustomed. Many suffer from insomnia as low as 6,000 feet, though personally I am not affected below about 10,000 feet.

In times of acute depression one harks back to a previous existence, and lets the mind browse on memories; the conversation of friends, music, the theatre, gardens, and holiday crowds. Movement, events; here things happen with the gigantic inertia of geological epochs. One even dares to look forward to a time when one will enjoy such phantasias again. Possibly it is only a harmless delusion that these things have anything to do with life at all: but if so, most of us happily share that delusion. After all, these are the things one was brought up to reckon with; whereas romantic scenery, adventure, the violence of Nature, and playing a lone hand, were rare fruits to be tasted judiciously, not swallowed whole. Those who envy the plant-hunter his free, careless life are apt to forget this; they forget that he has renounced many of the things which make life pleasant. He may have chosen the wiser part; and at any rate he *had* the choice, a choice which falls to few men. But people who envy him are often thinking of the results rather than of the slow and usually painful steps which led to those results. The only existence they know of which can be compared with the plant-hunter's life is their own annual summer holiday, when for a short time they can turn their back on the shams and formalities of civilisation, and shun all men except one or two boon companions. And if the weather is bad, how bored they are! But at the end of a fortnight in the wilds, how many men would be willing to stay on? Some, of course; probably not many. After all, do we not enjoy a change just because it *is* a change ? Even the most exhilarating holiday palls at last, and we are glad to return to our accustomed bondage, to see the friends we are used to, to do the safe everyday things once more! Though we are not aware of it, our dislike of solitude is at bottom *fear*, and we seek the society of our fellow-creatures because in the midst of the herd we feel *safe*. It seems easier to die in the sunlight, and together, than in the darkness, alone, as wild beasts die. Plant hunting, then, may be a wonderful life, but it certainly is not the life most men picture it to be. It is a life's work, and, like all work worthy of the name, it involves responsibility and toil. However, let us drop philosophy, and continue our scramble.

To descend an unexplored gulley connecting the ice shelf with the main valley is to risk trouble. Sooner or later the gulley will end in a cliff. However, on this occasion I had no difficulty, and presently found myself on a tall scree, with a straight descent into the valley. On the scree I noticed tuffets of a dwarf Rhododendron, with pairs of pale pink flowers borne stiffly on long stalks. The plants were scattered, never forming a continuous carpet like most of the dwarf Rhododendrons, though that might have been the fault of the scree. This was 'Pink Baby' (*R. pumilum*), a plant of the Eastern Himalaya, to which I shall have occasion to refer again. So absorbed was I with this find that I did not at first notice several other remarkable plants on the scree. There was in fact a threadbare carpet of dwarf undershrubs, including Willow and Honeysuckle, clinging in strips to the otherwise naked surface, and woven into it were two plants of great charm. The first was a species of Gaultheria, whose flowers were so small as to be scarcely visible; the other a creeping Rowan (Pyrus). But it was not till the Autumn, when I saw both plants in fruit, that I realised how good they were. By that time the wee flowers of the Gaultheria had given place to large 'berries' of a pure and delicious rose colour; and the short flowering stems which grew stiffly upright, like sprigs of moss, crowded with needle leaves, bore many rosy 'berries'. *G. procumbens*, which is common on mossy banks in the Fir forest, and *G. nummarioides*, which is found in drier country, are rather similar in habit, but more prostrate; also the 'berries' of the former are bright cyanide blue, those of the latter black. As for the Pyrus, its numerous clusters of reddened berries presently turned snow white, beading the crinkly black stems with moonstones.

Descending the scree now as quickly as possible, I reached the path in the valley up which I had started in the morning, and pushing through the Rhododendron bushes, hastened down to my hut. Chokara was waiting for me. There was a bright fire burning; my pyjamas, solignified with the wood smoke of weeks, were warm; and seating myself, I let Chokara unlace my boots while I stripped off my wet shirt. Then Laphai appeared with the table-cloth, and by the time I had changed into dry clothes, tea was steaming on the table. The plants were laid out on the bed and forgotten for half an hour, while I drank cup after cup of foaming hot tea, and ate toasted chuppatties.

I have mentioned a dozen plants found during a typical day's work, but it is obvious that one cannot always be finding new species. There must be *some* limit, over a limited area; sometimes several days pass without a single new plant being added to the collection. Why is this plant so common and that one so rare? How do all these new species come to be here, and here only? Why are they not also like the majority, found either in Sikkim to the west or Yunnan to the east? During the long days of wandering, as one looks at the scenery, the flowers, and the rocks, these and many other problems present themselves for solution; but the answers do not come while you wait, neither in the excitement of the climb, nor in the quiet of the hut, nor in the long, often sleepless hours of night. Not that day, nor the the next, nor perhaps at any time. One sees, and records. And yet an answer to some minor problem, or a working hypothesis which will cover a host of observed facts, may leap into the mind at any moment, anywhere.

But during the actual climbing, you *must* concentrate on what you are doing, and think *ahead*, or disaster is certain. I do not now mean climbing in the technical sense of climbing a chimney or crossing a glacier, but being out on these mountains at all, especially alone. Direction, rock and snow surfaces, and above all weather, have to be reckoned with. There is no morning paper with its weather forecast; but that is of no consequence. You can easily forecast it yourself, because it is always either unsettled, or downright bad. Plant hunting rarely involves serious climbing; mostly it is marching and scrambling. But the risk of losing one's way, or of being injured by falling rocks, or tumbling over a cliff, or getting into a fix, is an ever-present menace. Of course, such risks become a part of your life; you do not think of them, though common prudence makes you careful. Your aim is to be bold, but not rash, cautious, but not fearful. Again, the sheer physical labour of climbing day after day and week after week above 12,000 feet in a country where the earth's crust is on edge, dulls the senses. One's impressions are neither so numerous nor so vivid as they become in stimulating society; nor, on the other hand, are they so fleeting. Yet whatever the dangers and hardships of the plant-hunter's life, he too has his reward. Often and often I have stood in a friend's garden in England looking at some child of the snows, glowing with health and vigour, which had taxed me to the uttermost farthing, and said to myself: "It was worth it!"

7　The Road to Rima

EARLY in July I was ready to cross the Diphuk La, and go down to the Lohit river, which flows out of Zayul, through the Mishmi Hills, to the Assam valley. This would be my shortest route back to India and I proposed to follow it in the Winter, if the Indian Government raised no objection. Meanwhile a reconnaissance of the route as far as the Lohit would be an advantage. A study of the alpine flora had shown me that, as already recorded, the Irrawaddy–Lohit divide was an important climatic barrier. On the far side of this range, therefore, I expected to find a flora different from that of the Seinghku valley; and by going now and finding many of the plants in bloom, I should know which to collect seed of in November.

There was also the lure of exploration. The Diphuk La had been crossed only once before by white men. In December 1913, Captain B. E. A. Pritchard, of the Intelligence Branch, Indian Army, and Captain Waterfield, crossed the Diphuk La from the Assam side, and eventually reached Fort Hertz. They did not, however, live to tell their story: Captain Pritchard was drowned in the Taron a few months later in the course of the same journey, and Captain Waterfield was killed in the war.

To a botanist, however, the Lohit–Irrawaddy divide was virgin territory, and anything I might collect would be of interest. As early as June 13 three Tibetans had crossed the pass and come down the Seinghku valley with salt for our village; thus it would be easy to cross now. But it was not so easy to find transport, though the Tibetans had promised to supply it. However, on July 6, the Tibetans came along with some yak and took me up to the last bothies, situated within sight of the pass at an altitude of 12,000 feet. This was a delightful spot at the junction of two streams, and here, at High Camp, I spent four strenuous days before finally setting out for the Lohit.

The main stream now divides for the last time. The western branch pierces the limestone belt, which trends northwards, and the angle between the two streams is blocked by a limestone peak over 16,000 feet high. At its foot is a large moraine, supporting a last clump of Fir-trees. Long stone chutes slant up for 3,000 feet to the ice shelf, with the jagged crests and spires of the divide beyond. These slopes are knee deep in Rhododendron scrub, and at their base wash yellow seas of *R. telopeum*, over which rock the flaming flowers of 'Scarlet Letter' (*R. sanguineum* variety); for the ground is broken up where the big moraine boulders have been piled in heaps, and the surging Rhododendrons chop and change here. 'Scarlet Letter' sprawls, but not untidily. The numerous ascending stems rise a foot above the rocks in a compact body, each stem bearing a rosette of leaves, dark green above, silver washed below, upon which the seven-flowered trusses ride. When the flowers open towards the end of June it is as if a crater had opened to reveal pools of red-hot lava.

About the same time that 'Scarlet Letter' broke into violent eruption, *R. suaveolens*, the first of the three 'Lapponicum' Rhododendrons, opened its buds, a film of bright purple spreading over the crooked brooms. The flowers are deliciously, though not powerfully scented. I placed some in a tin box, and carried them back to camp. When the box was opened I noticed a sweet perfume, which scented the whole hut. Fragrance is not a common feature of Rhododendrons and is particularly rare in these twiggy alpines, which are more commonly aromatic owing to the presence of oil in the leaves. The second 'Lapponicum' to flower, early in July, was a more bushy species, *R. rupicola* with flowers stained the colour of plum-juice. Lastly came the midget 'Lapponicum,' *R. microphyllum*, with tiny bronzed leaves and lavender-violet flowers borne at the ends of wiry twigs. On the alpine moorland, at an altitude of 14,000 feet, the three 'Lapponicums' often covered the ice shelf knee-deep; and early in July the fells were a rippling lake of purple and violet where the breeze ruffled the broom tops. Elsewhere the rosy purple *R. riparium*, perhaps the most gregarious of the 'Saluenense' Rhododendrons, mingled with the 'Lapponicums'. Rhododendrons of the 'Lapponicum' type, though rare on the wet ranges, are abundant in the interior, where the climate is drier and colder. In the Mishmi Hills I did not find one. In Tibet, on the other hand, and in far Western China, hundreds of square miles of windy fell are awash in the shallow 'Lapponicum Sea'.

The north face of the valley above my camp was a steep and stony slope, here broadly striped with Rhododendron scrub, there divided by a narrow band of bald gravel, rasped daily by falling stones. The south face, on the other hand, was precipitous and only some of the chimneys were climbable. Where gravel predominated 'Pink Baby' (*R. pumilum*) grew in tuffets, with 'Limestone Rose'. This last—*R. calciphila*—formed tight mats studded with large rose-pink flowers, which, instead of being hoisted clear of the tiny brittle leaves, almost cuddle them. It is confined to limestone screes, and flowers late in June, but is not at its best till July, when *R. riparium* is over.

In the dips and downs of the slope were tanglewood thickets of a large 'Lacteum' Rhododendron notable for its long narrow leaves, buff beneath, recalling those of *R. Beesianum*, and large spherical trusses of white or blush flowers. It is a tree rather than a shrub, especially on the other side of the range, where it grows abundantly in the Fir forest; the stout copper-red trunk, with its tattered thin bark flying, sweeps up from the ground in a bold curve. The branches are so twisted and interlaced that though it attained a height of no more than twelve or fifteen feet, they brought the straying trusses together into one fierce storm of flower.

Related to this, but more gnarled and lowly, rising less than three feet above the boulders which it clasped, with smaller leaves, bronzed beneath, and paler flowers, was *R. sigillatum*. It furnished a generous coat of green over the rough ground, where it broke in waves of ochre and *rose du Barri*, flecked with blobs of white foam. It is a gregarious plant, forming many a thicket by itself. Other species which formed tanglements and thickets were *R. pruniflorum*, *R. hypolepidotum*, *R. myiagrum*, and *R. horœum*.

Thus even in the second week in July there were many Rhododendrons in bloom at High Camp. Above 14,000 feet plants are scarce; and between 15,000 and 16,000 feet the rocks were practically naked, though the snow-line exceeds 16,000 feet. That is to say, there is an alpine belt some 15,000 feet deep which is a frozen desert. What probably happened was this. As the ice retreated, the flora crept up the mountain in its wake, occupying the devastated area. But no plants have yet succeeded in compressing their life history into a period short enough to occupy the last belt, though the mountains are now clear of ice. On the Tibetan inland ranges north of the Tsangpo I found a varied alpine flora at 17,000 feet and a fair number of alpines at 18,000 feet, where the snowline was little less than 19,000 feet. On the other hand, in the Mishmi Hills, which show no sign of recent glaciation, the blank belt occurs as low as 13,000 to 14,000 feet, the snow lying too long above 13,000 feet to give the plants a start in the Spring.

The base of the limestone cliff which crowned a long grassy slope, gay with Irises and Primulas and clumps of Slipper Orchid, was covered with a stiff pile of dwarf shrubs, including *Cotoneaster microphylla*, Lonicera, Barberry, Juniper, Ephedra, Daphne, Cassiope, and *Rhododendron lepidotum*. Higher up in the glare of light reflected from the crushed limestone and snow were many wizened shrubs and bunched or cushioned flowers. There was no easy way up the cliff. I tried to claw my way up the face but did not get very far. I tried one of the many chimneys, and found two plants of the violet *Primula euchaites*, but was stopped by an overhanging rock. Finally I found a way up, and crossing the ridge at a height of 15,000 feet, descended a long scree on the other side. In the gravel at the top were stuck the small carmine pincushions of *Androsace phœoblephara* with clots of the mauve *Primula Genestieriana*; and in fruit was *Solms-Laubachia pulcherrima*. Other good plants here, both of them confined to the limestone, were the congested crimson-flowered *Primula cycliophylla*, one of the woody-stemmed rock Primulas which, alas, are never likely to grace an English garden, the absurd little *P. moschata*, besides species of Ypsilandra.

The upper end of the Seinghku valley was indeed an enchanting garden of wild flowers. The brisk stream, lined with a robust form of *Primula sikkimensis*, both yellow-flowered and milk white, rattled between gravel banks where waved ruby, turquoise, and amethyst Poppies. There were meadows of violet Irises and white Anemones, spotted Nomocharis, golden Trollius, and blue Primulas; and everywhere grew Rhododendrons, foaming with blossom. Indeed there were more Rhododendrons than all other woody plants put together, this being the dominant association. Imagine a Scotch glen purple with Heather; then let there be at least a dozen different kinds of Heather, including small trees and bushes, with flowers of all colours from burning scarlet to palest pink and white, and you may form some idea of the Rhododendrons in the Seinghku valley.

On the afternoon of July 10 a party of Nung and Lisu coolies arrived from the Nam Tamai to join my porter corps; and the Tibetans agreed to start for the Lohit next day. The Nungs went straight up to the meadow to dig for the bulbs of a Fritillaria which they cook and eat, and returned to camp at dusk.

The following day we began the ascent to the pass with ten coolies and two bullocks. The bullocks would not or could not climb the steepest step, so halfway up they were exchanged for yak, which did eventually reach the pass, where men took over their loads.

At 13,000 feet, I noticed a sheaf of tall yellow Poppies growing amongst the scrub—just half a dozen of them. This was a peculiarly graceful variety of *Meconopsis pseudo-integrifolia*, the Lampshade Poppy, which is common in Tibet, and in Western China; but it was a rare plant here. The valley now rose very sharply with long screes slanting back on either side and great hummocks of worn rock bulging up on either side of the pass. The steep grassy slope was violet with the posies of *Primula chamœthauma*, and tight clumps of *Omphalogramma Souliei*.

However, I was anxious to reach the pass and see what lay the other side of the great range, so I hurried on, panting and blowing. At last I found myself in the snow at the top of the Irrawaddy–Lohit divide. One more effort and breathless with excitement, I reached the far edge and looked over into Zayul! But the view was disappointing. Lofty mountains rose abruptly in the foreground and cut off the middle distance; all I saw was the head of a narrow valley with a lake of clouded jade lying in a basin surrounded by heaps of stones and backed by stark cliffs. The view was particularly grim because no trees were visible, and the rocks were bare. The first thousand feet of descent to the lake was almost precipitous. Below the upper lake and just above the first clumps of Silver Fir was a second smaller lake; the glaciers had left their mark even more deeply engraved on this side than on the Burma side.

A rough descent brought us to a meadow where the stream cut across the limestone belt, some 2,500 feet below the pass; and here we camped. The meadow was filled with flowers by no means the same as those commonly met with on the other side. Abundant here were *Anemone rupicola* and the speckled yellow form of *Nomocharis nana* (var. *lutea* ?). There was also an immense Rheum—the Rhubarb Rheum—just unpacking its pentagonal leaves. Scattered about on the flat stony sands where the stream wandered about stood the ten-foot-high skeletons of last year's plants; and lower down the valley this year's inflorescences were spouting in cauliflower fountains from their leafy nests.

Another interesting find was *Primula sinopurpurea*; and I noticed the starry clusters of *P. bella*; *P. involucrata Wardii* paddled in the brook[1]; and *P. chamœthauma* carpeted the grass slopes. More whimsical was the fact that *P. melanodonta*, which is incredibly abundant on the other side, was not seen here at all!

I could get no certain information as to how long it would take us to reach the Lohit: some said one thing, others said another. Actually it took us six days, and we did not see a village, nor a hut, nor even so much as a bothy the whole way. As it was two days' march from the Tibetan village to High Camp, it is altogether eight marches from the last village on the Burma side to the first village in Zayul, through totally uninhabited country. Even at the southern end of the range, crossing the low Kronjawng pass from Fort Hertz, it is a seven days' march from village to village: which will give some idea of how shunned this country really is. Nor is it much more thickly populated on the other side of the range. In fact there is, on the borders of Burma, Assam, and Tibet, a tract of country which if it were flat would cover 10,000 square miles with a population of considerably less than one per square mile. Actually, of course, owing to its mountainous nature, the area is much greater than this.

During the next four days we continued down the right bank of the Di Chu, as the river is called, passing from the high alpine region, through meadow and scrub, into Fir forest; and thence into mixed Conifer forest. Below the more aggressively glaciated cirque the valley was flat and marshy. There was no trace of a path and for miles we squelched through bogs, where Irises grew in drifts amongst cushions of *Rhododendron suaveolens*, and waded through streams. There was no grazing for cattle here, the ground was far too soft. Myriads of mosquitoes and sand-flies made night hideous even at this altitude. On an outcrop of limestone I found *Cypripedium tibeticum*, together with another red Slipper Orchid. Then the stream dropped over a ledge, and we reached a moraine clothed with forest. Here were Silver Firs, and magnificent red-barked Birch-trees, with *Rhododendron Beesianum*. Just below, an immense snow bridge gave safe passage over the Di Chu, and here *Rhododendron riparium* was flowering brightly. The bottom of the valley was filled with dense thickets of Rhododendron and other shrubs, and the farther we descended, the more

---

[1] *P. Wardii* of gardens; *P. involucrata Wardii* of the *Botanical Magazine* (tab. 9149); *P. yargongensis* of orthodox botany. And yet there are not three Primulas, but one Primula.

THE UPPER SEINGHKU VALLEY IN JUNE.   ALTITUDE 11,000–12,000 FEET.
FROM RIVER CAMP.

THE LOHIT RIVER JUST BELOW RIMA.

pronounced became the difference between the flora on the Burma side and on the Zayul side.

On the third night we camped opposite to a hot spring famous for being the haunt of takin (*Budorcas taxicolor*). In a little grass hut three Tibetan hunters sat cutting up an animal they had just shot, and smoking the meat. We bought some from them and found it delicious, like beef. But perhaps that was because we had had no meat, except chicken, for three months. There was an open sward amongst the Fir-trees here, but still we saw no sign of grazing. One reason for this is that the climb up from the Lohit into the Di Chu valley is difficult, if not impossible for cattle; and no yak can live below 7,000 feet. Nor is there any arable land in the Di Chu valley, as there is in the Seinghku valley. The valley grew steeper and narrower, the cliffs so sheer that every side stream tumbled pell-mell over the cliff. As for the Di Chu, it had become a formidable torrent bounding down a steep crooked stairway overhung with big-leafed tree Rhododendrons. Huge angular blocks of granite which had toppled off the cliffs lay about, many of them crowned with the snow-white *Rhododendron manipurense*, or with the cinnamon-leafed *R. crinigerum*. Forest not only filled the glen, but ascended some way up the north flank as well; the south flank, however, was bush clad, except where falling stones had mowed a clean stripe through the coverts. The bush consisted largely of *Rhododendron rhaibocarpum*, *R. pruniflorum*, and the hardy-looking aromatic-leafed *R. brevistylum*, now in full bloom. The flowers of this last vary, white or pink with a bold purple flash at the base; and though small, are borne freely in large trusses. This shrub seems to grow anywhere, in the forest or in the open, on the raw scree, or by the river, and looks as hard as nails; flowering so late in the Summer—it was still in fine bloom when we returned ten days later—it should prove valuable in English gardens.

Far from widening as we descended, the towering cliffs of the Di Chu now drew in closer than ever, pressing on the baffled river, whose roar echoed to heaven. The glen was reduced to a slit in the mountains some 3,000 feet deep and we had great difficulty in crossing the numerous torrents which poured through the slotted cliff. But from the hot spring there was at least a definite trail to follow. Below the spring there were no obvious marks of ice action; but owing to the narrowness of the gorge and the height and steepness of the walls, even in mid-July a big snowdrift remained as low as 8,000 feet.

For two days we descended through mixed Conifer forest, where grew gigantic Picea and Tsuga-trees, with Silver Fir, Juniper, and scattered Larch: and from all the trees waved the pale-green cobwebs of Lichen; not Moss as in the temperate rain forest. There grew here, too, a magnificent tree Rhododendron allied to *R. Thomsoni*, but the flowers were long since over. The smooth tawny bole shone like plate-glass, supporting a fine head of gnarled and twisted branches, which carried immense bunches of fruit amongst the long slim leaves. Beneath the big trees, which included besides Conifers and Rhododendrons, Maple, Oak, Poplar, and Birch, grew shrubs and small trees in great variety: *Rosa Moyesii, Lonicera Webbiana* and other species, Rowan, Cherry, billowy clouds of Philadelphus and Deutzia, Jasmine, Euonymus, *Ilex dipyrena,* Cotoneaster, Enkianthus, and Ribes, to mention only a few. The Honeysuckles were particularly numerous and conspicuous, just as species of Acer had been in the Seinghku valley. Out in the open there was a neat small-leafed bush covered with fragrant cream-white flowers, followed later by plum-coloured fruits. This was *Lonicera tsarongensis.* Hardly any of these shrubs grew on the Burma side of the range; but many of them I had found on the dry ranges of southern Tibet! In spite of some Bamboo, the forest was much more open than the rain forest, and flowers grew freely amongst the undergrowth of Ferns: worthy of note were the handsome blood-orange *Primula chungensis, Pyrola uniflora,* and *Souliea vaginata,* species of Thalictrum, Podophyllum, Rodgersia, and Impatiens.

More Rhododendrons appeared in fruit, including *R. triflorum* and *R. oleifolium,* a species resembling *R. bullatum, R. megacalyx,* and a 'Boothii' species with strikingly handsome silver-fringed bud scales; most of these do not cross the range, and in fact I found ten species in the Di Chu valley which I did not see in the Seinghku valley! Several of the Seinghku species also did not cross over to this side. None of these Di Chu species were in flower, however, so it is not possible to name them with certainty until they flower in England.

When we halted on the evening of July 15, it seemed almost uncomfortably warm compared with what we had been accustomed to for the last six weeks; actually the temperature fell to 58° F. in the night. Huge Conifers cast a deep gloom over the riotous river. Across the other side, above the fringe of Rhododendrons which dragged their leaves in the white water, the gaunt granite cliffs towered up smoothly out of sight; and the air was filled with spray and thunder. We had a pleasant camp here on a sandbank, the tropical trees throwing queer shadows in the dancing firelight. It was the last of the forest.

Next morning we started at dawn, and in two hours emerged from the forest and from the gorge into a wide-mouthed valley. The torrent plunged furiously down, and we found ourselves high and dry on a steep dislocated face with Pine-trees and *Rhododendron arboreum* scattered amongst rocks and parched grass. A narrow path climbed dizzily, swung over the next ridge, crossed a gulch by a ledge of rock, and clawed round a precipice. Now we could see the mountains across the Lohit, and presently, after a fine scramble, we reached the tortured crest of a spur whence the whole valley came into view; far below us, the river flowed in a deep trench, flanked high up by wide terraces. We could see few signs of cultivation, or indeed of vegetation either.

At last we reached a terrace covered with high Grass and Pine-trees; there was a water-hole here, but the water was foul, the colour of stout, without its flavour; the Tibetans drank it, though it was not good for them. From here a path descended on either flank of the spur, that on the up-river side going to Rima, that on the down-river side to Kahao, a small Tibetan village which we could see on a terrace above the river. We made for the latter, descending a thousand feet by a breakneck path to a wooden bridge over the Di Chu; and half an hour later we reached Kahao.

The day which had begun in bright sunshine ended with pouring rain, a storm coming up the valley while we were pitching our tents. Just then a party of Mishmis appeared on their way to Rima, and stopped to gaze at us in astonishment. The leader, addressing me in Hindustani, asked me if I understood 'Assam language,' and when I replied that I did, he seemed pleased. Oddly enough he was the only Mishmi I met who did speak Hindustani, and from him I gleaned some useful information which proved surprisingly accurate. He told me it was fifteen marches to Sadiya, that the path lay on the other side of the river, and that I could get Mishmi coolies for the journey, the first Mishmi village being three marches from Kahao. So favourable were the chances of success in fact, that I then and there wrote a letter to the Political Officer in Sadiya informing him of my proposed journey and asking him to send a guide to meet me in Kahao at the beginning of November. I gave this letter to the headman with instructions to have it forwarded from village to village. This was done, and the letter, written on July 21, reached Sadiya in September.

From above, Kahao had looked quite a large village, and it was in fact surrounded by Rice-fields. But several of the buildings were granaries not houses, and five or six of the houses were uninhabited owing to a recent epidemic which had carried off most of the people of the district! Only three families were left; and when six of my coolies went off to Rima on their own business, leaving me to replace them as best I could, Kahao could only supply three men. The net result of all this was that I had to remain five days in Kahao, while my men scoured the valley for food and coolies, going north as far as Rima and south as far as the next village called Dong, more than a day's march away. Even so we could only buy a little inferior rice and some *tsamba*; but as the numerous delays had greatly depleted my resources, I was glad to get even that, helped out with an occasional scraggy fowl, or a stale fish. I also learnt that we would have to return the same way as we had come, that being the only way. There is a difficult pass above the village of Dong, which crosses the range close to the Diphuk La; it joins the branch valley at the head of the Seinghku just above my High Camp, but is only used by hunters.

The Lohit, like all the rivers of Eastern Tibet, flows due south roughly parallel to the Irrawaddy divide. Thirty miles below, it suddenly swings to the west, and after describing a semi-circle of small radius northwards, the long-pent-up water bursts out into the plain of Assam in a devastating flood. As one of the principal streams of the Brahmaputra it may therefore fitly be compared with Nam Tamai on the other side of the divide, which is one of the principal streams of the Irrawaddy. Both flow at an altitude of 2,000 to 4,000 feet. But what a contrast in their valleys! Instead of the dense hill jungle of the Tamai, draped with epiphytes, open Pine forest; instead of the varied evergreen Indo-Malayan trees, a hard metallic-leafed scrub fringing the river, and lining the deep ravines; instead of Bamboo groves, naked rock, Bracken and Grass, with scattered bushes! And then— Rice-fields!

However, I found Kahao irksome, even for five days. The heat was severe, the thermometer often registering 95° F. in my tent, and infinite torment of blood-sucking flies, day and night, robbed me of sleep. The weather was erratic as well it might be in such a trough! In the early morning a dense white mist lay over the river, but this was soon dispersed, the sun came out, and the temperature rose. At midday, without warning, a furious gale sprang up from the south; all the afternoon it blew with ceaseless violence, until just after dark, when it blew itself out. The first day I was caught unawares, and the wind blew my tent down; after that I weighted the ropes with stones. When it rained, the wind was less boisterous, though the valley was hardly more pleasant; but sooner or later the wind tore the clouds to tatters till the turquoise lining of the Tibetan sky shone through in a dozen places.

In the warm scented Pine forest, and amongst the rank Grass, thousands of grasshoppers planed and jumped, and there were many other insects also, expecially beetles, wasps, and flies, most of them small. I made a collection of insects, and was lucky enough to find an interesting new grasshopper, which has been named *Podisma wardi*.

Almost every day bands of Mishmi youths passed us on their way to Rima, whither they migrate to work, leaving their women and children behind to weed the fields. The climate of the Mishmi Hills is appalling. During the horribly wet Summer months while the crops are growing, there is little enough for the young men to do, nor is there enough food left to go round. Last year's stock of grain is almost finished: this year's will not be ready till August. So the young men seek food abroad. In the Winter they migrate by whole families, in the opposite direction; that is to say, down the Lohit valley to Assam, where they are employed by Indian contractors to cut cane.

The Mishmi are short, muscular, almost naked savages with simian features, and long hair tied in a knot on top of the head. It is difficult to say just what colour their skin is, so dirty are they; but it appears to be a sort of light coppery brown. They dress very simply. From a cord round the waist a flap of cloth hangs over double, one half being pulled under between the legs and fastened by the cord behind. Over this is worn a sporran, or a short skirt, open down one side. A sack-like jacket, reaching to the knee, with holes for head and arms, and a long scarf thrown negligently over the shoulders, complete the dress. The ears are pierced for large gypsy rings; hence the Tibetan name for the Mishmi—*Na*. The usual short knife is carried over the shoulder in a flat wooden scabbard bound with wire rungs on the open side, and raw hide straps support both knife and bear- or monkey-skin bag. Seldom have I come across a hill tribe so uncouth and so unsophisticated as the Mishmi. They fled at sight of a camera, and eyed me from a distance with dark suspicion. Except from that one man who had been to Sadiya, and was quite worldly, I could get no information of any sort from them. They would not open their mouths, and on any attempt to fraternise, they edged away from me, keeping close to one another like sheep. No tribe in the Irrawaddy basin bears any resemblance to the Mishmi; and eighteen months later I was to learn how difficult they are to deal with.

The only trees in the valley are *Pinus khasia* and a hard-leafed Oak; a little higher up the valley even these disappear. The flora is indeed strongly zerophytic. Many of the bushes and shrubs have the under-leaf surface whitened with long silken or woolly hairs, no doubt a special adaptation to the unfriendly climate. A few species owed their pallor to a coating of wax, or to a short stiff pile, e.g. species of Oak, Willow, and Clematis. But the greater number are silvery or fleecy.

Amongst the shrubs, *Rosa bracteata* and *Ceratostigma Griffithii* were in flower, and I noticed also species of Ilex, Pieris, Desmodium, Sophora, and Ailanthus. Most of them had leaves of that lustreless green often associated with a dry, windy climate.

On July 22 we started on the return journey to the Seinghku. It was terribly hot on the blistering granite cliffs, and I was much relieved when at last we reached the edge of the forest and camped by the torrent 3,000 feet above the Lohit; we had had nothing to drink since breakfast, even the water-hole being dry.

During the next two days we made the same stages as on the downward trip, camping at the hot springs on the 24th. On an immense boulder overhanging the river, *Rhododendron manipurense* was still in bloom, its cold white trumpets gleaming amongst the dark foliage. It is one of the last species to flower, and I have seen it lasting well into August.

Most of the Rhododendrons missing from the other side of the range were found hereabouts, that is to say between 7,000 and 10,000 feet. Another interesting plant was the 'Tsangpo Lily' or 'Pink Martagon,' found amongst the rocks and the Pines; but it was not common. I discovered this Lily growing in the gorge of the Tsangpo in 1924, and many plants were raised from the seeds I brought back; but no christening has yet taken place, so the last new Lily is still known by a number, like a convict. It appears to be closely allied to *Lilium Ducharteri*.

75

The violet mops of *Primula capitata* had also opened out, and *Pyrola uniflora* grew in the leaf-mould. Bushes of Syringa (Philadelphus), Honeysuckle, and pink Deutzia were smothered in blossom; and the weather being fine, we were able to halt in the middle of the day for a cup of tea and a rest under the spreading trees. At the hot spring the Lisu hunters of my party finding no Tibetans in residence, decided to slay a takin. Before it was dark they left the camp, and creeping across the flimsy bridge, took up position, with their cross-bows ready. It was a cloudy night but a full moon showed up occasionally, and one could make out shapes a few yards away. They returned about midnight, and early next morning begged me to stay here a day as they said they had shot three takin, two of which had got away. To this I agreed, and off they went once more to trail the wounded beasts, while others brought in the one certain victim. It was a young female. According to the men's story, a whole herd had come down to the spring to drink, and the hunters seized their opportunity and plugged poisoned arrows into the three nearest before the alarm was given. But if two others were wounded, they were never found, and it is to be feared they died miserably.

I went over to the scene of the ambush, and found the hot spring just above the river, on the edge of the Fir forest. The limpid water wells up under granite boulders into a natural basin at the foot of the slope. It was just the right temperature for a bath, being sufficiently cooled by several cold streams flowing over the surface of the rocks, and it had a faint smell, suggestive of sulphur. All around the black mud was trampled bare by the takin which came down to drink, though elsewhere hundreds of purple Roscoeas grew on the open slopes. Radiating from this spot are narrow lanes through the dense screen of Rhododendron, which lead to the barer crags and screes, where the takin dwell. No amount of persecution seems to keep them away from this spot. For years they must have furnished a steady supply of meat and skins to the Tibetan hunters, who own the rights. The Mishmi do not hunt in this valley, and it was a lucky chance that brought me here with Lisu and Nung hunters, who seized the opportunity to poach.

I spent the rest of the day botanising on the south screes, round the base of which grew dense thickets of *Rhododendron rhaibocarpum*, *R. pruniflorum*, and *R. brevistylum*, the last two in full bloom. Thanks to the variations of colour, *R. brevistylum* was a brave sight, pale beneath the trees, darker in the open. Rather higher up on the scree, *R. riparium* and the aromatic 'Cephalanthum' formed a shorter scrub; and above these again, plump bushes of *R. crinigerum* and another dwarfer species hugged the barren face. Though not more than a foot high, this dwarf had been completely overwhelmed with blossom earlier in the year; but the bushes were older than they looked. A stubble of earlier years' bud scales bearded the short thick stems which ended in rosettes of narrow leaves (K.W. 7184).

This type of Rhododendron, which is characteristic of a somewhat dry alpine climate, makes very slow growth.

The most interesting Rhododendron on the scree was a bush intermediate in character between *R. rhaibocarpum* and the species just mentioned. It was undoubtedly a hybrid. I found half a dozen specimens which had flowered freely; subsequently they set seed (K.W. 7190).

The day's halt here, though pleasant to me, was not relished by my Zayul coolies, who threatened to come out on strike unless I paid them immediately. Of course, I refused to do that, so they decided to trust me. We marched again the following day, tramping through meadows where the Rhubarb Rheum towered six feet high, amongst Poppies, Primulas, Asters, and coloured Louseworts; and many a plant was fawned on and foiled by the wiry stems of a Codonopsis, whose sickly yellow tubes sulked in the sunshine. Further on the violet Iris shadows lay across the bog.

On July 27 we camped on the moraine close to the last clump of Fir-trees, and that night the fine weather broke up. In the morning we could hardly get the fire to burn, so wet was everything, and the morning was well advanced before we started for the pass. Near the top we met a Lisu coming down: he wore the scarlet turban of Government, so I knew that he came from Fort Hertz with letters. He also carried a bag of money for me; but he brought no news of my promised rations.

After crossing the pass, High Camp was reached in less than two hours. Here the sun was shining brightly, and I halted to drink a cup of tea and to read my mail; latest news from home May 10, a lot about the General Strike, and a copy of the *British Gazette*.

It was pleasant to look down the Seinghku valley again, and see the familiar shapes of the mountains. The alpine turf glittered with flowers. Here spangled with the gold of Potentilla, there lurid with patches of crimson Lousewort, or deep blue with Gentians, or violet with pigmy Primulas. *Rhododendron campylogynum* was in flower, and tall yellow Cremanthodiums fluttered in the breeze. Out of the wind grew clusters of Salvia, wine-red Nomocharis, and prickly Poppies.

In the evening we walked down the valley to my old hut. After three weeks' absence it smelt of mould, and the roof leaked; but when we had lit the fire it grew cosy again.

We stayed here a day, and then moved down to the lower camp. The crossing of the torrent, now bridgeless and enormously swollen, was rather risky, but we waded over three at a time, holding hands.

Everything was growing rankly, but there was little in flower that I had not already seen. However, on one of the screes two notable plants were secured. High up in the raw gravel, above the dense thickets of blue-berried *Gaultheria Hookeri*, a frail Primula was flowering. *P. siphonantha*, as it is called, was indeed a waif; the scape, hardly more than four inches high, springs from a tiny rosette of downy leaves, and bears two or three, rarely more, pallid violet flowers, so delicate that you would never suspect that they are capable of facing the wind and rain at 11,000 feet! There were not more than a few hundred plants in the whole gulley, and I saw it nowhere else; but it looked like the ghost of *P. Cawdoriana*, a plant collected in Tibet which has bloomed in England, and been rewarded by the Royal Horticultural Society for valour; practically a posthumous award! Alas! it is dead now, at any rate, as *P. siphonantha* will soon be; for they belong to the lovely but unhappy 'Soldanella' section, which are too homesick to live away from their beloved alps.

The second plant, which grew at the base of the scree, was a dwarf Hypericum forming footstools a yard through, studded all over with brass yellow flowers; a fine rock-plant if it could keep its form in cultivation.

We were now back in the Burmese monsoon, and it poured with rain incessantly. When we awoke on July 31, we noticed fresh snow on the mountain-tops, but that soon melted. Our snow bridge had gone, and the muffled thudding of great boulders being rolled along in the coffee-coloured torrent was awe-inspiring. Every few minutes a new sound broke on the ear—the plop of stones as they slithered down the slope into the river which was violently undermining the opposite scree, where two months before I had first seen the Tea Rose Primula. Tons of rock and earth were thrown into the torrent while I watched, till even its fury was momentarily sobered and its headlong course checked.

Things boded ill for the last march to the village; nor were our apprehensions ill-founded. In places the bank was completely washed away, and we had to climb high up the precipitous face, cutting our way through the dense leech-infested undergrowth. Elsewhere the path was itself a channel for the flood-water which threatened to sweep us into the main river! The Bamboo forest below was a bog, and the meadow above the village was crawling with leeches. Thus my attention was fully occupied, and I had little leisure to collect plants. A few, however, thrust themselves into notice, one of the most interesting being *Rhododendron vaccinioides*, already referred to. Much more exciting was *R. Taggianum*, a tall leggy shrub, growing on an Alder-tree, overhanging the river. The flowers, in clusters of three, were long since over—probably it was a Winter-flowering species, but it needed only a glance at the three-inch capsules, and at the equally long style, to convince me that here was a fine 'Maddeni' Rhododendron, one of the big trumpet-flowered group. This diagnosis was confirmed by the large calyx, with crimson scales thickly clustered round its base and wandering off like star-dust on to the green leafy lobes. *R. Taggianum* is probably a rare plant, and this was the only specimen I saw in the Seinghku valley, at an altitude of 7,000 to 8,000 feet, in the temperate rain forest. Probably it is not very hardy.

I found another puzzle of a 'Maddeni' a thousand feet higher up, and having no name for it am forced to include it amongst the convicts—K.W.

7606. It also was a solitary epiphyte, growing on an Oak-tree, and its claim to notoriety lay chiefly in the fact that the style was shorter than the capsule—a most freakish thing. The umbels are four-flowered, as commonly in the 'Ciliicalyx' group to which it belongs.

The meadows round the village were a rank wilderness of flowers, including clumps of salmon-pink Hedychium, and yellow Cnicus, like a dwarf Thistle on a pole (for it grew twelve feet high). But further investigations into the local flora were postponed until a more favourable occasion; for when I reached Haita I was kept busy for some time pulling off the leeches which crawled and sucked all over me.

8 The March to Fort Hertz

BACK in my hut after two months' absence, I found the roof leaking like a sieve, the floor a bog, and a smell of mould everywhere. The river was raging down, and a terrible din rose as great boulders were shaken together; the previous day the heavy timber cantilever bridge, which had stood for years, was carried away, and we were cut off from Haiia!

The first thing to do was to put my hut in order; fresh leaves were gathered, and slipped in under the leaks; and a bamboo floor laid down. Although this was often awash, it was better than paddling about in the mud. Two days later the Tibetans threw a temporary bridge of poles across the river, and communication with the local tradesmen was re-established. I was now able to buy a fowl, or a few eggs, or even a piece of smoked goat, or beef. Best of all, I could sometimes get potatoes. Milk and butter were always available, and I had a daily supply. But coolies for transport I could not get. There was hardly anyone left in the village; the Tibetans were nearly all up the valley with their flocks, or they had gone to Rima. Those who were left behind had work to do, weeding the fields, or scaring monkeys and deer away from the ripening crops after dark. Several 'Elephant' Bamboos about eight feet high and split in half at the top were stuck in the ground. A line was attached to one half, and the separate lines were all attached to a master line, which was pulled from a small hut perched high up on the slope. In this hut someone kept vigil all night; every twenty minutes he tugged on the master line, and all the split bamboos started to clack loudly. Sometimes a whole family occupied one of these cabins for the season.

Although monkeys were said to be plentiful, I only once saw any by day. Birds, however, were abundant, and in astonishing variety. Insects swarmed in overwhelming numbers, and in the mud around my hut many brightly coloured Lycinidae—small butterflies about the size of our chalk blues—were always to be found, wet or fine. Only when the sun shone, which was not often, did the more gorgeous swallow-tails put in an appearance; and as soon as the rain came they took cover.

It continued to rain, with only short pauses, for the next ten days. Whenever I went outside my hut I returned covered with leeches. The inside had horrors of its own, for there was always a plague of sand-flies at night. Indeed more than once I wished myself back in the Alps.

The days slipped by quickly enough, and I found plenty of work to do;

and when sitting in the hut became too unbearable, I could always go out (braving the leeches) and collect plants.

A big rough-leafed Begonia grew on the cliff near my camp and was now in bloom; though the pink flowers are small, they are borne in such a rosy cloud above the harsh and handsome foliage, that I was quite pleased with the plant. You could grate nutmegs on the leaves. On the earth banks a pale violet Chirita with leaves mottled like a Lungwort was common; and from high up in the trees huge orange sprays of *Dendrobium fimbriatum* peeped out.

Another interesting plant was a climbing Raspberry which quite smothered some of the big trees. It looked like one of those devils which, once they get into a garden, can never be got out of it again; so I was not tempted to collect seed of it.

Looking back on the excursion to the Lohit, I felt well satisfied. True, I had not found a large number of new plants in flower, though I had marked down ten or twelve more Rhododendrons for seed; but I had confirmed what the alpine flora and the late glaciation of the Seinghku valley between them had already made me suspect. The Irrawaddy–Lohit divide is a first-class barrier, comparable to the Himalaya; that is to say, it separates two distinct floral regions.

Now since a dry mountain flora is found on the Lohit side, and the typical dry region alpine Rhododendrons are more abundant on that side than on the Burma side, one must suppose that they have spread from there to the Burma side; in other words, the Seinghku valley is becoming progressively drier. Lack of precipitation would of course account for the shrinking of the glaciers; but how are we to account for the lesser precipitation?

From the Diphuk La the atmosphere becomes steadily drier and the rainfall less as one proceeds towards the Lohit, and steadily wetter with a greater rainfall as one proceeds down to the Tamai.

The valley of the Di Chu is about thirty miles long, or rather longer than the Seinghku. It is clearly divisible into three sections. (i) An upper ice-worn portion, from the Diphuk La to the hot springs, all bogs and boulders, with lakes at the head; about fourteen miles. On this stretch the limestone belt is crossed. (ii) The lower, forested, water-worn gorge, from the hot springs to the end of the forest; about twelve miles. (iii) The funnel-shaped granite mouth, where the cliffs are covered with thin Pine forest; about four miles. The valley is entirely uninhabited, there is neither grazing nor arable land. The Diphuk La is little used except by the Zayul Tibetans and those of Haita, who traffic in salt and tea.

Another result of my trip had been to open the way to Assam. Once over the Diphuk La in November, I had merely to follow the Lohit, and sooner or later, without crossing another pass, I must reach the plains. It was not, perhaps, quite as simple as that; but no great difficulty need be anticipated.

It was now the second week of August. In another month I could begin harvesting seeds. Meanwhile why not enjoy a rest and change of air by the Nam Tamai? It would be hot down the valley, of course; but then I need do nothing. Both my mail and supply were due from Fort Hertz. So I decided to go down the path and meet them. We packed up, stored the bulk of the kit in the headman's house, and on August 11 marched down the leech-infested Seinghku valley. Grossness had descended upon the jungle. An overpowering smell arose from the fœtid mould, which was erupting in loathsome-looking Toadstools and clumps of sad leafless Orchids. But there were also masses of Begonias with red, yellow, or white flowers, and strings of scarlet Æschynanthus trailing from the trees. Here and there a sheaf of purple pouting *Aeginetia indica* had sprung up.

Then came a break in the rains. By day, an oppressive sticky heat troubled us; at night, the stored-up electricity was loosed over the ragged ranges, and the many-echoed slam of thunder drowned even the rage of the river. A party of starving Nungs, who had been up the valley digging for roots, passed us.

Arrived at the Adung confluence on August 12, I decided to rest a few days. It was a glorious evening, but myriads of insects made life intolerable. The chirping of crickets, the hoot of an owl, the bark of a muntjac away in the forest sounded terrifying in the hot darkness.

I awoke late next morning. The sun was shining brightly, and everything was very still. For several minutes I lay in bed, drugged with sleeplessness, collecting my wits. Something was wrong, of that I felt sure. The silence became oppressive. Why had I woken? Generally I woke when Chokara came in to light the fire, or when Laphai brought tea. I glanced at the table—everything was exactly as I had left it. No one had been inside the hut; yet it was certainly late.

I raised my voice. Chokara appeared, and began to tidy the hut. "Call Laphai," I said lazily.

"He has gone, Sahib."

This hardly penetrated my brain. I supposed he had gone out shooting.

"All right, call Maung Ba."

"He's gone too; they both went in the night."

So that was that. My staff had deserted. They had packed their belongings, taken as much food as they could carry, and turned back along the path which led to Fort Hertz and civilisation. Chokara and I were alone in the jungle.

The day was intensely hot. One sweated continuously, and the sweat rolled down face and back and chest in rivulets. The glutinous air could not hold any more moisture. After taking thought, I decided to return to Fort Hertz. But first, to find coolies. In the evening two natives appeared, and I sent them off for help. Their fellow Nungs had mostly fled into the jungle, and were living on such roots and fruits as they could find. The villages were empty.

However, next morning my messengers returned with five others, and having reduced the kit to the barest necessities, we started in the afternoon for Fort Hertz. The cane bridge over the Seinghku river was in a terrible state of disrepair, but we got across safely, and by dusk had covered the first stage. Altogether the six stages down the Nam Tamai were done in three and a half days of strenuous marching. Starting soon after dawn, and halting at sunset, we rested only for two hours in the hottest part of the day. But it was a strain. The heat, which made me feel sick, the ceaseless torture of insects day and night, the plodding up and down over steep spurs, along a narrow muddy path, overgrown with jungle, almost persuaded me to give up the struggle and return to my alpine camp. But there was the difficulty that we had no food; the truants had helped themselves to what remained of the rations in no niggard fashion. Rice we must have, not only for the three remaining months in the Seinghku valley, but for the journey to Assam as well. Better to go through with it, and ensure my supply; at the same time I must get assistance—Chokara single-handed was not to be borne. I worked out a time-table. If I left Fort Hertz on September 1, and did single stages all the way back, I could easily reach my camp by the last week in September, even allowing for halts to change coolies. That gave me time enough, so I decided to go on at all costs. I had lightened the burden of those long marches down the Tamai by botanising. Though there are never many flowers in the jungle, in the thickets grew Zingiberaceæ—species of Costus with snow-white flowers, and of Alpinia, besides several species of Hedychium gay with combinations of red and orange, like clusters of insects. Along the edge of the forest were ground Orchids, notable being an Odontochilus with yellow, and another with white flowers. A shady rock by the river way plastered with the large flat milky blooms of a Diplomeris; and every stream was choked with the lush leaves, glassy stems and vivid flowers of Impatiens. We required only seven coolies, but I had some difficulty in getting even these at the Tamai bridge, and it was midday, August 19, before we left the river, and turned our faces westwards, towards the long low ranges and the eerie darkness of the hill jungle. It is eight hard marches to the Mali river, slogging up and down several thousands of feet each day. Now the hill jungle stretched away from us, range beyond range, many days' journey in every direction. In the clammy embrace of the monsoon, when all the scuppers of the mountain gush, and the trees weep pitifully as the white mist soaks through the moss-bound branches, it is a shambles. A ferny carpet covers the soil, which is composed entirely of dead leaves, flowers, twigs, fruits, seeds, scales, and bark, cast off by the trees. Below this warm jacket, myriads of fine roots interlace to form a spongy network, which penetrates to the living rock. It is impossible to dig in the forest soil, without first using a knife; it is like trying to dig through a load of hay. The framework of the mountain, however, is never far below the surface, and just before you come to it, you find a layer of grit which the myriad roots have slowly loosened and torn off. Great numbers of insects and worms are everywhere at work churning up the soil, mixing the grit with the mould, and feeding on the fruits and seeds which fall from the trees. Fungi of all kinds spread their mycelium over the skeletons of leaves, and wrap round every piece of fallen timber. Many of these are not visible by day; but in the dead of night you may see the leaves and twigs which carpet the ground lit up with a soft phosphorescent radiance, caused by a Fungus. Elsewhere, however, the hidden mycelium manifests itself in warts and pimples which break out on the dead wood; or in toadstools of gorgeous colour, but flushed and spotted as though swept by some awful contagion; others more gruesome, with pale gills, strike at the living tree itself. Everything that goes down into the abyss is set upon by a horde of ravenous plants and insects, none the less dangerous because they work slowly; and everything that is set upon perishes. The wonder is that any seed escapes to germinate!

In the Irrawaddy forest one may pick up hundreds of fruits, hard or soft, including those of Magnolia, Myristica, Illicium, Castanopsis, Quercus, Schima, Dipterocarpus, Parinarium, Bauhinia, Ficus, Michelia, Garcinia, and a great many other trees; almost every seed examined will have a tiny puncture, and on cutting it open, a wee grub is seen curled up inside, taking the place of the embryo plant. What happened was this. An insect laid its egg inside while the fruit was still on the tree. The seed swelled, and at last when the fruit was ripe the grub emerged from the egg and began to eat a home for itself. The fruit falls to the ground, the grub, having eaten the embryo plant, chews its way out, and burrows into the earth. In the Spring it emerges again as a full-grown insect, and returns to the same tree whence it started. Probably it pays for its board and lodging by pollinating the flowers.

Thus the soil becomes a festering hot-bed of transformation. Life is ever multiplying itself, ever changing. Death succeeds life, life death, in never-ending motion; round and round, until they seem the same thing, or at any rate parts of one thing. The dead are mixed with the mould, which is found to contain the wing-cases of beetles, small Gasteropod shells, and other hard skeleton parts. All is grist to the mill. For this is the workshop of the jungle. From this ghetto spring the solid wooden pillars, with their props and buttresses, which support the green roof a hundred feet above our heads. Rarely does a living tree fall in the hill jungle, save when the mountain sloughs a portion of its skin, which peels off the steep rock face, and goes sliding and splintering into the valley, carrying the forest with it in one grand ruin. When a tree is uprooted, as may happen during a storm, it is often so well stayed by creepers that it cannot fall without either pulling down the trees to which it is bound, or breaking its bonds. Thus it stands, leaning for support against the surrounding trees, until at last the strained rigging parts, and its weight brings it crashing down. Such a tree, with its coils of creepers lying in every direction and its massive branches, is a formidable obstacle across the path. Only when such a tree is laid low does one get an idea of the size of these forest giants. Then, too, one begins to realise the third estate of the forest —the hanging gardens. So overlain is the roof with epiphytes, plant growing on plant, that it becomes utterly impossible to distinguish the tree itself from its attendant vegetation, which hides leaves, flowers, fruits, even the very bark; while if the dome of the tree is covered with creepers, the confusion is worse. In the Burmese hill jungle the commonest epiphytes are Ferns, Orchids, Zingiberaceæ (Hedychium, Globba), Arisæma and other Araceæ, Æschynanthus, Lysionotus, Rhododendrons, Ficus, Agapetes, Pentapterygium, Desmogyne, and Begonia. These flourish, and overflow the branches and boles of the big trees in a boundless flood, intent only on the struggle for light, food, and water, doing nothing in return for the support which helps them to obtain these necessities. Every nook and cranny of the tree not already occupied is covered with a layer of moss, or of Filmy Fern, or lichen. Hardly anywhere is the bark exposed, unless it is so smooth that no soil can gather on it, or so easily cast off, that no plant can obtain good anchorage. So heavy is the pressure of life, that the very leaves of the trees are sometimes encrusted with Mosses and Lichens. This is very conspicuous on a species of Myristica.

While the big trees of the hill jungle are staged by a rigging of creepers, those of the sub-tropical jungle are often supported by thin wooden buttresses, which radiate from the base of the trunk like planks on edge—the so-called plank-buttress. These are rarely met with in the upper forest. More common are the prop-like roots, or flying-buttresses, which spring from the lower part of the trunk of Pandanus, or the stilt roots let down from the branches of Ficus.

In spite of the hidden death which lurks in the mould, death by fungus, death from strangulation and smothering by rivals, death from pressure of population, above all death from a vast army of hungry insects, the forest could not survive but for those same insects which seem to be so destructive. Insects pollinate the flowers which produce the seeds on which their offspring feed. It is probable that certain insects are associated all through their changeful life with certain plants. This is known to be true of the Fig, which is visited and pollinated by certain Hymenopterous insects.

The Figs form a vast family, many species of which are found in the Irrawaddy jungle, though few of them are edible. One frequently sees bunches of Figs hanging from the tree-trunks. In the temperate zone, trees bear their fruit either on the current year's shoots, or on last year's, but not on older wood. It is otherwise in the hills, where the air is always saturated. There any part of the tree may bear fruit, and often does. The crust of bark which confines the seething juices within, splits open to release the pent-up forces, even as the face of the earth is ripped open by the molten rock compressed beneath. It cannot be said that fat trunks and rounded limbs, breaking out in bunches of fruit, as though erupting in monstrous spots, are objects of beauty; but beautiful or not, there was one tree subject to this exorbitant fructification which was always welcome. This was a species of Garcinia, whose branches were knobbly with yellow fruits the size of nectarines, and tart, but delicious to hot and tired men. The Nungs like other dwellers in the jungle have much empirical knowledge of the uses of fruits, leaves, roots, bark, and other forest produce. First and foremost they know what is wholesome and what is poisonous, and that is important in a land where famine stalks abroad. It is also important to know when and where to find food in the forest. I have seen them collecting the seeds and shoots of Bamboo, various kinds of Fungi, the big tubers of Dioscorea, and the fruits of *Ficus Cunia*, Saurauja, Garcinia, and Rubus. Most of these I have myself eaten and enjoyed; only when it comes to frogs, lizards, snails and even snakes, have I declined. Then again the leaves and bark of certain trees are used to poison fish, others as dyes, or medicines; and other useful products are known.

The hill jungle though poor in undergrowth—except Bamboo, which often grows so thickly as to be impenetrable—is rich in lianas. Some of these have flattened stems, two inches wide and almost as thin as ribbon. Such band-climbers, however, are always concertina-pleated, thus using at least twice the amount of material they need to reach the roof, if stretched out. Other lianas are twisted like a corkscrew; both devices assist the young climber to hold on to its support, and prevent side slip. But how is it done? There is only one means by which it can be accomplished, and that is by unequal growth on each side of the band alternately. First, the outer side of the band grows faster than the inner side, so that a curve is formed; then the inner side starts to grow, outstrips the outer side, and reverses the curve; and so it goes on to and fro. But it is not caused by pressure or contact, for how could such regular waving be brought about by that means! A helical spiral one can understand; there the turning stem is in contact throughout its growing end with a rigid, vertical stem, round which it winds itself coil by coil. Not so the bandclimber. When the pleat has reached a certain size, it is reversed; the inner side speeds up its growth, the outer side slows down its growth, and another pleat is added.

Then there are lianas whose stems are stuck all over with warts ending in prickles, or with dwarf shoots, or pedicels, which turn themselves into hooks or springs. All these appendages grapple amongst the branches overhead, supporting the stem on its long climb upwards to the light; not till it reaches the light does it bear leaves and flowers. But the band-liana, even when it has reached the roof, does not straighten itself out. The stem,

Meconopsis violacea ON THE BURMA FRONTIER,
11,000–12,000 FEET. FLOWERS VIOLET. JULY.

LOHIT VALLEY BETWEEN RIMA AND THE ASSAM FRONTIER,
3,000 FEET.

once soft and flexible, is now lignified; it is no longer capable of growth and resists pressure or tension. Yet this great excess of wood amidst the scaffolding of the jungle is of no use to the plant, once it has attained the open. Rather is it an embarrassment, since it means so much further to lift water and move supplies.

Inside the jungle leafless lianas lie about in loose coils like whipcord, but following them with the eye we notice that presently they climb up and up towards the roof, till they are lost in the gloom. When they have reached the top, the corkscrew lianas often relax their grip, or perhaps the support dies, choked in their embrace; then the coils sag down, adding to the tackle below. From outside, however, we get a different impression; for in the hill jungle it is often possible to look down on to the leafy roof from a neighbouring ridge. Now we see a fountain of creeper splashing over the tops of several trees in a mixed wave of flowers and foliage; but it is often impossible to be sure which leaves and flowers belong to the creeper and which to the several trees involved!

Although few trees fall in the battle, many are killed where they stand, not swiftly, but smothered, limb by limb, or strangled. For these lianas and lazy epiphytes are the enemies of trees. Some epiphytes, species of Ficus for example, though harmless enough at the beginning, presently grow so large that they overshadow the host altogether. Then enlarging their hold, gradually they crush the life out of it and take its place, no longer as epiphytes, but standing on the ground on their own roots. Everywhere climber and epiphyte are harassing the tree which gives them support, cutting off the light, harbouring insects, and generally making themselves a burden to their host. Gradually the tall tree pines and sickens; one by one its limbs perish. Fungi and insects, skirmishing on the flanks, are ready to pour into any wound, however caused. Once they are within the citadel, it is only a question of time before the last spark of life goes out from the tree. Thus, the forest giants perish, assailed on all sides by enemies, weaker than themselves, but in numbers irresistible; and a hundred seedlings spring up to compete for it place.

In the abyss where the dead trunks of trees lie in their green shrouds of fern and moss, and the great gaunt Bamboo stems groan together in the wind, hundreds of seedlings are growing. No matter that the insects have destroyed millions of fruits and seeds; many have escaped. The younger generation are pushing sturdily upwards, beneath the shade of their parents. There is not room for half of them, nor yet a quarter, perhaps for no more than one or two as they grow bigger. But now they are playing a grim sort of musical chairs, with their lives as stake. When a gap occurs in the forest, one tree may take its place. At present all are growing up together, in harmony; as they grow, the harmony becomes more and more strained. At last they begin to crowd their parents and rivals. Perhaps there is no vacancy yet and all are doomed to die; perhaps there is one vacancy, and one is chosen—many were called, and are now rejected. It seems just luck *which* is chosen!

Thus the tree can afford to throw its offspring to the worms by thousands, if the worms do something for it in return. Seeds and seedling are doomed, anyhow, and the parent is unmoved. Every other plant or potential plant is its rival and must fend for itself. There is no quarter.

Undergrowth, lianas, trees, and epiphytes together comprise the hill jungle, where every plant strives, first to live, secondly to reproduce its kind. But the plants are already so crowded that they are standing on each other's shoulders. The greater the number of the dead and dying, the greater the number of the living; such is the paradox of the jungle.

After crossing the first range we dropped down 4,000 feet into the valley, crossed the next range, and doing a double march, on August 21 found ourselves the same evening wading through the swamps of the Tisang river. We got covered with leeches here, and the sand-flies were terrible. As a result of exposure and poisoning by infinite torment of flies, I was taken violently sick in the night. At the Tisang we fell in with a runner from Fort Hertz carrying my mail; but he brought no news of our supply.

Next day we had to wade for miles across the flooded valley of the Tisang, so what with the awful heat, and sickness, I could only go slowly, stopping often to rest. It is not nice to be ill in the jungle, with no white man to hold your hand, and to know that you must keep moving at all costs, or fare worse. To rest in a swamp such as the Tisang valley in August is to invite disaster. However, after a night's sleep I felt much better, and able to face the biggest climb of all in good humour. We were now only five stages from Fort Hertz and I expected to do the distance in four days.

Half-way up the mountain we at last met our supply train on its way to our rescue; five coolies, each carrying a 60 lb. bag, four of rice and one of flour. I told them to dump the loads at the Nam Tamai bridge, and we would pick them up on our return.

The monsoon had started blowing again, and we had an uncomfortably wet march. On the ridge-top, 6,169 feet above sea-level, a raw wind drove the rain full in our faces. Several notable plants were in flower, the most notable of all being a scarlet-flowered bush Rhododendron! This on August 23! Though past its prime it was still a brave sight, with the rain scudding across the serried crests of the hills, and the troughs between packed with mist. It could not have opened its flowers before August 1, which of course is very late indeed for a Rhododendron, but it belongs to a type, which, in the Burmese jungle usually *does* flower late; in fact the rainy season is well begun before *Rhododendron facetum* and its allies fire the hillsides. They are all smallish trees occurring scattered amidst forests of Oaks, Magnolias, Bucklandia, Schima, Castonopsis, and Eugenia. In the damp gloom to come suddenly on a glowing flame such as this is a joy; it wrings from us a shout of delight. The ground beneath is red as though strewn with hot cinders.

Four years previously, in November 1922, I had crossed this pass on the overland journey from China to India, and had noticed this same Rhododendron. It was not then in flower of course, but I collected seed of it (K.W. 5533), and it is in cultivation. Now I had the flowers to match. The corolla is a hot glossy scarlet tattooed all over with tiny crimson quavers, rather fleshy, and pinched in at the base to form five honey-pockets. The chubby trusses pack more than a dozen flowers, which blaze out fiercely amongst the dark-green leaves.

The 'Irroratum' Rhododendrons, as a class, are not too hardy. But the plant just described, coming from an exposed position on the ridge at 6,000 feet altitude might prove more Spartan than most in constitution. That remains to be proved; its flower-buds at least should escape injury by Jack Frost!

Further along the ridge, growing only on the trees, was a charming dwarf Begonia (B. Hymenophylloides), whose white virginal flowers possessed a certain quality of freshness rarely seen in the jungle during the rains. This plant is even more remarkable for the strange beauty of its filmy leaves. They are exquisitely thin, narrow oval in shape, but with the end drawn out into a long drip tip. The plant clings closely to the tree-trunk, woven in amongst Mosses and Ferns, each leaf pointing straight downwards; and as the fine rain filters through the forest and clogs the beds of moss, it rolls down the trunk and drips steadily from the tips of the Begonia leaves. These leaves depart as widely from the usual 'elephant's ears' as do the strap-shaped leaves of B. rhoëphila which grows in the rocky stream-bed not far away.

One more plant, seen on this ridge, deserves mention. The long thread-like stems cling to a tree for support, sending roots in amongst the rough bark at intervals. The small leaves resemble green glass tubes filled with liqueur, and the solitary flowers which hang loosely against the trunk, gash the bark with vivid scarlet wounds.

Another double march, and we stood next afternoon on the last ridge, overlooking the emerald plain of Hkamti Long. That same evening we reached the Mali river. Much of the plain was flooded, so next day I hired a canoe to take me to Putao, which is close to the fort. But the sun came out and bludgeoned us all into a state of coma, so that we made slow progress against the strong current. At last I could stand it no longer, and disembarked to walk across the paddy-fields. These, however, were knee deep in water, and it took me rather longer to wade the last four miles than it took the canoe to paddle twice that distance against the current. However, here I was, having covered fifteen stages through the hill jungle in ten and a half days, at the worst season of the year; one hundred and fifty miles, going all out.

It was hot and clammy on the plain, not much more than a thousand feet above sea level, and closely invested by mountains, and I was glad to lie in a long chair during the worst heat of the day. It was pleasant to sleep in a bed again, and to have regular meals—I dined and breakfasted with the Superintendent, who was at headquarters for the rainy season.

Shortly after my arrival, some Nungs turned up from the Nam Tamai, bringing my truant servants in custody! It appeared that Maung Ba and Laphai, hearing of my whirlwind march down the valley, and believing me to be in pursuit of them, turned aside to a Nung village in the mountain, where they were hospitably received. Next day, having robbed their host of some money he kept under the floor, they took to the road again; it being reported that we had passed. But the Nungs discovering the theft, pursued and captured them, and conducted them in to Fort Hertz. The man who had been robbed then brought a case against them, they were convicted of theft, and discharged as first offenders! The headman recovered his money, and received a further reward from me. I recovered the articles which the pilferers had seized before their flight, and they all lived happily ever afterwards. At least I suppose so; there seems no reason why not. And that was the end of Maung Ba and Laphai so far as I was concerned!

Meanwhile I had acquired two more servants, the raw material this time; Nungs, fresh from the jungle. One, a smart little fellow named Pyi, was a sort of catch-'em-alive-oh! or local policeman lent me by the Superintendent: the other, whom I installed as cook, was about as familiar with white men as he was with white elephants. However, with Chokara, Pyi, and Fat behind me, I felt I could face the world again.

Having purchased stores for the journey, we left Fort Hertz again on September 2 after six days' rest. Travelling down the Mali by boat, we reached the edge of the plain in a few hours. The clouds, low and shredded, were dragging over the dismal hills, and it rained without ceasing.

The journey to the Nam Tamai furnished an incident. Though the Monsoon had started afresh, it did not rain every day, or at least not all day every day, and when it did not rain it was oppressively hot, and in the jungle we were plagued by bees. The day we left the Tisang river behind us was particularly hot, and arrived at the hut in the late afternoon, I mounted the ladder, and stretching myself out on the springy bamboo floor, prepared to rest. The coolies were squatting by their loads outside, too exhausted to move, my men were lighting a fire in the adjoining shack, preparatory to making me some tea. I had been lying down only a few minutes, when I heard a startled cry; at the same instant there came to my ears a crack, followed by a dull tearing sound. I sprang to my feet. Once long ago in the Maru country I had heard a similar sound. My mind jumped back to one hot afternoon on the frontier before the war, and vaguely, almost unconsciously, I understood. In two strides I was across the room, and out of the door—seconds only had elapsed since the warning, and already the veranda was tilted at an alarming angle; the ladder which had been leaning against it was gone. But I did not stop to consider that. Taking the veranda in my stride, I stepped over the low railing and jumped the six feet to the ground, where I landed in a heap; and as I jumped, the hut crashed behind me. When I picked myself up in a cloud of dust, there was no hut; it had collapsed flat like a house of cards. Whether an earth tremor had passed through the hills, or whether the immense weight of thatch, soaked by the recent rains, had at last proved too much for the central beam, weakened by the mining of white ants, it was impossible to say. Anyhow, I had escaped a peculiarly unpleasant death by a miracle.

The jungly native hut is a big heavy barn, with massive beams to support a vast deal of Grass or Palm thatch, the shaggy eaves projecting far below the stunted walls. Walls and floor, of split bamboo mat, are flimsy enough, but the roof is upheld by the great central beam, which runs the length of the hut, supported on powerful pillars. If that goes, all goes. Once I saw the framework of a Maru hut crumple up like so much brown-paper when struck by a hill typhoon.

There were more coolies available now, so we went on without a halt. I even tried to do a double march, but the girl coolies all shammed lame in protest, so it came to nothing. Much to their chagrin I dismissed them and substituted young men who volunteered for service. On September 17 we reached the Seinghku-Adung confluence, and the Nungs said they could not go any further. It would have taken several days to find coolies in this wilderness, so I said they must go on to my base camp—it was only two marches. Finally they agreed to do so.

Up to this point we had come through fairly unscathed from enemy bites, but once in the Seinghku valley, first sand-flies and then leeches attacked us. On September 19, in the course of the last march, we halted for lunch on the Rhododendron ridge. Amongst the smooth-leafed Rhododendrons I noticed a solitary big-leafed tree bulging with large trusses of rust-red capsules. "This is *R. grande*." I said to myself confidently. "I may as well get a specimen, though." So I sent one of the men up to lop off a branch. Imagine my surprise when, on looking closely at leaf and capsule, I found it was not *R. grande* at all, or even closely related to it but one of the 'Irroratum' Rhododendrons—*not R. tanastylum*! The biggest leaves secured were a foot long and six inches wide! This tree was fifty feet high, and stuffed almost to bursting with fruits; perched on the knife-edge ridge, it must have been a never-to-be-forgotten sight in full bloom! Sometime in the course of the next twenty years it may flower in Britain! and, should the flowers turn out to be glowing scarlet, like those of *R. facetum*, this nameless Rhododendron will astonish the next generation. But perhaps someone will have gone to the Seinghku valley and told us all about it before then.

Near the village, beneath a gigantic Oak, I picked up the butter-golden corollas of a Rhododendron, but the plant itself was high up out of sight. Several times in the course of the next few days I was tantalised by the sight of butter pools in the forest where this species had strewn its flowers, but peep as I would, always the plant was screened behind dense foliage overhead. Nor could I see which tree to hack down, or climb; though so great was their girth that neither plan was reasonable. Not till September 25 did I find that a small 'Maddeni' Rhododendron in fruit, which had been under observation since June, now glittered with the same colour. The flowers are small for a 'Maddeni', borne in trusses of four to six, scentless, and of a glossy quince-yellow in bright light, though more butter-gold in the depths of the forest. This is *R. chrysolepis*, a charming little plant though possibly not very hardy.

In the home paddock, where the grass had grown three feet high, we ran into thousands of famished leeches, and the almost naked coolies arrived in camp with arms and legs striped like a Bengal tiger. The headman was so covered with blood, which streamed down his face, as to be almost unrecognisable. The meadow, because they had not cut the grass, harboured all kinds of loathsome life, besides leeches. I had cherished a fond hope that by mid-September conditions would have improved. Vain delusion! My hut was a sty, full of earwigs, cockroaches, and all uncharitableness. It was mouldy, and it stank; the roof leaked, the floor was littered with leaves, mostly from the roof, and the wind moaned through the log walls. However, when the fire had been lit and the roof repaired, I began to cheer up, though the fire smoked evilly because the wood was wet, and the rain still beat in at all angles.

Next day the Nung coolies had to depart, as we could not feed them. The girls took half their wages in beads, which were doled out by Chokara. Knowing the exact value of beads to Nung damsels, he was much more frugal than I would have been. Nevertheless, the girls were well pleased with their bargain.

9   Through the Back Door

BY the end of October I had harvested my seeds and was ready to start for India. Sanction had been obtained from the Indian Government, the only condition being, that I must be self-contained as far as the Tidding river, since no supplies were available *en route*. In other words, if things went wrong, I need not look to the Government for assistance. After working out a time-table, I decided to ration myself for three weeks. From Haita to Kahao, of course, I could get nothing, as the Di Chu valley was uninhabited. At Kahao I reckoned on getting supplies from Rima, sufficient to take me to the Tidding river at any rate.

Including my collections and rations, I had twenty loads; a tent and all surplus stores were jettisoned at my base camp. On October 27 the coolies paraded, and after inspecting them, I gave them a cash advance and some rice. I bought a goat from the Tibetans; and we parted on excellent terms. October 28 was a glorious day, not a cloud in the sky; the lull before the storm.

When we started up the valley next morning the sky was completely overcast, and a light drizzle filled the air with moisture. An hour later we sat down to rest in the river-bed, and one of the Lisus, pointing to a tree, quietly strung his crossbow. I watched him take careful aim and then, *twang*! there was a flash of yellow in the tree-top, and the bird dropped dead, pierced through the heart; a marvellous shot. It was a long-tailed Trogon (female), and I took it for a specimen, promising to give it to the owner when I had skinned it, for of course he had shot it for food. In the evening I set to work, and never having skinned a Trogon before, I naturally supposed that my clumsiness accounted for several rents made. Had I known that a Trogon has a skin like wet blotting-paper I would never have undertaken the work at all. However I completed the task, and sent the specimen to the Natural History Museum where I learnt that it was a new species, which has been named *Ptyrotrogon wardi*. The next incident in the history of this remarkable long-tailed Trogon was its discovery in northern Tongking by Monsieur Delacour, in 1929! Monsieur Delacour secured several specimens, both male and female, so evidently it is not rare in Tongking. The male bird has the breast bright rose instead of yellow.

In the evening we reached Snowy Camp, and halted there for the night. There was no snow now, and the stream had shrunk to a rill. Next day it was raining steadily, and we went on to River Camp, and from there to

High Camp; by which time we were wet through and chilled to the bone.

The cold bare valley looked bleak indeed. The only flowers were Gentians, which glittered like splinters of blue ice on the steep lawns. There was no snow, except a film on the high peaks, but a curtain of grey mist spread itself over the landscape, and through this the shapeless mountains leered at us. Luckily we found a supply of dry firewood at High Camp. It froze sharply in the night, and the coolies, even huddled round a good fire, suffered terribly from the cold. Early next morning I went outside to look at the weather; it was snowing, but presently it ceased, and the clouds began to break up. There was no sign of snow on the pass itself, which was just visible. After a hurried breakfast we started. The coolies marched slowly, and though I had to stop and collect seeds, I reached the top first. The sight which greeted me filled me with dismay. On the Burma side, even at the summit, there was hardly any snow. Looking back down the Seinghku valley, one saw the familiar features of the mountains, the keen edges of schist, the fretted turrets of limestone, grey against the whiter clouds, and the long straight line of pale scree with darker stripes of Rhododendron. The view on the Tibetan side was utterly different. At first one could distinguish nothing; just blank whiteness. Then the upper lake appeared, shining dully like pewter, a thousand feet below, and a sombre grey cliff crystallised out of the mist. That was all. Not a tree, not a bush showed up; there was nothing else, except snow.

For some time I sat there in a numb fear, waiting for the coolies, and then, seeing them on the move again, I started down to stamp a trail. The snow had drifted against the steep face, and I sank in to my knees, kicking a path as best I could. When I reached the upper lake I looked back; a file of black dots was slowly descending the white wall. A pair of Brahminy duck rose from the lake as I approached but I saw no other sign of life. Descending to the lower lake, I waited for some of the others to come up, and presently Pyi and Fat appeared, leading the goat, and followed by two Lisus and two Nungs. We waited again for the main body, and then as they did not come, we decided to push on to a camping-place and light a fire.

Turning a corner, the first trees came into view; but the soft snow was deep and the descent was not easy. Late in the afternoon we reached the junction of two streams, a little below our camping-place in July, There were Fir-trees and Rhododendron-bushes here, affording some shelter from the cruel wind, so we decided to camp. Hastily collecting a few faggots, we lit a fire and warmed our hands. We had no hope of getting out of the snow before dark, though there was still an hour's daylight left.

We fully expected the sixteen coolies to arrive at any minute, but after half an hour I began to grow uneasy. Surely they would not linger once they were over the pass! Yet they might have halted by the first clump of trees and lit a fire! Twice I started off along the trail and up the snowbound slope to see if I could see them coming over the escarpment below the lake basin. There was no sign of them. I shouted again and again, but the cliffs flung back a mocking echo, which was lost in that cold white wilderness, and each time the ensuing silence was more horrible than before. Then I returned to our fire, where the torrent gurgled between the clinking ice jambs. Night had fallen.

Now I took stock of the position. We had no tent, or food (except the goat), but we had our bedding, so we made up our beds and tried to sleep. Luckily the weather was fine, though the sky was overcast. Very early next morning we got up, and after waiting an hour for the missing coolies, in case they had spent the night by the first clump of trees, one of the Lisus and I started up the valley to find out what had happened. At the lower lake there was no trace of them; and so vanished the last lingering hope that they might yet come. They had fled. The question was, what had they done with the kit? An awful feeling of despair came over me, and I sat down on a rock, staring at the leaden water and feeling very unhappy. Then to pass the time I set about looking for the dwarf 'Lapponicum' Rhododendron which grew amongst the granite tors, while my companion went on towards the pass; nor had he gone far when he came to the loads, flung down in a heap in the snow.

With the data now available it was easy to re-construct the crime. The sight of the snow, and still more, contact with it, had frightened the Nungs. As they were almost naked, this was intelligible. Arrived at the upper lake, some distance behind us, they had halted. Nothing was visible except snow, and deep snow, too; not a vestige of a tree even. Snow and rock, rock and snow. And the wind! Those girls! Had the sun shone and warmed them a little things might have been different. Had we been there, even, I would have persuaded, or bribed, or forced them to go on. But there was no sun, and we were out of sight. The sense of desolation in that silent valley was awful. The Nungs sat there, shivering with cold and the fear of death. Someone, bolder than the rest, hinted at flight, which for a Nung was daring enough. But they were urged now by something stronger than tribal law, or even tribal custom. Fear had them by the throat. Panic set in, and ran through the party like an epidemic. Their one desire was to be quit of the snow as soon as possible, and to light a fire, before they perished of cold. In front of them lay deep snow for an indefinite distance. But behind them! They had only descended fifteen hundred feet from the pass! They *knew* there was no snow on the Burma side, that there was a hut, and firewood waiting for them. It would be easy to reach High Camp before dark if they went immediately; probably they could reach River Camp. The last thing they wanted to do was to burden themselves with impedimenta; nor are the Nungs given to thieving. The meek, who have indeed inherited the earth, or what there is of it at the headwaters of the Irrawaddy, have inherited little else, and covet nothing. So they turned, and leaving the loads, hurried up the steep hill, with many a fearful back-ward glance, we may be sure; and our loads lay there in the snow just as they had been thrown down by the fugitives. The few things missing were just what people in such desperate straits as these Ishmaelites believed themselves to be, would commandeer without a twinge of conscience; a beggarly bag of rice, my Burberry—a few unconsidered trifles like that. They might save a life—several lives.

What was a bag of rice worth? Ten rupees or so. But to the Nungs it was worth its weight in gold. Unfortunately, however, in the peculiar circumstances in which we were now placed, a bag of rice might be worth its weight in gold to us too! One cannot eat gold, and we had to be rationed at least as far as the Lohit, and possibly further. We had in fact started with enough rice to last my two men and myself ten days on full rations; after that we must trust to luck. But now a very different complexion was put on the affair. The four staunch coolies had barely enough food to last them to the Lohit, and here we were one day out of our reckoning already, and goodness only knew how many more to follow!

However, I must confess that the sight of the loads lying there in the snow was a great relief to me. Look at it how one might, it was easier to go on than to retreat; and I began turning over a new scheme in my mind. Meanwhile, my companion, shouldering the last bag of rice, carried it back in triumph to our camp; while I abandoned the dump in disgust, in order to continue my search for the missing 'Lapponicum' Rhododendron. It occurred to me later that, but for this upset, I should never have got seed of it at all. It will be recalled that the two best 'Lapponicums' were stratified, *R. suaveolens* resting conformably on the swarth *R. rupicola* so to speak. *R. microphyllum*, however, was so rare that it could only be said to form pockets in the general mass of 'Lapponicums'. The inference was, it belonged rather to the Tibetan side of the range and had only just overflowed across the passes on to the Burma side; so now to find large deposits. This was accomplished with less trouble than might have been expected, considering the snow. I discovered, in fact, that *R. microphyllum* formed much of the thin scrub on the short broken cliffs above the lake; the tuffets growing in the crevices and amongst the tumbled rocks. These tuffets or brooms are small, compact and twiggy, the capsules in twos and threes amongst the crisp scale-backed leaves. It took me an hour to collect a few dozen (many being destroyed by Fungus), and with these I returned to camp. First we all had a meal, and then I held a council of ways and means. The gist of it was this: that the unaccompanied baggage being on our side of the pass, it was as easy to go on as to go back, but that we could not abandon it altogether, or only a very little of it. At all cost, the collection must be saved, and that meant food and bedding as well. There were seven of us, counting myself as a coolie; but this was an over-estimate, my coolie-power being not more than fifty per cent. that of the man trained from childhood to carry weights. Anyhow, seven men could not carry sixteen loads, *and* the luggage-in-advance per stage per day.

The first thing to do was to rescue the unaccompanied baggage; the second, to jettison what we did not actually need; the third, to withdraw horse, foot, and guns from our advance position in contact with the snow. If another storm came, the forward dump might be hopelessly cut off; though luckily the weather was improving. At the same time I could not forget that our temporary camp was at a height of 12,000 feet, and it was the month of November. The dump lay a thousand feet higher. Two marches down the valley, but not more than a thousand feet below us, was the hot spring, in the bosom of the Fir forest; there we would be safe even through the next storm.

Why, it may be asked, was there so much snow on the Tibetan side of the pass, and none on the Burma side? It is impossible to say; it was just luck. The interesting thing about these mountains is, that the weather never is the same; abnormal weather is the rule. Another year the position might be reversed, the Burma side be snowed up. Perhaps we were lucky not to find *both* sides under deep snow by the end of October! Had they been, the Nungs never would have crossed the pass!

My plan was very simple; namely that the seven of us should relay the loads down the valley as far as the hot spring, dump them there, and with light loads go on to Kahao for help. I had difficulty in conveying this plan to the men. With the exception of me, they all spoke Chingpaw, which was their *lingua franca*. My language was Hindustani, but none of them understood a word of that! However, in a mixture of Burmese, of which Pyi understood a little, and Chinese, of which one of the two Lisus understood a little, eked out with signs, I conveyed my meaning, and offered substantial rewards to those who stood by me. All promised to do so, and it was arranged that the six of them should go straight up to the dump and rescue the loads right away. Pyi and Fat were decently clad; but the other four were not, and before they started I divided my raiment—spare parts— amongst them.

Meanwhile, I was left in charge of the camp. I chopped firewood, cut out a nest for myself under the bushes, and collected Rhododendron seed. The dull afternoon dragged on, the violet dusk deepened. No sound broke the stillness, except the bicker of the stream forcing its way through the Tamarisk bushes, and the occasional clink of ice. Darkness fell with the sudden weight of an axe, and the frost hardened. I lit the lantern, and went up the path, the sugary snow crunching underfoot; but there was no sign or sound of the men. A thought struck me. Had *they* also turned tail? If so I was in a fix. I put the thought aside; no, it was not likely. Nevertheless, it kept recurring, and as the night grew darker and darker, I grew first uneasy, and then alarmed. Suddenly the goat bleated. Yes, I had the goat, and most of the rice! The goat was better dead than alive, being a nuisance on the march: but I was feeling so lonely that even its company was welcome, and it heralded the return of my companions, who presently staggered into camp with bulky loads.

Here we were, then, united once more. Fortune smiled on me again; and basking in that fickle smile, I slept warmly in my snuggery. With the rising of the sun on November 2 our stock also rose; for the weather turned gloriously fine. Further outlook settled for some days at least. The four coolies returned to the dump for the remaining things, Pyi and Fat rested, and I collected seeds and took photographs.

On November 3 we sorted the loads, jettisoned what we dared, made up our loads to include not only the most necessary, but also the most precious goods, dumped the remainder, and started down the valley.

My own load, though it did not weigh more than 30 lbs., proved a sufficient burden, but the weather was sunny and the path easy. What had been a bog in July was now firm ground. Early in the afternoon we reached a meadow and a moraine covered with huge Fir-trees, and halted. It must not, however, be imagined that the valley was forested; it was not. As on the Burma side, so here, the trees clung to the moraines in the bottom of the valley, though higher up on the flanks there might be scattered trees. Thus there were clumps of silver Fir on the steep rocky riser which separated the two lakes; on the moraine, at the junction of the two streams where we had lately been camping; and on the moraine where we were camping now. On this last mound there were also several big red-barked Birch-trees.

Next morning the four coolies returned to Camp 1; Pyi and Fat were given a rest; while I climbed a neighbouring gulley and collected more seed of *Rhododendron microphyllum, Meconopsis violacea*, and other plants. On the cliffs were clumps of vivid blue trumpet Gentian (*G. setulifolia*). The top of the ridge was strewn with angular slabs of rock, overlain by sugary snow. There was no extensive view, but I could see the Diphuk La away up at the head of the valley, surrounded by snowy peaks.

The four coolies did not return that night, but two Tibetans from Rima arrived instead, and next morning when my coolies got back from Camp 1, I persuaded two of them, together with the two Zayul Tibetans, to go straight on to the hot spring with loads; the other two returned to Camp 1 for the remaining loads, and we spent another day at Camp 2.

On the 6th, which was my birthday, the last two coolies arrived from Camp 1, and all five of us started for the hot spring, leaving behind what we could not carry; and next day two coolies again returned to Camp 2, while we stayed at the hot spring. These two rejoined us on November 8 and once more our party was united. All the loads were safe now at the hot spring, and we could put the rest of the plan into operation.

Meanwhile, I had been up on the cliffs across the river collecting seed of the Rhododendrons discovered in July. Snow still lay under the bushes, even round our camp, showing how severe the storm had been; and a thousand feet higher up on the scree it was so deep that all the dwarf Rhododendrons were buried.

At the hot spring we found two Tibetans skinning a takin, and bought some meat from them.

On November 9 we started again, with heavy loads, our intention being to march straight through to Kahao in three days. The rest of the baggage was stored in the bamboo shelter at the hot spring.

During the descent we met a number of Zayul men on their way to the Seinghku valley; they were much better clad than the Nungs, and carried heavy loads.

On the march I collected seed of several Rhododendrons which I had not seen in bloom, besides other plants, and making the same camps as in July, we reached the Lohit on the 11th, glad to be warm again. Arrived at Kahao, I was handed a letter from the Political Officer, Sadiya. A Mishmi had brought it ten days ago, the headman informed me, had waited two days, and then running short of food, had returned to his own village.

We were given an empty hut to live in, and I now tried to engage eight coolies to return to the hot springs and bring down my loads. Impossible! Kahao could only produce four, and my own men were in need of a rest; however, I engaged men to go in search of coolies. Four days passed. Another storm swept up the gorge, and raged furiously in the mountains. Almost every day Mishmis passed up the valley, carrying loads to Rima, but I could not persuade them to break their journey in order to fetch mine. I was getting desperate. Another serious problem presented itself; our rice supply was finished. While we were at the hot spring, the coolies' supply failed, and I had to feed them. Already eleven days had passed since we left Haita, and they had brought only a week's supply. With four extra mouths to feed, my own supply rapidly dwindled; and here we were at the end of our rations! I had a few stores, and a little flour left; but we were more than a fortnight's march from the nearest help, and moreover, there was not the slightest sign of our ever being able to start for Sadiya. We seemed to be held up indefinitely for lack of transport.

At last on the 16th I persuaded my four coolies to return to the hot spring with four Kahao coolies, and bring in the loads. They went off quite happily; and on the 21st I had the satisfaction of seeing all my kit once more and getting a square meal; for my stores had been left behind at the hot spring in order that the collections could be brought down.

Meanwhile, I had not been idle. All my seeds had been spread out to dry, and as they dried, I had packed and catalogued them.

I was impatient to start down the Lohit valley; but two more days passed before we finally got away, because food had to be prepared. However, on November 23 we really did start, with a mixed lot of coolies, Nungs, Lisus,

Mishmis, and men of Zayul, who for want of a better name may be called Tibetans.

For the first two marches the path was not bad, although there were awkward cliffs and corners. A succession of Pine-clad terraces, cut into blocks by streams, backed by bare granite cliffs, and truncated below by the turbulent Lohit, succeeded the rice-fields of Kahao. Large streams, like the Di Chu, have gnawed a passage for themselves through the cliffs; smaller ones leap down from the top. Thus the Dati Falls, which we saw on the second day, are 3,000 feet high, the cascade being in three joints, but there was not enough water coming down to be really impressive. The worst places were in the bed of the river. Here we had to dodge about amongst huge blocks of stone, and work hard for every yard gained, with the added risk of a nasty tumble. Some of the rock faces high up also proved thrilling, and there was one specially awkward cliff which we reached at dusk, and over which we had to climb above the swerving river in order to reach a camping-ground.

It was dark when we halted in the Pine forest that night. We lit big fires, and slept as we were on the ground. Next day we did a long march to the Dong river, where there are two huts, the first we had seen since leaving Kahao.

Just below the village of Dong a hill of earth and rocks, covered with trees, fills the valley. Looking northwards from its summit, one clearly sees the terraces on each side, marking the old high-level valley, with the river picking its way amongst their remains, and snow-clad peaks poking up their heads in the distance. Looking southwards on the other hand, one sees thick forest, and the spurs beginning to overlap. It is as though the upper Lohit valley had been ice worn, and we were standing on the moraine which marked the furthest extension of the glacier.

There was more cultivation round here than the population seemed to warrant. Descending abruptly from the hill, we reached the paddy terraces, and camped by the rope bridge. Here were several Tibetan huts on both banks.

On November 26, the headman visited me, bringing some eggs and a little rice, for which I gladly paid a rupee; but the morning was half spent before the local people arrived with slings to help us over the rope bridge. The crossing, which was a difficult one, took three hours; consequently we had hardly started down the right bank of the river than we had to halt for the night. The Lohit here raced through a deep trench, and the rope was suspended fifty feet above the water, the span being about eighty yards. After sliding a short distance down the inclined rope, one had to haul oneself two-thirds of the way across, owing to sag.

Below the rope bridge, the Pine forest ended, at least in the river-bed, though there were still Pine-trees higher up on the flanks of the gorge. With the change to a moister climate, jungle was beginning to appear, and we saw Palms, Tree Ferns, and a species of Pandanus for the first time. Walong, at the rope bridge, was the last Tibetan village; we now entered the Mishmi Hills. The Tibetan huts are log cabins built of Pine wood, of which there is an almost unlimited supply. Some of the trees too, though of no considerable girth, are upwards of 150 feet high, and very straight, with a fine head of branches. But owing to lack of water for irrigation, and to the rocky nature of the soil, the Lohit gorge is scarcely inhabited. A day's march below Walong, we reached the first Mishmi village, on the left bank, and camped opposite to it.

The Mishmi huts are something less solid than the Tibetan, being built of Bamboo, thatched with grass. The second day after leaving the rope bridge, we reached Sati at noon, and camped in the fields. The headman brought me a fowl, and promised coolies for the following day; so I paid off the four men who had come with me from the Seinghku, keeping only Pyi and Fat; the others then returned to Rima.

A tall white-flowered Aster was very abundant in thickets in the drier parts of the valley.

Near Sati we passed a granite boulder on which the following inscription was carved:

5th COY. 1st K.G.O. Sappers and Miners, 1912.

It marked the furthest point reached by the British expedition in 1913; and it was the first hint, not merely that we were in British territory, but even that white men had ever been in this valley before. The track immediately began to improve; it was still only a footpath, but expert engineers had obviously been at work on it. Here and there were stone revetments as solid as on the day they were built, fourteen years ago; but everything was now smothered in jungle.

At midday on November 30 we reached Mindzong, where the Ghalum river flows in, and the Lohit makes its big bend to the west. All the local Mishmi headmen brought presents of fowls and rice, for which of course I paid. After the stories I had heard about the Mishmis, they seemed quite amiable and pleasant folk, and I began to think them much maligned. But it happened that their friendliness was entirely due to the personal influence of the Political Officer in Sadiya. One thing I could not get them to do, and that was to start early in the mornings. Yet in spite of what we had bought, we were running short of rice, and it was important to push on as fast as possible; already we were two days down on the time-table from Kahao to Theronliang, apart from the twelve days lost owing to the breakdown on the Diphuk La.

Four more marches along an overgrown track, which involved a good deal of climbing, brought us to the mouth of the Delei river on December 4. Less than an hour previously we had crossed the Dou, both rivers flowing in from a horseshoe ring of high peaks to the north. The Sappers and Miners had thrown a wire-cable suspension bridge over the Delei, but this had long since collapsed from neglect. One cable had sagged, but from the other the Mishmis had managed to hang a Heath Robinson footway, across which I walked not without a qualm.

The Mishmis told me that we were now only three marches from the Assam frontier. The Mishmi Hills are 'unadministered territory,' though theoretically the tract is part of the province of Assam. The Zayul frontier has never been demarcated. As we were starting next day, an old chief came to me and whispered that we could reach Theronliang in two days if necessary.

On December 5 we marched for seven hours, and camped on the narrow path. The river, which is here flowing in a semicircle, was still very turbulent, and, owing to the overlapping spurs, we could not see any distance down the valley; but everything pointed to the fact that we were now close to the plains. As far as the Delei river, we had been passing through quite a number of villages; we also met parties of Mishmis and Tibetans, returning from Sadiya. Now we were sunk in another uninhabited tract. The jungle was very dense, one of the commonest sights being the long hanging scarlet ropes of *Thunbergia coccinea*. On the cliffs were Begonias, and there was a species of Phaius in flower.

Our last march was quite dramatic. At breakfast we finished the rice and flour. After marching for five hours we suddenly left the Lohit valley, crossed a spur, and descending abruptly, about one o'clock found ourselves by the Tidding river. Here we halted for lunch, and soon after starting again the Mishmi coolies wanted to halt for the night. I urged them on, however, and we marched for another two hours, wading ankle deep in water for several miles. At dusk we reached a suspension bridge over the Tidding river, and the coolies threw down their loads. I had no idea how far we were from Theronliang, my servants had gone on, and there I was left with the Mishmis, who refused to budge. However, one man offered to bring my servants back. I sat down on the bridge, feeling very tired and hungry, and dozed. It was now quite dark. Suddenly I sat up; a light was moving amongst the trees on the far bank; it disappeared, only to reappear again. It certainly did not belong to us; I had long since abandoned my hurricane-lamps for lack of oil. Five minutes later several men stepped on to the bridge and crossed over to me; Pyi, the *durwan* from Theronliang, carrying a lantern and the Mishmi messenger, were easily recognised. I was told that we were less than a mile from the bungalow, and the Mishmis promised to bring the loads on as soon as they had eaten their supper. So, lighting bamboo torches, which soon went out, we stumbled along the narrow path in almost total darkness, and soon reached Theronliang, the last bungalow in administered territory on the road to Rima! We had crossed the 'inner line'! What a joyful moment that was! First I had a hot bath. About ten o'clock Pyi brought me some food; and then I sat by a blazing fire, with no thought of bed till about 3 a.m.

Next morning to my disgust I learnt that we had to climb one more spur, 6,000 feet high, in order to reach Denning Post, on the edge of the plain. It was twenty-four miles to Denning, and we started too late to go through in the day. Just over the saddle, however, was another bungalow, called Dreyi; and I decided to spend the night there.

It was a long pull up the hill but the path was wide and properly graded; the coolies, however, followed the old Mishmi path, which went straight up the face. At last we reached the summit, where there is a notice board which says:

Tidding Saddle, 6,000 feet.

It might have added: 'This hill is dangerous to cyclists.'

Unfortunately, the sky had become overcast, spoiling the view up the Lohit valley; though I caught sight of the needle peak of Dapha Bum, which is over 15,000 feet high, some miles to the south. This is said to be visible from Sadiya.

It was late when we reached the saddle, and there was a bite in the air. Hardly had we begun the descent to the plain when there burst on us without warning one of the most amazing sights it has ever been my good fortune to see. The mountain is very steep on this side and the path slants to and fro in long wave-lengths, with a high bank on one side and an almost sheer drop on the other. The sun was now low down, and dead ahead; indeed we would have had it full in our eyes, but for a belt of cloud drawn tightly across the sky, its lower edge firm and hard like the sea rim. From behind this belt sprang a dazzling illumination. Right below us the hills ceased suddenly as though trimmed off with a knife, except where two long spurs flared sharply into the sunset; and there at our feet, stretching away league on league until it was swallowed up in the reeking embers of the winter's dusk, lay the plain of Assam! From this height the plain looked like a gigantic park, and across it brazenly lit by the rays which splashed out in a golden shower from behind the cloud wrack, a maze of rivers flowed to swell the Brahmaputra. The Lohit, which we had followed for so many days through the hills, rushing out of close confinement, is suddenly checked on the plain, and proceeds to spread itself out in a network of streams covering a wide expanse of barren sand. Now all these placid channels were caught in the flame of the setting sun, and shone like molten metal.

Northwards the view was cut off by ranges of mighty mountains, through which broke other great rivers, now sunk in the gloaming; but for the next half-hour while we slid to and fro like shuttles on the gigantic loom of the hill, we caught glimpses of this astonishing silted sea below, partly lit by enormous streaks of raw colour, trailed comet-like across the sky, partly in the deepening shadow of night. Gradually the whole scene faded into the grey mist as the air chilled.

103

Not till the stars came out could I tear myself away from the contemplation of the plains, and all that they meant; villages, towns, cities, life, movement, great crowds of people. After being buried alive in the mountains and the jungle for so many months, the revulsion of feeling on the threshold of civilisation leaves one at first a little breathless.

The colours faded and changed swiftly now. Hot crimson was succeeded by a cold indigo, indigo dimmed to grey, and night came just as we reached Dreyi, 5,160 feet, a windy bungalow perched on a spur overlooking the plain and the ranges which buttress the eastern end of the Himalaya.

The plain was steeped in milk-white mist next morning, but there was a fine view above, nevertheless, though it lacked colour. Four hours easy march brought us to Denning at the end of the cart-road, forty-five miles from Sadiya. There is a detachment of Military Police here, and a shop, where I was able to buy rice for my starving servants.

I at once got into touch with the Political Officer, Mr O'Callaghan, over the telephone, and started at 5.30 next morning, December 9, to walk to Sadiya. After walking twenty-four miles I reached the Digaru river, and waded across, and a mile further on I met O'Callaghan's car which he had sent out to meet me. Two hours later I reached Sadiya; and my journey was over.

I stayed several days with O'Callaghan, while packing and dispatching my seeds to England, and then left by train for the coast.

As a result of this journey down the Lohit, I decided to botanise on the difficult mountains of the Assam frontier as soon as arrangements could be made to return here. The Abor Hills were out of the question as the Indian Government would never consent to any European risking his life amongst those dangerous highlanders. But the Rima road offered a route to the high ranges via the Delei valley, and the Mishmis appeared to be friendly.

I talked over the project with O'Callaghan, and he offered me every assistance in his power, if the Indian Government were agreeable. Eventually, after a year in England I returned to Sadiya, this time accompanied by Mr H. M. Clutterbuck, and we set out together for the Mishmi Hills.

10　The Last Town in India— and Beyond

THE traveller bound for Assam leaves Calcutta in the afternoon by the Darjeeling mail, and after crossing the Ganges, reaches Santahar the same night. Here he changes into the Shillong mail, which is less comfortable, the broad gauge railway having given place to metre gauge. A night in the train, a morning on the dun-coloured level plain of Upper Bengal, with outcrops of low hills in the middle distance, and at noon he reaches another and greater river. How many people, gazing at that broad flood pushing vehemently between its wooded banks, ever pause to think of the mystery and romance associated with its name! One cannot dismiss it in a word, though that word be holy Brahmaputra! Turn, then, to the map of India and see how it rises, hundreds of miles away, behind the Himalaya; how it flows eastwards past the sacred city of Lhasa in a bed now a mile wide and 11,000 feet above sea level; how it then gradually grows narrower and deeper, while the mountains which threaten to entomb it grow ever higher; and how at last, restlessly seeking a way out, and finding itself trapped between snow peaks 25,000 feet high, it turns on them savagely, and with pent-up fury smashes its way clean through the Himalaya, in a gorge two hundred miles long and 10,000 feet deep! Emerging from the very bowels of the earth, the river, now called the Dihang, flows fast through the forest-clad outer ranges, where dwell the fierce fighting clans of the Abor tribe, until at last it empties itself into the funnel-shaped head of the Assam valley; and here at last being joined by the Lohit, it is transformed into the Brahmaputra of India. In the course of its great drive through the mountains the river, dropping 6,000 feet in a succession of wild cataracts, has swung right round until by the time the plains are reached it is flowing almost due west instead of due east! Nor has it reached the sea yet; it has still 600 miles to flow! In the last phase it joins Mother Ganges, which flows westwards along the southern foot of the Himalaya, just as the Tsangpo flows eastwards along the northern foot; and their mingled waters pour into the Bay of Bengal.

After crossing the Brahmaputra at Pandu by ferry steamer, the scene changes abruptly. At once the shining rice-fields of Bengal, with palm-shadowed villages, give place to jungle. We are in Assam, a mystic land with a long history of civilisations slowly dying in the heat and stupor of the all-conquering jungle. One dynasty was followed by another which in turn was overthrown. All that hot sleepy afternoon the train snores through the forest, and all the next night. Miles of orderly well-kept tea-gardens alternate with stretches of impenetrable jungle. High hills, dim in the lowland haze, loom up to the north. On the third day we reach Tinsukia, where the line forks. A branch line goes to Dibrugarh, on the Brahmaputra, the centre of the tea-planting industry; another branch goes towards the foothills, where coal and oil are found. But the main line continues eastwards towards the mountains which rise now flight by flight to the roof of the world. At last they come into view, brooding over the plain, ever calling as a lover; the first steps on that passionate climb to the Babylonian garden hung between heaven and earth.

What a thrill that sight gives the explorer as he gazes across to the outer line of blue hills wallowing in the mist! Those hills are his goal, mysterious, dangerous, blocking the way to the Forbidden Land; home of wild and lawless tribes, womb of mighty rivers, above all a garden of splendour where grow trees and flowers undreamed of by man.

At the head of the Assam valley, the Brahmaputra splits into three rivers; low gaps mark their passage through the barrier. Against the porcelain blue sky, the mountain rim is seen to dip sharply in the west, leaving a V-shaped notch, and there the Dihang comes bouncing out of the green hills. Some distance to the east, where the near mountains scrape the clouds, is another gap, through which the Lohit river suddenly bursts into view and spreads across the plain. Between these two, the Dihang in the west, and the Lohit in the east, is a third gap, whence issues the Dibang. This is the smallest river of them all, and the most mysterious. In those steep and trackless jungles, scored by a hundred shrill torrents, crouch the fierce Chulikata tribe who, like their surly cousins the Digaru Mishmis, dwell across the border; for all this vast tangle of mountains beyond the edge of the plain is 'un-administered territory.' There is no Pax Britannica here. The hill country is within the Indian Empire, but not of it; its inhabitants are left to their own devices, save that a watchful eye is kept on them—and on their neighbours on the other side.

These three rivers then, yoked together where they pour their waters down to the plains, form the Brahmaputra which the tourist, who visits Gauhati or Shillong, crosses at Pandu, 300 miles down-stream.

Where the Brahmaputra is born, at the apex of the plain, it is only 600 feet above sea level, and 600 miles from the sea; yet with such force do the three rivers rush together, that for some distance the Brahmaputra is pushed along at a fair speed.

The Assam railway ends at Saikhoa Ghat on the left bank of the Lohit, twenty miles above its junction with the Dibang at Kobo. Five miles up-stream on the opposite bank, a line of huts, seen mistily amongst the trees, marks the position of Sadiya, the last town in India. Here we are on the

Map 3

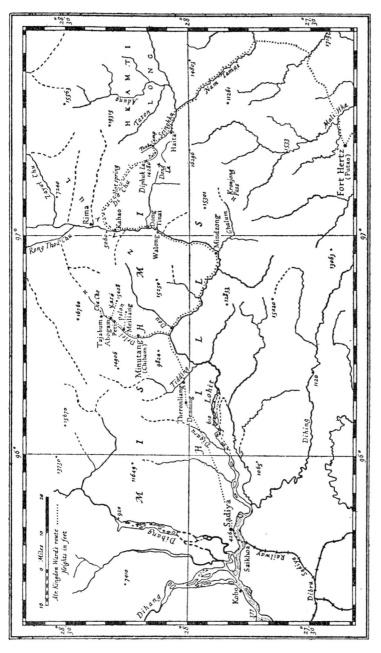

The Mishmi Hills

edge of adventure, with the Rima road running out from the bazaar towards the distant curved hills. We are now in a 'political area,' the Sadiya Frontier Tract. The Political Officer, who keeps watch and ward over the tribes, is monarch of all he surveys. For the traveller, it is not just a matter of crossing the Lohit to Sadiya, engaging coolies, and marching off. In the first place, no man, European or Asiatic, is allowed inside the frontier tract at all, without the Political Officer's permission; in the second place, the country we are bound for lies beyond the frontier, and no white man is permitted to cross what is known as the 'inner line' (that is, to enter 'unadministered territory') without express permission from the Indian Government, which for obvious reasons is very rarely granted. The days when a white man could go anywhere or do anything are over for ever, at least on the Indian Frontier. A hundred years ago, exploring was easier in this respect at least, that no one troubled to say you nay. But in these days of safety first, when empires have to conserve their capital of accumulated glory and live on the interest, called prestige, a white man who is prepared to run risks in the pursuit of knowledge is not merely discouraged; he is prevented. A secret journey on the Frontier is of course impossible, even if it were advisable; no man is more in the limelight than a European on the Indian Frontier, east or west. A criminal fleeing from justice hides in a crowd, not in a wilderness, where he is as plain as a bee in a bonnet.

However, thanks to the goodwill of the Political Officer, and to my friends in the India Office, I obtained permission for Mr H. M. Clutterbuck and myself to botanise in the Mishmi Hills; for the Mishmis, though they have one or two murders on their conscience, and are on the whole an unpleasant folk, are considered harmless. After due preparation Clutterbuck and I, with a Kashmiri servant named Luso, who had been with the Roosevelts in Central Asia, and was highly recommended to me by them, left Sadiya on March 1, 1928. Most of the kit had been sent on in advance to the foot of the hills by elephant and bullock cart: and now we ourselves were bowling along the Rima road in the Political Officer's car. But the Rima road, being a mud *bund* across the swampy plain, is a road only in the dry weather; and recent rain had left its mark in places. Before we had done twenty miles we were bogged axle deep, but by unloading the car and pushing, we got out of the slough. We walked the last twelve miles to Denning on the following day. It was pleasant in the shade of the jungle. The Coral trees (*Erythrina indica*) were in bloom, and glowed blood red against the tinsel blue of the mountains, which showed mistily between the trees. Little time was wasted at Denning Post, though I collected several ground Orchids here, including a quaint pigmy Odontochilus. We were also joined by a Mishmi interpreter named Hablam, always known as Hubble-Bubble, who spoke a little Hindustani. During a violent thunderstorm we crossed the first range of hills, to Theronliang, where our baggage and rations were awaiting us. Here coolies were scarce, and it took us a week to get the loads properly made up and everything forwarded to the Delei bridge, three days' march up the Lohit. Then we plunged into 'unadministered territory'; and the hills and the jungle swallowed us up for eight months.

At Delei *mukh* we camped for a fortnight while our kit was being gradually moved two marches up the Delei valley to a large Mishmi village called Minutang. We had over fifty loads, two-thirds of which comprised rations, rice, flour, and tinned provisions, for we had to carry all our food with us; and there were never more than six or eight coolies available at a time. Then rain put a stop to all movement for several days; the track along the cliffs of the Delei being so dangerous that the coolies dared not risk it except in fine weather.

At first sight the jungle presents such confusion that it seems quite hopeless to try and unravel the tangle, or to recognise species. Inside, nothing is visible, outside nothing is attainable. But the botanist has re-course to indirect methods of identification. After a storm, fallen fruits and flowers tell their own tale; birds, parrots especially, visit certain trees, and a good pair of fieldglasses will resolve much that is obscure. The two most conspicuous trees here were *Derris robusta* and *Acrocarpus fraxinifolius*. Both were in flower. The former usually grew high up on the steep flanks of the mountain, where its domes of scented white blossom hung like cloud-puffs. The latter was common along the riverside, and its bronze flowers strewed the ground, and matched the young leaves, which were just breaking, so closely as to be hardly distinguishable from them. *Engel-hardtia spicata*, two species of Sterculia, and Stereospermum are as readily recognised by their fruit, even when on the tree. Monocotyledonous trees, such as Palms and Pandanus, as well as the Palm-like Araliaceæ, *Trevesia palmata* and Brassaiopsis for example, are recognised on sight by their habit; while the enormous fidgety leaves of *Pterospermum acerifolium*, deep green above, but continually displaying their white under-surface as the breeze flicks them over, are unmistakable.

In the fourth week of March came heavy rain; but early in April we were able to move up the Delei valley in fine weather. Two long and difficult marches partly in the river-bed, partly on the cliff face, where we hung on as best we could above the violently swerving river, climbing up and down by means of shaky ladders and doubtful creepers, brought us to Minutang, a large village scattered up the slope in a bay of the hills. Minutang is about 3,250 feet above sea level, and 1,000 feet above the river. Round the back of us ran a high ridge, its upper slopes covered with temperate rain forest; and it was towards this ridge that I lifed my eyes.

Our main object, however, was to continue as far as possible up the valley, and we immediately began engaging coolies to move our loads another two stages to Meiliang. There were rumours that the Mishmis were anxious to prevent our advance, and that if we ignored the stories of disease and famine which they circulated assiduously, they would oppose us with more material means.

It was the agricultural season, and women and children were busy in the fields from dawn to dusk, weeding, hoeing, planting, and burning. Almost every hut had its own patch of opium Poppy, and there were good crops of Peas and Sweet Potatoes. These however, were side lines; Maize is the principal crop in the lower Delei; Barley is grown higher up.

The Mishmi hut is long, low, and dark, built of bamboo and thatched with grass. It is raised a few feet off the ground on piles, the space underneath being used as a pig sty, while under the eaves baskets are suspended for the family fowls. At the front end is a neat, well finished porch, and at the back is another door. Along one side are several small open windows and a peculiarity of the Mishmi hut is a fence or screen of bamboo up which Beans are grown. Thus seated inside the hut at an open window, one can observe without being seen.

Although we were able to buy Peas and Sweet Potatoes, on which we chiefly lived for the next five weeks, it was rarely that we could buy a fowl. When a Mishmi falls ill, he slays a fowl and eats certain parts of it, hoping thereby to cure himself. Thus a fowl is a potential drug in case of disease, and is consequently valuable. We had better luck with eggs, and when available they were cheap. We observed, however, that they were always what at home are called eggs, or shop eggs, not new-laid eggs, or even fresh eggs. Some were high-explosive, but Luso learnt to explode these harmlessly in the rear of the cook-house; the rest were just—eggs.

The Mishmis who live higher up the valley also keep a few humped cattle and mithun. It was amusing to see them swimming cattle across the Delei river, just below the remains of the bridge on the Rima road, attached to a long line; they were generally hauled ashore upside-down, and then left to empty the water out of their insides as best they could. On the cultivated slopes around Minutang were Peach-trees, Bananas, clumps of Bamboo, a few stunted Palms and the universal tree *Albizzia Julibrissin,* now in full bloom. This last was used as a shade-tree for crops. As usual in cultivated areas, there was plenty of secondary growth in the neighbourhood and this comprised a wild tangle of shrubs and bushes, small trees, and climbing plants, far too thick to penetrate. Amongst interesting plants were *Edgeworthia Gardneri,* the lovely pink-flowered *Luculia gratissima, Buddleia asiatica,* species of Coriaria, Saurauja and Jasminum, and a fine big-leafed Gaultheria bearing uncommonly large cream-coloured flowers, with rosy cheeks. The flowers were far larger than those of any known Gaultheria. The crimson hairs on the young foliage, and the handsome flowers, make this shrub most attractive. Seed sent to England germinated readily, and many plants have been raised; but it is doubtful whether it will prove hardy.

Not far above us rose the ridge, all shining with the spring colours of temperate rain forest. Our camp faced west, beneath us was the deep gorge of the Delei river, and beyond that, separating the Delei and Tidding valleys, rose long bumpy spurs, whose highest visible peaks were covered with snow. Behind us, a comparatively easy gradient, mostly arable land, slanted up to a low wooded ridge which then tilted up more sharply towards a peak called Atsin; to north and south the mountain knot flung out long arms which held us in close embrace.

I was now eager to reach the temperate forest belt, and the obvious route was directly up the slope to the ridge and then along the ridge itself. After a few preliminary reconnaissances, Clutterbuck—or to call him by the pet name I had invented for him, Buttercup—and I started for a long climb on April 11. It was a fine, sunny day in the loveliest season of the year. Throughout April and May the rain forest is a blaze of Rhododendrons of all colours. Here grow the big-leafed trees which form more than half the forest. They bloom while yet the silken buds of deciduous trees are erupting fountains of infant leaves, and the chubby catkins of Corylopsis are dangling from unfledged twigs. The Alps are still sleeping under snow; but with the first rush of the warm monsoon rain a frill of blossom creeps along the raw edges of the cliff and a higher tide of colour rises in the forest.

We found many plants this day. Just over the brow of the ridge the sheltered face was covered with primæval forest, rich in species. *Magnolia rostrata*, quite leafless, was conspicuous here, and a big Podocarpus, with long silver-striped bayonet leaves.

On the ridge many Rhododendrons were crowded together. There was *R. tanastylum* with flowers of daring purple, rasped with clusters of darker stars, giving it a sort of blackberry-and-apple colour, or in some lights, crushed strawberry. To be seen at its best, this species needs a strong light; and the flowers last well. There was Big Bill Thomsoni (*R. Griffithianum*—a Sikkim plant), with astonishing leaves a foot long and half a foot wide. The flower-buds, in trusses of three or four, have a hint of pink in them, but the huge flower opens virginal white. 'Big Bill' is a large shrub, sometimes almost a tree, with smooth tawny purple bark and weirdly contorted branches. There was *R. stenaulum*, a gawky tree with a stout copper-red bole, almost like glass, and a crown of branches which had burst into a foam of white flower. As a forest tree it is at its worst. The pinched flowers in floppy trusses, for all their elegance and fragrance, fall too quickly; the commonplace leaves crowded at the ends of the bare branches, and the tattered bark, also help to make it look shabby. Even so, seen from the outside across a glen, it appeared as a dome of soft blossom. But grown on a sunny or windswept ridge, the leggy-looking tree becomes a solid shrub with a firm outline; then, when a mantle of blossom surrounds the whole, with the scarlet of old leaves, and the purple plumes of the newly born, this Rhododendron takes on a very different appearance.

The only common epiphytic Rhododendron in flower was the beautiful *R. dendricola*, a small bushy shrub, almost as much at home on rocks as on trees. The flowers, in trusses of four, are white, not the puritanical white so often seen, but a festive, almost cream white, with a splash of canary yellow at the base, and a wealth of fragrance.

The Mishmis of Minutang were on the whole friendly. They have more dealings with Sadiya than those from farther up the valley, and are not quite so uncouth. Indeed they live a rather different, sub-tropical, instead of temperate existence.

On April 18, in spite of epidemics and deaths and threats, we moved on again, and on the 19th reached Meiliang. The path, now high above the river, was difficult, and though the distance on the map looked ridiculously small, the second day's march was long and arduous. We saw many Podocarpus-trees, all males; not a solitary female could I discover! At Meiliang we pitched our camp in a meadow, a pleasant site by the path, but some distance from the village. The *Gam* of Meiliang, who was quite pleasant-looking for a Mishmi, greeted us, and we promptly bought him over as a possible ally in the event of trouble. He was the first efficient man we had met, and he produced coolies for us with incredible promptness; but perhaps that was because he was anxious to get rid of us. Against this must be set the fact that, though we were only one march from Peti, he succeeded in making two marches of it.

As usual, the loads were sent ahead as fast as possible; and while we were waiting to move, I climbed the ridge and collected plants in the forest. A new crop of Rhododendrons greeted me here—*R. aureum*, terra-cotta stemmed, grey leafed, golden flowered, on the open ridge, and *R. sperabile* dangling blood-red bells amongst narrow white-backed leaves, in the forest. But the best was a thin shrub with golden-whiskered heads of gamboge flowers, a plant closely related to the rare Bhutan species, *R. Boothii*. This plant, named *R. mishmiense*, will delight the heart of the horticulturist, and it delighted no less the heart of the botanist. It is a well-known fact that most flowers are, or prefer to be, cross-pollinated; that is to say, they prefer pollen from a different flower, or even from a different plant, rather than self-pollen from the surrounding stamens, to reach the stigma. Such cross-pollination is usually effected by insects, and it ensures stronger offspring. Most Rhododendrons are almost invariably cross-pollinated, and there are various devices to further this; but never have I seen a mechanism quite so certain and neat as that of *R. mishmiense*. The following brief description will explain the trick. The flat corolla faces an approaching insect like the dial of a clock. The three upper lobes are spotted with burnt sienna, and there are two broad furry bands reaching from the base of the shallow tube half-way up the limb. The ten stamens are about equal in length; nine of them with filaments hairy for half their height, form a continuous pallisade round the front and flanks of the barrel-shaped ovary, the long hairs of adjacent filaments being entangled with each other, thus completely blocking access to the ovary. The tenth and uppermost stamen is free, being kinked at the base and bent back, so as to lie against the face of the corolla. Its filament also is hairy, but all the way up instead of only half-way, and the filaments to right and left of it are also rather more hairy than the remaining seven; these three being in contact with the furry bands on the corolla already mentioned. The detachment of the tenth stamen from its fellows is cunningly effected by a projecting knob on the disc beneath the ovary; the filament which springs from its base being pushed outwards and kinked by the bulge, thus leaving a tiny passage on either side through the staminal pallisade. Honey is secreted as usual by the disc, between the pallisade and the ovary, but at the back only, and is squeezed through the two little ports on either side of the tenth stamen, thus reaching the back or upper part of the corolla—XII o'clock on the clockface. Thus the honey-drop lies at the bottom of the tube, with the spots just overhead, enclosed by the furry bands. Finally the short style is bent sharply down, and sticks out through the front portion of the fence, presenting its large butt to the oncoming insect. So much for the mechanism. The agent is an insect visitor, probably a bee. Bees visit flowers chiefly for honey. The brown spots on the upper half of the corolla attract the insect, which goes straight for the place where the honey-drop lies at the bottom of the flower. The first thing it touches and indeed stands on, is the butt of the stigma; as it thrusts its head into the flower, its legs claw amongst the stamens for further support, wiping off the pollen which is in long strings, convenient for entangling in the hairy legs of the bee. The bee gets its honey, and goes to another flower. As before, the first thing it touches is the stigma, and on that it wipes off some of the pollen it is carrying. And so the game goes on. Thus cross-pollination is always effected, so long as bees visit the flowers. And if by some unhappy chance they did not, the pollen threads would still trail over their own stigma and effect self-pollination, which is better than none.

On the ridge above our camp were several fine species of Calanthe. One had amethyst flowers, deliciously fragrant; another had the five outer petals apple-green, the lip canary-yellow, a charming combination; and this also was fragrant. These were the two commonest ground Orchids in the temperate forest, and they grew together in colonies, both flowering in April. A third species, flowering at the same time, had chocolated red flowers, and was not so attractive as the other two. In August a white-flowered species was in bloom. But the most magnificent plant here was a species of Æschynanthus, a climbing epiphyte with thick leathery leaves and vermilion flowers in large heads. From a little distance it looked like a Rhododendron. Another flowering plant of the undergrowth was a species of Disporum, sometimes with cream, sometimes with amethyst flowers. Apart from the plants mentioned, there are few spring flowering plants in the depth of the temperate rain forest. Along the open ridges, however, and in clearings, Violets and other flowers are common.

At 8,000–9,000 feet, we found *Rhododendron sinogrande* in full bloom on April 25. The almost regular 10-lobed flowers are cream with a small deep crimson flash at the base, and are compressed into big spherical trusses.

By April 26 we were on the move again. And now the valley began to change in character. The mountains became terrifically steep. The river plunged through a deep winding gorge, and every flank stream dropped over a high cliff. We saw some beautiful cascades, with pale blue Irises growing on the spray-drenched rock. Fields of Barley appeared, and we passed through several villages, finally reaching Peti on the 27th. Then rain put an end to our activities for five days.

Peti stood on a terrace some height above the river, which here split up into two big streams. The junction, which we called Watersmeet, was a turmoil backed by huge snow-clad peaks.

In order to keep an eye on us, apparently, the Mishmis chose for us a camping-ground in the midst of cultivation; and the people being engaged in agriculture, we were always the centre of an interested throng. It is doubtful if we were ever popular; but thinking that we were only paying a short visit, the Mishmis of Peti, though surly, were not openly hostile. They were a different type altogether from those we had met further down the valley, and their simian features did not inspire confidence. As befitted a tribe who live a hard life, they were dressed in woollen cloth, of Tibetan manufacture, and the skins of wild animals. Just above the village a wooden post was driven into the ground, and from this hung a warrior's cane helmet. This I learnt was a memorial to a murdered man. When I had persuaded the *Gam* of Meiliang to let me take his photograph, he chose to stand by this obelisk; and though he never confessed to me, I had dark suspicions. He always wore a necklace of human teeth, which obviously were not his own.

Feverish activity prevailed in the fields, but such strenuousness was confined to women and children. The Poppy capsules were being scratched for the juice, wiped off on to a dirty rag; before the end of May the Barley crop had been harvested; and women went about the fields with a pointed stick in one hand and a bag of seeds in the other, sowing Maize, which ripens in September.

While waiting for coolies, we explored the forest, ascending to 9,000 feet, on May 5. On the rocky ridge we found many tree Rhododendrons in full bloom, the most abundant being *R. crinigerum*, with pinkish purple flowers. Other common species were *R. sidereum* (sulphur), *R. arizelum* (ivory), and *R. sino-grande* (cream). It was wonderful to look down on the green forest and to see all these hundreds of bright foam clots tossed about on a heaving sea, amidst flashes of bronze and silver from the breaking leaves. Since April a gale of colour had swept over the ridges, as the bush

Rhododendrons seethed into bloom; and now the whole temperate rain forest was responding to the call of spring. *Quercus semiserrata* was very common lower down, and red-leafed saplings were springing up everywhere. *Magnolia rostrata* was in full leaf; and the only leafless tree was *Quercus lamellosa*. Another wonderful sight on the ridge was *Viburnum Wardii*, a mound of starry white sea foam.

On this excursion Buttercup and I got separated in the forest, and during the descent I found myself on the wrong ridge. This mistake landed me in trouble; first I was involved in the forest undergrowth and towards dusk, when at last I emerged from the forest, in the much worse secondary growth which covered the slope below. As a result I did not reach camp till after dark.

On May 8 we started again up the valley, our object being to camp near the pass, not more than three days' march, as we reckoned it. The river above Watersmeet was a roaring torrent; we were still high above it, but could often see it thundering through the gorge below. As for the path, it was a mere ledge high up on the rock face, with terrifying cliffs where we had to climb down shaky ladders forty or fifty feet high, holding on to roots and creepers. On the cliff, which was overgrown with shrubs, I found the golden Leycesteria, a solitary plant with long hanging racemes of golden-yellow flowers, and large auricled stipules at the base of the leaves.

In the afternoon we reached a cultivated platform by the riverside; a score of Mishmis were engaged in fixing a rope, made of twisted Bamboo strips, across the river. The crossing was effected next day. Large cane rings are threaded on the rope, and seated in one of these the victim hauls and kicks his way over. As the river was fifty yards wide, some idea of the strength and agility necessary to do this may be surmised. The loads were pulled across by means of a line; and so were Buttercup and I.

On the far side were a few huts, the last in the valley. Our coolies, however, did not halt here, but crossed the next ravine by a flimsy bridge, awash in the cataract, climbed a thousand feet up the opposite cliff, and dumped us down on a ledge of rock where there was hardly room to turn round! We decided at once that this was no place for a base camp; and as the Mishmis flatly refused to take us any further up the valley, or to find any other camping-ground, we demanded to be taken back to Peti. But the Mishmis refused that also, saying they had no rations. Here was a deadlock. The best way out seemed to be to cut the Gordian knot and this I threatened to do. "If," I said, "we cannot return to the village, neither shall you. Either carry our loads, or stay here with us; I am going to cut the rope bridge." With that I seized a knife from Hubble, and telling Buttercup what I proposed to do, set out for the bridge. Arrived there, I sat down to wait. It was a fine day, and piping hot; there was not an atom of shade. After a vigil lasting two hours, three Mishmis appeared on the cliff path above me; they were not carrying loads, and I promptly cut the rope near its support. It slipped into the rushing torrent, and was instantly drawn down stream under the far bank.

Then I started back for camp.

I had hardly got half-way when I met Buttercup on his way to rejoin me. He told me an amazing story; how the Mishmis had obstinately refused to do anything; how at last when even his patience was exhausted a youth had said, "Well, if you will cut my hair I'll go!" and how at that everyone had suddenly decided to go! Then the Mishmis had picked up their loads and raced down the hill. At Tajabum—the two huts previously mentioned —they had bought a little food; and now they were coming along as quickly as possible. Then I told Buttercup that I had cut the bridge. It was vain to regret it now; it was done, and we must make the best of a bad job. Both Sim, the headman, and Hubble were carrying loads, as two of the coolies had sneaked away before the settlement was reached; it was them I had seen on the path, which led to my cutting the bridge!

When the Mishmis arrived, at first they could hardly believe their eyes; but when the truth dawned on them that the bridge really was cut, there was a scene. Sim looked grave; and we waited for what was to come next. There was a minute's tension, and then Hubble created a happy diversion by falling down in a sort of fit; he had taken an overdose of opium. At once the medicine man came forward, sprinkled flour over him, and muttered incantations. As for us, we pitched our tents by the river, and waited to hear what the Mishmis had to say about it. This they said next morning, Sim delivering himself to the following effect. We had cut the bridge, so we could just stay where we were and stew in our own juice. As for him, he and his friends would march down the right bank of the river, make a bridge lower down, cross, and cut the bridge on the other side. So "Bah! to you, Hah! Hah! to you"; and much more. Then all the young men drew their knives, and slashed down their shelters, and kicked out their fires, in an orgy of spite, which serious though the position was for us, made us laugh.

The Mishmis tramped off, and we were left alone. Of course I was sorry now I had cut the rope. We were no better, and probably, worse off. Yet I was not altogether chastened in spirit. In an impasse there comes a time when I must do something. It may be the wrong thing, as now; but it is something, and if it is the wrong thing one suffers and does not squeal about it. One is made that way, or not, and it can't be helped. Besides, it was worth while to be involved in a mess like this to see how coolly Buttercup took it. Nothing ever ruffled him, and he was full of sound advice; in fact to discuss a problem with him during these dark days was to rob it of half its difficulty. Luso was staunch too; and Hubble, though partly responsible for the deadlock, was indispensable.

At midday we discovered that though the Mishmis had departed they had left one of their number behind to negotiate with us. After all they were not fools. In the first place they had not yet been paid. In the second, they wanted a bridge here. In the third, to leave us here indefinitely might result in reprisals. So they decided to open the matter with us again. We asked the liaison officer what he proposed to do. He replied that if we would pay for a new bridge—we had agreed to pay for the old one before it was cut—he would get it put up and call the coolies back. We agreed to this, and off he went. The following evening he re-appeared on the other bank of the river with two cronies, and more bridging material; and by the third day a new length had been woven into the cut rope, and it was back in position! Meanwhile, I decided to take a look at the valley beyond our late camp, so early one morning I started off. I crossed the torrent by the flimsy bridge dryshod, climbed the cliff, and followed the path up the shoulder. After ascending about 2,000 feet I came out on to an open rocky meadow hillside. The path continued through forest, alternating with open rock faces, where I found my first Primula—*P. alta*, a species closely resembling *P. denticulata*, in almost ripe seed. Unfortunately, a thick rain mist was blowing up, which spoilt the view. Even so I could see to the head of the valley, and almost make out the pass. The one certain thing now was, that the Delei valley was a water-worn gorge, forested to its head; that it never had been glaciated; and that the stream rose from a spur, though a high one, and not from the main prolongation of the Himalaya. This was disappointing, but it was too late to alter our plans now.

On the return journey I collected in the dim sodden depths of the forest a huge Arisaema with a chocolate spathe, silver banded, like a monk's cowl, and a spadix like the proboscis of a tapir, drawn out into an immensely long flexible whip, which trailed several feet along the ground. Altogether a queer plant, one of nature's monstrosities.

I reached the torrent late in the afternoon, and found to my consternation that I could not get across the bridge. This consisted only of a couple of Bamboos, which bent under one's weight, and one more for a hand-rail. Owing to the rain, and still more to the melting snow, the torrent was enormously swollen, and a huge wave swept right over the bridge, almost swamping the rail too. I made several efforts to cross, but soon realised that it would be suicidal, so tremendous was the rush of water. I searched for a spar, and finding a small pole tried to push it across and fix it in position, to strengthen the bridge; but the other end being free, it was instantly torn from my grasp and sent hurtling down the cataract. There was nothing for it but to wait, which I did with the best patience I could muster; being wet through, I was soon shivering in the blast of cold air which the torrent forced before it through the ravine; I thought, however, that it would be better to wait here till nightfall, in case help came. Meanwhile, not having eaten for eight hours, I ate my lunch ration. At the end of an hour I noticed that the stream had risen; but as the snow would presently cease melting, if it had not already done so, I might expect it to start shrinking after dark. However, it looked as though I would have to make a night of it

And just then came relief, in the shape of two Mishmis who appeared on the opposite bank. One of them tried to cross, but shook his head, made signs to me, and disappeared. Ten minutes later he returned with a long Bamboo and a coil of creeper. Pushing the Bamboo across, he flung me a length of creeper; then he lashed his end, and I did the same to my end; and behold! a Bamboo bridge level with the top of the wave which took the strain off the flimsy hand-rail. In a twinkling one of the Mishmis slipped across and took my rucksack, and now came my turn. I will not pretend that it was a very wonderful bridge, or that I was not frightend; but it was safe if I kept cool, and anyhow the alternative to risking it was an extremely unpleasant night. So I went straight at it, and was surprised to find myself sliding safely over in my nailed boots, keeping my balance by means of the twanging hand-rail.

It was now dark and we hastened back to camp, arriving just as Buttercup was setting out to succour me, with food, matches, and other comforts. My rescue I owed entirely to his native wit; for noticing a discolouration and rise in the main river, no sooner was I overdue than he concluded that I had been cut off by the torrent, and sent the two Mishmis to help me. Buttercup reported that the Mishmi coolies had all returned, and that half the loads had been slung over the river. We were to march next morning.

When next morning came it was raining steadily. To our surprise, however, the Mishmis stood by their bargain. The prudence of carrying loads over such a dangerous trail in the rain might be open to question, but there was no question of the Mishmis' good faith. Anyhow, we supposed they knew their own business best, and if they could go, we could.

So we packed up, and crossed the river. At midday the rearguard lifted their loads, and we saw the last of that fatal bridge which had cost us so much trouble and anxiety, to say nothing of money. We never saw it again.

The climb back through the gorge was a nightmare. We were covered with leeches, and Buttercup was bitten in the ankle. The wound poisoned, as also did several others, and for months refused to heal. From June on he was practically a cripple, and it was not till he reached England again that he really recovered from his first experience of leech-bites! As for me, I had been through the same experience years before on the Burma frontier; and, being to some extent immunised, I got off more lightly now.

At dusk, tired, soaked to the skin, itching with bites, and sick with the sense of failure, we reached Peti. But by the time the tents had been run up, and we had changed our clothes, and lit the stove, and drunk some hot tea which Luso made for us, we felt better able to face life. We had lost the first round; but we were warming to the fight.

MISHMI ROPE BRIDGE, DELEI VALLEY.

TEMPERATE RAIN FOREST WITH LARCH, OAK, AND
Rhododendron bullatum, MISHMI HILLS, 10,000 FEET.

11　The Temperate Rain Forest

THAT type of forest to which the name temperate rain forest is properly given lies between the upper limit of hill cultivation, at about 6,000 feet altitude, and the level at which Rhododendrons and Conifers begin to mass themselves together to the exclusion of other trees; which change, though gradual, is completely effected at about 9,000 feet. Above that the forest is again evergreen. Where the mountains do not much exceed 7,000 feet in height, there is no true temperate forest, and the mountain-tops are clothed with what may be called hill jungle. It is not till they average 12,000 or 14,000 feet, and the full sequence from sub-tropical jungle in the valleys to alpine meadow on the heights is developed, that a real temperate forest exists.

Nor is this distinction a mere convenience. It is a matter of common knowledge that a particular plant association corresponds, not to a certain fixed altitude, but to relative altitude; altitude, in fact, is only one of many factors which influence the type of vegetation. The nature of the surrounding vegetation also influences it. Thus, the 7,000 feet contour in the eastern Himalaya, though everywhere characterised by forest, is not everywhere characterised by the same type of forest. Southwards, where the hill ranges rise from a sea of Indo-Malayan jungle, they themselves tend to be covered with the same jungle even at considerable altitudes. Northwards, where the mountains are in contact with a temperate flora, they are themselves inclined to support temperate forest as low down as possible. The line where hill jungle meets temperate forest is an ever-shifting battleground. In the deep damp river gorges, the subtropical jungle is so aggressive that it pushes far beyond the tropic; on the high ranges, the temperate forest is equally aggressive. One of the chief characteristics of the temperate forest is its variety. It contains a fair sprinkling of deciduous trees mixed with Conifers, not all of one kind. The Rhododendrons also, of which there are many species, are scattered, especially at the lower levels; though above 9,000 feet they begin to band themselves together. Thus the temperate forest is composed neither entirely of broad-leafed trees like the jungle below, nor entirely of Conifers like the high forest belt. It is neither entirely evergreen nor entirely deciduous. Above all, inside the forest, no two trees in contact are alike. The bulk of the evergreen trees are found amongst the following genera: Tsuga, Juniperus, Quercus, Ilex, Schima, Cinnamomum, Podocarpus, Castanopsis, Illicium, Michelia, Pinus, and Rhododendron. Shrubs include the red-stemmed *Mahonia calamicaulis* and the prickly *Brassaiopsis speciosa*. Familiar deciduous trees met with are species of Acer, Betula, Magnolia, Larix, Populus, Alnus, Pyrus, and Bucklandia, amongst the larger trees; Eriobotrya, Enkianthus, Corylopsis, Viburnum, Sorbus, Heptapleurum, and *Gamblea ciliata* amongst the smaller; a bare list which, though far from exhausting the trees met with in the temperate forest, will give some idea of their variety.

It is at the two seasonal changes, Spring and Autumn, that the temperate forest is most gay with colour. In Summer the blanket of cloud which muffles it like a cloak, and the scolding rain, impress on it a drab uniformity. In Winter for three months it sleeps; though not much snow falls, nor does it lie over-long. But with the dawn of Spring the temperate forest awakens, and puts on fine raiment; and in the Autumn, after the tyranny of the monsoon, it breaks up into an archipelago of vivid colours sprinkled over a broad green sea.

No one who has only seen the temperate forest quick with the promise of life in April, or smouldering with the reflection of drawn fires in September, can form any idea of what a hell it is during the monsoon. Now the very trees which a month ago were the most brilliant, seem to shrink into themselves as though appalled by the cold fury of the storm. The temperate rain forest exists, of course, by reason of the monsoon; but during the ordeal it is not a pretty sight. In the rainy season the trees put aside all display, and work hard that they may survive as individuals, and as a race.

The rain forest is certainly the last place in which to camp in Summer. Far better is it to be in the alps, out in the open air, free from the drip and gloom. But in the Mishmi Hills we had no choice. We could not reach the alps by the main valley, because the torrents were unbridged, and rising every day with the melting of the snow. The Mishmis, who have no traffic with the Tibetans on the other side of the range, refused to take us beyond the last village. Then finding that we had no intention of leaving the Delei valley, they became more surly than ever. It was no use counting on them to solve our difficulty, and whatever we wanted done, the sooner we persuaded them to do it the better. We therefore decided to attack the peak immediately above the village, having observed a path going up the shoulder in that direction. This peak, called Kaso, 15,400 feet high, stood at the head of a deep ravine which separated us from the next village. Unfortunately, the path went up the far ridge, so that we had to cross the torrent before beginning to climb. On a cold and cheerless May day, we started out from Peti to explore the path and seek a camping-ground. Above the lip of the gorge the ascent began in earnest, a steep and slippery path leading us through cultivation and high grass; then, passing through a belt of forest, we emerged on to the ridge. On the north side thick forest came right up to the brow, but the south face was almost bare of trees, clothed instead with grass and clumps of Piptanthus whose bright sulphur-yellow blossom had attracted our attention from below. Presently the ridge became precipitous, demanding hand- and foot-hold, so that we began to question whether the coolies really could carry our loads up such places; but the path was still there. At 8,000 feet, where we met with the first specimens of *Larix Griffithii*, a soft blue-green in its young foliage, the whole mountain was covered with thick forest. Conspicuous trees were Tsuga, *Magnolia rostrata* and *M. globosa*, species of Oak, and innumerable Rhododendrons, chiefly bushes growing along the rocky crest of the ridge, and on the cliffs. Tree Rhododendrons, such as *R. sino-grande*, also began to mingle with the other forest trees. Dense tangles of Bamboo, Enkianthus, Holly (*Ilex nothofagifolia*), *Rhododendron manipurense*, and *R. Keysii* crowded up to the brow of the ridge.

Again the ascent became exceedingly steep, and we found ourselves in the very depths of the temperate rain forest. At about 10,000 feet altitude, the ridge shrugged a shoulder; and here, where the Fir-forest began, we decided to pitch our tents in the only possible place we had seen. But what should we do for water? Further exploration along the ridge undertaken by Buttercup, who spent a night there, revealed a trickle about half a mile from the proposed camping site; but this source, which became known as Buttercup's Well, never yielded much.

The nearer we approached the alps the more broken became the ridge. Enormous slabs of rock, heaved up by some titanic convulsion as it seemed, and flung down anyhow, blocked the way, leaving a cave where a dozen men might shelter. Then the whole ridge became a confused ruin of shattered towers, ragged cliffs and broken buttresses, beneath which on either side yawned the open mouths of gullies. A mile and a half below, the white ribbon of the Delei river swerved through the hills and everywhere, trying in vain to hide the ruin, surged a dense tangle of bush Rhododendron, vivid with colour. The violent beauty of the scene took our breath away.

Of the further exploration of the ridge, I shall speak later. My present purpose is to describe the temperate forest. But first, of the events which led up to our camping in the forest at all.

After our failure to reach the head of the Delei valley, it seemed as though the Mishmis would do no more for us. But by the time we had explored the hunter's path up the ridge they were more reasonable; and the *Gam* grumblingly promised us coolies to carry a camp up to our site; having in vain tried to dissuade us from going on the pretext that there was no water on the ridge. After five days steady rain it turned fine again and on May 29 the coolies carried our loads up. We were very worried lest they should not be able to complete the climb in a day, knowing that once we let them go, they would not return. But, in spite of their 50-lb. loads, they made light work of what we regarded as a pretty severe test. However it was with a sigh of relief that we at last pitched our tents on the shoulder. We were now at the upper limit of the temperate forest, where it passes into Rhododendron-Conifer forest. Gigantic trees, chiefly *Juniperus recurva* and *Abies Webbiana*, towered above us. Sheltering beneath these came a more varied lower story, some forty or fifty feet high, chiefly composed of tree Rhododendrons, including *R. sino-grande*, *R. lanigerum*, and *R. arizelum*, whose enormous outspread leaves cast a deep gloom over the ridge. On these, the rain beat with a noise like the roll of kettle-drums.

It is in the middle temperate forest that the Magnolias, *M. Campbellii*, *M. globosa*, and *M. rostrata*, are found scattered. This forest forms a continuous belt from Sikkim in the west to Yunnan in the east, south of the line of great peaks, with the three Magnolias distributed almost from end to end. *M. Campbellii* is a comparatively well-known tree in the milder gardens of Britain; it has even seeded in Ireland. Discovered by Hooker in Sikkim ninety years ago, it has been gradually traced eastwards as far as the China frontier. It is common at the headwaters of the Irrawaddy, and also in the Mishmi Hills.

The discovery of *M. rostrata* on the Burma-China frontier was greeted with wild enthusiasm in horticultural circles. Here at last was the Queen of Magnolias! Alas for the frailty of human observation and the credulity of the most level-headed men! The pæans chanted in praise of *M. rostrata* were based on a complete fallacy! It will be many years yet before it flowers in Britain—the largest plants are hardly twelve years old; and when it does, there will be weeping and gnashing of teeth. For, truth to tell, the flowers are ridiculously small, and are utterly dwarfed, and almost entirely hidden by the immense leaves. Moreover, they are fugitive, lasting perhaps ten days under the most favourable conditions, but scarcely a week in their native forests, exposed as they are to the storms which herald the break of the monsoon. *M. rostrata* does indeed deserve praise. It is a fine strapping clean-limbed tree, straight as a dart, upwards of eighty feet high with huge leaves eighteen inches long by twelve wide. When covered with its erect red cones, six inches high, it is almost startlingly beautiful; but it is not what it was thought to be.

M. rostrata, the only one of the three not found in Sikkim, is found as far west as the great gorge of the Tsangpo, across the Assam frontier ranges, and the Burmese Oberland, to the Salween Valley. In Burma it is found as far south as Hpimaw. Except for the occurrence of this species in the province of Pemako, which surrounds the sheared-off end of the Himalaya where the Tsangpo pounds its way through the mountains, there are no Magnolias known from Tibet; they are trees of the rain forest. Although nowhere very common, and never gregarious, one cannot climb these mountains without coming across isolated specimens of *M. rostrata*. Its leaves and fruits betray it; rarely its poor flowers. In early April it is still leafless, its slender, smooth, silver-grey stem shooting up like a pillar amongst the gnarled and bearded Oaks, Maples, and Birch-trees, which surround it. About mid-April, the long pointed leaf-buds begin to crack and open, accompanied by a gentle rain of bud scales. By early May the leaves, growing quickly, are almost full size, and when the white flowers open in the second week of May, they are already swallowed up and hidden amongst the leaves. If the flowers opened early, before the leaves, *M. rostrata* might be less discouraging. But the flower-buds are terminal, opening last of all, and being closely supported by huge platforms of leaves, are invisible except from above.

Of course, in these steep mountains, one may view the tree under the most favourable conditions. Forest often grows right up to the brow of a ridge, leaving the other face bare; and if the Magnolia is in the forefront, there is a chance of looking down on to it. Seedlings spring up in the artificial clearings made for *Coptis Teeta*, along with those of *M. Campbellii*. One glorious tree I caught sight of in the Mishmi Hills. It was still in full foliage at the end of October, and every branch ended in a tall cone. In bloom it must have been a delightful spectacle: at least one could have seen the flowers!

M. rostrata is not found quite so low down as *M. Campbellii* nor quite so high up as *M. globosa*.

This last is a big shrub, or more commonly a small tree, scattered on the steepest forested slopes, amongst big-leafed Rhododendrons, Tsuga, and other trees. It is the latest of all to flower, for its globular milk-white blooms do not open before the middle of June. Although the tree is then in full foliage, the flowers show up moderately well amongst the silky leaves. *M. globosa* remains in flower about a fortnight. The fruits are dumpy and short, bright red, and hang down when ripe. Sometimes it forms a bush amongst the very thick scrub covering a broken cliff, growing gregariously at about 10,000 feet altitude; and this is its most effective form. The leaves are still quite green at the end of October. In the Spring they are covered with long champagne yellow silky hairs.

M. Campbellii stands in a class by itself. It is incomparably the finest of all Magnolias, at least in the wild state. The Tibet road through Sikkim might have been designed specially to enable travellers to see it in its *locus classicus*. The road cleaves to the face of the cliff, winding round and round, ever ascending towards the distant snows, while the valley fades beneath us. At last the air grows colder, for it is only March, and we reach the zone of Oaks and Rhododendrons. Everything is padded in moss; long wisps of it swing from the branches of the trees. A thin mist floats ghost-like through the dripping forest. Suddenly round a corner, we come on the first Magnolia in full bloom. It is just below us and we look right into the heart of the tree, spouting with blossom. The sight overwhelms us. After that we see scores of trees, some with glowing pink, others with ivory-white flowers. From our giddy ledge we look down over the wide waves of the forest beating against the cliff, where the Magnolia blooms toss like white horses, or lie like a fleet of pink water-lilies riding at anchor in a green surf. It is the only precocious species of the three; in Sikkim at least the flowers are practically over before the leaves appear.

The eastern form of *M. Campbellii* (syn. *M. mollicomata*) is both common and widely distributed. It is a big tree. Specimens in the Seinghku valley were over 100 feet high. It tends to grow gregariously, perhaps half a dozen specimens together, and others within hail. In the Delei valley it was confined to certain waterlogged hollows on the ridge where the Bamboos grew most thickly; here it was associated with *Acer Campbellii*, a species of Cinnamomum and *M. rostrata*. It appears to flower later than the Sikkim form; in the Seinghku valley there were still flowers on the tree, which of course was in full leaf, on June 1; the immense accumulations of snow may have retarded it. The flowers of the eastern form, as far as I am aware, are always white or flushed purple; never pink.

Of the leaf-fall of these trees little is known; probably it is as variable as their flowering. *M. Campbellii* on Polon ridge above the Delei valley was in full leaf and shining with silver silken flower-buds at the end of October, after particularly vicious weather. *M. rostrata* and *M. globosa* retain their foliage at least as late. Probably none of them are stripped before December, and the end may come quickly.

It would seem that none of the Magnolias flower over two consecutive years; at least one never finds a tree with both fruit beneath and flowers overhead. The fruits of Magnolias, with the exception of *M. rostrata*, once they have fallen, are quickly destroyed by grubs and Fungi; but the large and peculiar cones of *M. rostrata* lie on the ground for at least a year, little affected by pests or weather. They have a strong and peculiar scent, not unpleasant; and are one of the most characteristic objects to be picked up in the temperate forest of the North-East Frontier.

The zone of Magnolias overlaps the zone of big-leafed Rhododendrons. These, with various Araliaceæ, form the lower canopy of the forest. They grow gregariously, a single species such as *R. sino-grande* sometimes forming more than fifty per cent. of the forest. These Rhododendrons however reach their greatest development where the forest trees themselves are gregarious, and will be dealt with later.

Welcome for their bright autumn colouring are the Maples. *Acer Wardii* is a small rounded tree with three-pronged leaves, the prongs drawn out into long tails and the finely serrate margin bright red. It is abundant both in the Mishmi Hills and in the Seinghku valley, growing on the windy ridge with Viburnum, and Ilex, and Rhododendron. The hanging clusters of greenish flowers, produced in May, are followed in October by bunches of red wings; and the bright-green leaves, beaded on the margin with red, are the first to colour in September, when they turn orange and scarlet. In the Mishmi Hills too is found *Acer Campbellii*, a large tree with big palmate leaves and straw-coloured fruits, with purple stains on the widely divergent wings. The most beautiful of the Maples however is *Acer sikkimense,* more shrub than tree, and in Sikkim said to be always epiphytic. I saw only one plant in the Seinghku valley, alone on a bare ridge. Its simple polished leaves, borne on pillar-box red shoots, are quite unlike those of an ordinary Maple, and the flowers open early. By May it is in fruit, long tassels of narrow red blades swinging from every shoot. In October these tassels, now six inches long, are still there, a dimmer red, nor have the leaves changed colour. *Acer sikkimense,* which grows about ten feet high, streaming with long ruby tails, composed of very small fruits, was one of the most gracious and ornamental shrubs I saw.

Growing on the same ridge, and also to be accounted a tree of the temperate rain forest, is the new *Eriobotrya Wardii,* already described, a tree allied to the Japanese Loquat (*E. japonica*) but more closely to the Indian *E. elliptica.* It is a tall slender pale-barked tree with large obovate leaves, and smooth, ovoid potato-coloured fruits as big as a walnut, which hang on the tree for a year; but the flesh is hard and inedible. This Loquat is found on the lower rocky ridges of the Seinghku valley, with *Pinus excelsa.* It is not rare, neither is it abundant, being scattered through the forest.

As for Conifers, few species definitely belong to this zone. Conifers are peculiarly fitted to withstand extremes of climate, and are usually unable to withstand extremes of climate, and are usually unable to compete on level terms with broad-leafed trees. Conifer forests occur above the temperate rain forest, on the outer hill ranges. They also grow gregariously at quite low altitudes on the inner ranges. In the rain forest the only abundant Conifer is a species of Tsuga, which in the Mishmi Hills is often a dominant tree round about 9,000 feet. It is, in fact, the first conspicuous Conifer met with. More interesting is a species of Podocarpus, which we found at 7,000 feet in the Mishmi Hills. It grows only in the depths of the forest, occurring with some frequency where the conditions are to its liking; but I saw only male specimens, which produced flowers freely in April. It is a handsome though sombre tree, medium-sized, or even big, with rough fissured bark, and harsh narrow leaves, six inches long, the under surface silvered on either side of the midrib. *Taxus Wallichii,* which is hardly distinguishable from our English Yew, is another scattered Conifer of the rain forest; but it reaches no great size; and the only Pine seems to be *P. excelsa* which is found in Nam Tamai valley, as well as in the neighbouring Seinghku valley. This beautiful tree becomes almost gregarious in the gorge of the Tsangpo; and still further west, in Gharwal, it leaves the rain forest altogether and forms its own forest at 12,000 feet altitude. Holly-trees, on the other hand, are common in every type of forest right up to the alpine region, though most of them are quite unlike our English Holly to look at. One of the most remarkable species is *Ilex nothofagifolia,* a small tree of tabular habit, each limb branching in one plane after the manner of a Cedar. The twigs are bloated with a skin composed of innumerable corky warts, and bear tufts of tiny dark green leaves, which completely cover the flat framework. These leaves are spoon-shaped, with toothed edge, and are borne on short stalks. Rows of sessile chocolate flowers appear along the shoots in May, followed in October by small bright scarlet berries, sewn on like beads. Whole branches are embroidered with them. This is what one sees in a close up. The common view is rather different, for this Holly lurks in the deepest, darkest, gloomiest depths of the rain forest, where it falls a victim to the all-devouring moss. Its crippled trunk, growing indeed erect but half limbless, flings out a few flat branches to one side or the other, often in echelon, which make the tree look deformed. These green lustre plates are draped and festooned with Moss which swathes its victim in deadly embrace, gradually choking the life out of it.

Ilex nothofagifolia seems to stand between the devil and the deep sea. It shrinks from the light. In the darkness it is smothered. It is not a rare tree, but well-grown specimens are rare, and in the grip of the moss it can neither flower freely, nor set fertile seed; the creeping, crawling death spreads its net over it until at last, perhaps after many years, it succumbs. It has been condemned to death in its own home. Plant-hunters have been accused before now of exterminating plants. Here at least is an example of the reverse; a plant snatched from the jaws of death at the hands of ruthless Nature, and given a fresh lease of life in a new land!

I saw many trees in the forests of the Burmese Oberland, but not half a dozen of them flowered and fruited in 1926. In the Mishmi Hills it is less common, though I saw finer specimens there. It is worth noting that the berries last till the following spring, being probably hidden from the prying eyes of birds; in fact I was able to collect some 1927 seed in June 1928!

The name '*nothofagifolia*' recalls the fact that this Holly has leaves something like one of the Southern Beeches, *Nothofagus Dombeyi*; originally it had been regarded as a mere variety of *I. intricata*, though no one who had seen the two growing wild would ever suppose that they had anything to do with each other.

There is another small-leafed Holly which forms ample bushes on rocks and old tree-stumps along the open ridge. It has polished Box-like leaves and larger berries than *I. nothofagifolia*, lifted clear of the foliage on slender but stiff stalks. It looks the sort of shrub one could cut back and back without damaging it; such stuff as hedges are made of. This Holly however appears only at the topmost limit of the temperate forest and belongs rather to the next higher belt. Other species, found in the Fir forest and above, even to the alpine region, will be mentioned later.

The temperate rain forest is fairly open, and not difficult to penetrate. Thanks to the shade cast by the heavy roof of foliage, there is not much undergrowth. Light retards growth; but green plants require a certain depth of light in order to grow at all. In the jungle, though the light is as dim, yet there is a much more favourable growing temperature, which encourages the development of thin climbing plants capable of reaching the roof quickly. Perching plants seek the light in their own way. The denseness of the tropical jungle is largely caused by the sagging coils of ribbon and rope climbers, and by the immense growth of flowerless plants and of foliage; as already remarked, warmth and moisture and darkness are peculiarly favourable to the growth of vegetative organs such as leaves, at the expense of flowers, which are children of light.

But in the temperate rain forest, not only is there a distinct check to active growth in Winter, but the temperature never reaches the optimum for plant growth. Consequently climbing plants at least are conspicuous by their absence. Moisture and darkness do indeed favour the growth of herbaceous plants; but in the absence of heat, they are of small size. Occasionally, in the temperate forest, Bamboos may grow so thickly as to cause obstruction, or one may come on a belt of broad-leafed Arundinaria, or of solid Cane (Phyllostachys), not tall but thick-set, through which it is necessary to hack one's way; or of Rhododendron. But generally it will be found that, where the undergrowth is dense, light is streaming in through a gap in the roof, as on a ridge, or in a clearing. So long as one keeps to the depths of the forest one can get through with a minimum of cutting. Normally the undergrowth, which is almost entirely herbaceous, is discreet. Ferns, species of Strobilanthes, always gregarious, Violets, Begonias, Oxalis, Thalictrum, Paris, and Dog's Mercury, contribute to a threadbare carpet. Amongst flowering plants, Monocotyledons predominate; they include species of Arisæma with hooded cowls, various Orchids, and Liliaceæ. The Ferns, though in some variety are usually of small size; and extensive areas are often covered with one or two species. Scattered shrubs, such as Ribes, Osmanthus, Rosa, and of course Rhododendron, help to fill up the wide spaces between the big trees. That the association is an 'open' one is further attested by the large number of seedling trees which spring up everywhere—Acer, Magnolia, Rhododendron, Quercus, and higher up, Abies. Only a small proportion of these will eventually survive, of course. But there are many dead trees to be replaced, and more are dying. in some places we noticed large areas of dead Bamboo, which had probably flowered the previous year and then died down. The epiphytic flora however, being mostly small and herbaceous, is not so much affected by the temperature factor; and the humidity, which is what chiefly concerns perching plants, being relatively as great as it is in the tropical valleys, epiphytes are rampant.

But if the forest is easy to penetrate, the steepness of the face and the rude obstruction caused by the bare skeleton of the mountain thrust through the thin flesh, more than balks the climber. Streams gnawing hungrily into the face, score deep grooves which are clogged with a richer growth. But always they reveal the foundations of the hills, and plunging wildly amongst the cliffs of the upper forest, at last cascade hundreds of feet into the main valley.

Thus while it is impossible to climb the flanks of the hills, one can generally follow up the crest of a spur, however steep; and although this involves great toil, for no spur ever continues in a steady ascent to the main range, but rises and falls in a long line of crests and dips, yet in the end one may succeed in passing the last belt of trees and reaching the open country beyond.

The temperate forest is always moist. Except for a short time in Winter, the trees stand with their heads in a cool Turkish bath and their toes in a wet sponge. The outer hills intercept all the clouds and condense all the moisture which these lofty areas draw up from the plains lying at their feet. Even during that lull in the monsoon which, coming in July or August, coincides with the hottest time of the year, the rain forest remains cool and moist. In early Winter, when the plains are already steeped in sunshine, the foot-hills are busy mopping up the dregs of the south-west monsoon and filtering out the moisture from the backwash as the wind changes. Then comes snow. But in the rain forest the snow is soft and yielding, ready to melt at a glance from the sun, and to disappear altogether when a warm breath from the valley blows upon it.

In Winter some of the trees, after colouring brilliantly shed their leaves. Only those trees which are well exposed to the weather, as on the crest of a ridge, colour well; lower down in the safe depths of the forest the leaves fade bleakly and crumple up. Last to shed their leaves are the Magnolias.

In April the temperate forest is once more full of colour, as the bare trees break into new foliage, some red, some vinous, some amber, some gold, or silver. But here are no carpets of Primroses and Anemones, flowering before the new fledged trees can throw a shade over the forest; no Bluebells sheeting the June glades. Instead there are species of Calanthe; tall white Lilies (*Lilium giganteum*); and the quaint Arisæmas. There is no colour here as there is in an English wood; all the colour has gone into the trees.

It is in the temperate forest that the Rhododendrons first begin to dominate the scene, and the zone of Magnolias is also the beginning of the zone of big-leafed tree Rhododendrons. At this season, when the scattered deciduous trees are robing themselves afresh, the flame of scarlet Rhododendrons breaks out like incendiary fires, closely followed by the more delicate pinks and soft daffodil yellows of the woolly-leafed trees. Lastly, the big scale-leafed species shatter the gloom with the clear arctic radiance of their white trumpet flowers.

The outer hill ranges are entirely forest clad. All the spurs which buttress the main range from 6,000 feet to 12,000 feet are heavily wooded. From high up on one of these lofty ridges one can look out across the chasm on either side, to spur beyond spur, rising sharply from the abyss. If we plunge down the flank for a short distance, following one of the gutters which collect water from above, we shall soon find a stream sliding and clattering down the smooth tilted rock slabs. We cannot follow it far without warning, for it suddenly disappears and we shrink back from the edge of a terrific precipice to find ourselves staring across the gulf to the mountains opposite, framed between lean trees.

Once leave the safe crest of the spur and you become involved amongst the cliffs; yet so well concealed by bushes are they, and screened by forest trees, that you do not suspect anything, though you are standing on the very brink of a precipice! Sometimes on a south face the escarpment is broken up into a chaos of rocks, swamped beneath an ocean of small trees, shrubs, bushes, and climbing plants. Such tanglewood is impenetrable; it requires hours of cutting and climbing to force a way through the dense growth which includes species of Rhododendron, Ilex, Viburnum, Acer, Quercus, and Taxus; together with climbing plants such as Clematis, Schizandra, Zanthoxylum, Holboellia, and Akebia, The tanglewood includes, besides stunted trees which grow full size within the shelter of the forest, shrubs and bushes, and especially woody climbing plants which grow nowhere else except along the open ridge; it is in fact a small plant association.

Where the forest faces due north, it grows more luxuriantly than where it faces south. Aspect has great influence on the appearance of the vegetation, and even on the type of vegetation; in the forest region, and in the lower alps, that is to say between 7,000 and 12,000 feet, it has a maximum effect. On north slopes there is of course less sunshine. At 7,000 feet that has a direct effect: at 12,000 feet it has an indirect effect, for here where sunshine is scarce, the snow lingers long after it has disappeared from the south face, directly exposed to the warm air from the plains. Within the temperate forest belt, many a south slope exposed at midsummer to a vertical sun, is covered with nothing but Bracken and grass, with scattered trees of Pine, or Alder or Oak, and clumps of low bushes.

It was, then, to this forest that we committed ourselves at the beginning of the monsoon. Here we spent six weeks. Our camp comprised our two tents and an open bark-roofed shelter, where we could have our meals and work by the fire; a sort of dug-out under a tree, roofed with bark and tarpaulins, where Luso lived, and cooked our meals; and another ruder shelter where Hubble lived. After Hubble's desertion this last was used for drying paper, and a sort of vestal fire was kept burning night and day. The orders on this point were explicit, and were so faithfully carried out that, the fire being by this time out of control underground (where the vegetable earth was smouldering like a volcano), one day set fire to hut, paper, and all!

Immediately after our arrival here, in the few days left to us before the rains broke, we pushed our explorations up the ridge, quickly passing from the temperate forest into the Rhododendron forest, and thence into the Fir forest. These preliminary skirmishes had but one object—the conquest of Kaso, and a clear way to the alps. Not that we had any ambition to climb Kaso; its botanical conquest was all we desired. From hard by our camp, which stood on the very brink of the ridge, we had a perfect view of our mountain before the rain came. In the dawn, Kaso peak glowered at us across the cloud-filled gulf, now beckoning us on, now mocking us. Very gradually its grim cliffs and screes wore through the snow-fields. With longing eyes we followed the wide sweep of our ridge as it curved in a steep semicircle round the head of the gulf; we marked where the trees stopped, the humped alpine ridge beyond that, and the ebbing snow-line. After the rains broke, we rarely had a glimpse of Kaso.

It is scarcely light when the clouds in the valley begin to heave restlessly, and to rise; presently the mist is flying by us on the wings of the wind. Half an hour later down comes the chilled rain in drenching sheets. Often it rained for days and nights with a pitiless resolution, as though it never would stop. But sometimes, just before sunset, even when the weather was at its worst, there came a lull. The valley below us would empty itself of cloud as though by magic, and the mountains across the way would loom up all greasy with mist in the blue dusk. But this glimpse too was brief, and the rain curtain was quickly rung down again. Sometimes just before dawn the peaks were clear.

As we sat in our summer-house by the smoking fire, with the clouds driving like fine spray over us, we would look down the steep slope, and see the twisted trunks of the trees, the interlacing branches of those just below, and then against the white bank of mist, the rounded tops of those still lower; all seen through waving curtains of moss. And staring thus into the heart of the forest the scene changed in our minds, and we imagined ourselves in some fairyland under the depths of the sea. A pale green light shone through the canopy of leaves, and against the milk-white mist loomed strange forms. The fan-shaped growth of the Tsuga-trees became branching coral, with the angular red boughs of the Rhododendrons for stems. The banners of moss hanging from every tree, swayed gently by the breeze, were ribbons of weed plucked by an idle current; the dark Junipers were sinister growths from the bed of the ocean, dripping with mournful weed. The fantastic leaves of Aralia spread themselves out like hands against the ghostly background, till they also stiffened into lobes of coral, and the bare tops of the Larches which peeped up in the offing were but the broken masts of sunken ships whose keels lay rotting in the ooze. In the greenish gloom, lit only by a pale phosphorescence, as though some shaft of light from a world beyond seeking its way had been caught and held captive, and in the faintly threatening silence which wrapped the forest, one sensed the underworld of the ocean. But the silence was unnatural, and listening, one became aware presently of a dull distant roar, as of waves breaking on a barrier reef. It was the torrent in the valley, 6,000 feet below.

Then the rain came down again, and drummed on the great leaves and dripped off the moss tails; the dark mournful Junipers wept ceaselessly, and the whole scene dissolved in tears. The monotonous drip from the trees tolled a knell through the dark and twisted aisles of the forest.

The ghostly white corollas of the Rhododendrons, perched high up in the trees, drop silently one by one; wads of moss fall softly, branches crack, and crumple on the mossy mattress, as the giants of the forest shed their dying limbs. Then the scuppers of the mountain gush, and the voice of the torrent rises a semitone, shrilling like a band-saw. And in the cool moisture everything grows, and grows, and grows.

12   Up the Ridge

WHEN we first pitched our tents under the spreading and gnarled boughs of the Rhododendrons at the end of May the ridge was dry and the weather fine; thus the water problem was serious. That it had rained continuously for a week was of no help, for water slid off that ridge as it does off a house-roof. As soon as we arrived, we rigged up canvas baths; but our immediate necessity was to discover a water-supply which would last us until the next rain came. To tide over the first day we had brought up two petrol tins full of water; but these lasted no time, and the search for a spring was vigorously pursued from the beginning. The Mishmis shook their heads and said there wasn't any water; but we thought we knew better. At any rate, there was Buttercup's Well, less than a mile along the ridge. Here a film of water slithered over the rock beneath a carpet of moss; and though we stripped off the carpet and directed as much of the water as we could control into a bucket, we found that there was not enough flow to fill an ordinary bucket in a day.

Some distance farther along the ridge the trail passed beneath a high cliff from which water dripped in half a dozen places. By an arrangement of bark ducts we easily directed several of these trickles into a common stream at the base of the cliff, and a bucket was soon filled. But there remained the difficulty that the water cliff was some distance from camp, and on the far side of the Rocks, where the ridge turned a somersault and the interruption was surmounted by means of an awkward chimney. Descending this chimney with a petrol can full of water on one's back was certainly difficult, but Aquarius Hubble made such heavy weather of it that a trip to the water cliff and back invariably occupied him a whole day! We left a bucket permanently at the cliff, and it was always overflowing when we passed on our way to the Alps; but not much water found its way to camp. However, we need not die of thirst; it was merely that we had to forgo washing.

In order to increase our water ration, I decided to explore the precipitous flanks of the ridge directly below our camp; though I had little hope of finding a spring less than a thousand feet below the crest, since the earth absorbed water like a sponge. But there I was wrong. True, on the south face I did not find water within a thousand feet—though I found *Magnolia globosa*. But on the north face I found it with quite unexpected ease. The earth did indeed absorb water like a sponge; but like a sponge also it filled, and yielded up the excess at no great distance below the crest. On these steep faces, for all their covering of forest, there is only a veneer of soil, and the naked rock is never far below the surface. The trees in fact, and especially the Rhododendrons, are mostly shallow rooted, and their roots are often exposed at the surface. When grown in the open in England, it is important to note that in the Summer they will sometimes need a top dressing of leaves to keep them cool and moist.

Descending one of the shallow grooves which line the face, I followed it down a short distance and presently found sweet water trickling from under the rock. The groove quickly became a ditch, and the ditch a gully: and only a couple of hundred feet below the crest of the ridge the trickle had swollen to an audible stream. The forest was quite open here, consisting chiefly of big Rhododendrons, Tsuga, and *Magnolia globosa*; but so steep was the face, that it would be no easy matter to lug a canful of water up to camp. However it had to be done, and anyhow here was water within reach, whatever the weather. Of course the monsoon broke a few days later, and for the rest of our stay we suffered from too much water. No need to seek distractedly for pools and springs and trickles now! No need to lug heavy cans of precious liquid up heart-breaking slopes! Henceforth the canvas tanks were full, pressed down, and running over; and we were hard put to it to keep the vital spark in fires which had to be fed on wet wood, in the teeth of the inquisitive rain mist.

But to return to the spring. The ditches, not yet carved to the depth of gulleys, were filled with all manner of herbaceous plants. At the call of the warm Summer rain they awoke, a rank growth of annuals, to be mown down again by the Autumn gales, and at last to be crushed into oblivion by the snow which for three months burdens the Rhododendron forest. But the banks of the ditches and the moss-covered rocks which everywhere peep through the torn lining of forest, were crowded with clumps of a handsome Primula whose finely cut leaves, glistening in the dusk, and whose bold heads of rosy purple flowers, with frilled edges, gave a hint of carnations. Although six inches high, in its much divided leaves, with winged petiole, this plant was curiously like little *P. eucyclia*. The sturdy stems of *Primula Normaniana*, however, rise boldly from a plump crown of leaves, and the mop heads peep over a green lace collar of bracts. There are often a dozen flowers in a mop, some of which have a crimson, others a yellow eye, just as in *P. eucyclia*. This may be a condition of age, but it has nothing to do with 'pin-eyed' and 'thrum-eyed' flowers. In October the leaves turned bright scarlet, and mature plants are as handsome in fruit as in flower.

P. Normaniana proved to be the most abundant forest Primula met with, colonies being found as low down as 8,000 feet. It flowers throughout June on moss-covered rocks and earth banks, in an atmosphere heavy with moisture, and in semi-darkness beneath the dense canopy of Rhododendron foliage. The zone of Spruce and Magnolias marks its lowest limit.

At the Rocks I found a clump of the Chinese *Primula septemloba*. The woolly foliage of this plant is always attractive, especially while the young seven-pointed umbrella is raising and opening itself slowly on its hairy handle. But the pinched tubular flowers, of a rather crude purple, are disappointing. Nevertheless, it was interesting to find this plant so far west, forming an obvious link with the Himalayan *P. geraniifolia;* indeed it may be questioned whether we are justified any longer in regarding *P. septemloba* and *P. geraniifolia* as distinct.

Lower down the water gulley, where the banded gneiss was exposed, Buttercup discovered a second woodland Primula, which at first sight looked something like *P. sikkimensis;* though that is not a woodland plant. But when it flowered, which it did early in July, it turned out to be neither *P. sikkimensis*, nor even a near relative, but one of the 'Candelabra' Primulas. Now the 'Candelabras' are no more forest plants than are the 'Sikkimenses', but, like them, usually grow in meadows; and in fact I did find this plant later on in meadow-clad gullies at least 2,000 feet higher up; but as it was incapable of setting a single seed there, its freedom did not seem of much advantage to it. On the other hand it set abundant fertile seed in the forest.

P. polonensis, as it is named, had the 'Sikkimensis' type of flower and inflorescence seen in *P. prenantha,* but is actually much more closely allied to the Tibetan *P. Morsheadiana.* Both the last named, however, are alpine plants, whereas *P. polonensis* is not, though perhaps it would like to be. The scape rises from a crown of hearty, rather Primrose-like leaves, and produces in solemn succession two, and even three, tiers of drooping intensely butter-golden flowers. A feature of this sleek, but hardy-looking Primula is its immense fibrous root system, very different from the few stout stays produced by *P. Morsheadiana.*

P. polonensis evidently had a secret passion for *P. Normaniana,* which was shyly reciprocated. The two were never apart. The yellow-flowered one did indeed refuse to follow its love into the most abysmal depths; it struck at 9,000 feet. Likewise the pink-flowered one would not follow its mate into the rarefied atmosphere of the empyrean, where, as I have said, *P. polonensis* met with no matrimonial success. But within legitimate limits, the two always grew together. If a forest ditch contained *P. Normaniana* it also contained *P. polonensis.* Yet so jealous were they, that nothing would induce them to share each other's ground. *P. Normaniana* was always at the upper end of the ditch; *P. polonensis* always below. In like manner *P. lacerata* and *P. obconica* share their home in the Burmese Beyond.

We first found *P. polonensis* growing on the edge of the naked rock in the Tsuga forest, some way down our water gulley; the stream at this point leapt over a high precipice, leaving a window in the screen of foliage through which the light streamed in. But at higher levels it shunned the light of day quite as much as did *P. Normaniana.*

When the water problem had been solved, we turned out attention to

Rhododendron sino-grande AND BAMBOO THICKET,
MISHMI HILLS, ASSAM FRONTIER, 9,000 FEET.
FLOWERS PALE YELLOW.

Magnolia rostrata IN BUD. RAIN FOREST, MISHMI HILLS,
8,000 FEET. FLOWERS WHITE. MAY.

the rough trail which led to Kaso. Our camp was pitched at a height of about 10,000 feet; the forest ended at about 12,500. But to reach the alpine region was not quite so simple as it sounds. The distance, measured along the ridge, was no more than six miles; but that included much more than a mere ascent of 2,500 feet. The ridge rose and fell, though the fact was well concealed by the mantle of forest; the dark spires of the Fir-trees seemed to rise in an almost unbroken succession. In several places it was thrown into violent fits, and the rough track dodged to this side and to that in a vain endeavour to avoid these eruptions; but sometimes we had to climb over them. The rain, too, made the going worse; and the nature of the trail did not encourage speed. I once did the trip to the end of the forest in three hours; but usually it took us longer than that. We had a theory that we came down much faster than we went up. But what with the climbing involved even during the descent, and the fact that by that time we were tired, I doubt if there was much difference. Anyway five or six hours is a good big slice out of a day's work, though luckily there were always plants to collect along the ridge itself before ever we reached the Alps; and the higher we went, the more there was to collect.

For nearly half a mile, to the Rocks, the trail kept along the crest of the ridge, without any serious climbing. The forest here was fairly open, and consisted as usual of Abies with *Rhododendron sino-grande* and *R. arizelum* in about equal proportions. Two other big-leafed tree Rhododendrons, neither of which I saw in flower, were less common. One of them, with a thin bronze pelt, like goldbeaters' skin, stretched tightly over the lower leaf surface, was *R. fulvoides*, related to *R. lacteum*. The other had grey woolly leaves and immense trusses of woolly fruit. Withered specimens of flowers looked purple. This was *R. lanigerum*; in April or May it must be just one immense cushion of wool and blossom.

Clumps of *Cœlogyne ocellata* perched up in the trees were a mass of white dabbled with egg yellow; but there were hardly any ground flowers yet. Then came the Rocks, and for the next mile the ridge was in a fluster, here piled up into proud towers, there thrown down in ruins. The path stuck grimly to the crest as long as possible, but at the water cliff we were thrust right off the ridge by a sabre-toothed rock. We had to drop down under the cliff, and climb up to the top again by a vile track, pushing through a dense grove of Bamboo, and then shoulder our way along a knife-edge, thickly overgrown with bushes, to the Look Out.

Along this portion of the route were many beautiful shrubs; and the most beautiful of all, in June, were *Rhododendron cinnabarinum* and *R. chœtomallum*, the one a red-hot mass of flowers, and the other, all burnt sienna and scalding blood. *R. cinnabarinum* was indeed one of the commonest shrubs in the upper forest, often forming impenetrable thickets by itself; but it grew only on the cliffs in the full light of day. Equally common was the pink 'Barbatum' with the cinnamon leaves, a free-flowering shrub with a vertical range which kept it in flower from April to July. Then there was *R. deleiense* with smoke-grey leaves and buttons of pinkish flowers; these four species making up more than half the Rhododendron scrub at this altitude. But there were other shrubs too. A small broad-leafed Holly which in October bore a profusion to tiny scarlet berries, much liked by birds, grew with the cherry-flowered Enkianthus, and with another shrub handsomer still—*Viburnum Wardii*. In full bloom this last is one of the most beautiful of the smaller trees. It is a deciduous species, with rugose leaves which in exposed places colour warmly in September. In April the whole tree-top is wreathed in snow-white lace, which spills over the crinkled green leaves in flocculent corymbs; at the same time many of the big-leafed Rhododendrons are in flower, and the middle forest zone is an ever-changing sea of beryl and amber.

Viburnum Wardii, however, has not proved an easy plant to introduce. Good flowering specimens are rare, and the fruits have a disconcerting way of ripening quite suddenly. At first yellow, rosy-cheeked, and hard, in a night their flesh turns to black pulp, and is quickly eaten by birds. Even so the fruits are firmly attached, and some remain on the tree. But the collector's troubles are not over yet. Presently he finds that of every hundred fruits laboriously gathered (each containing only one seed) the contents of nearly half have been devoured by a grub from within, leaving only the dead shell.

Meanwhile, we were making our camp as comfortable as possible, cutting down trees, collecting firewood, and improving paths. We spread the extra tent over the roof of our summer-house, and awaited the monsoon with more confidence. Aquarius Hubble complained bitterly at having to carry water; so on June 2, after heavy rain in the night which filled our reservoirs, we let him go down to the valley to buy food.

The following evening we were sitting by the fire in the summer-house when a branch snapped loudly. Buttercup looked round. Out of the tail of his eye he saw something move in the forest. "I thought it was a man," he said. "It must have been a shadow, or else Luso." Nevertheless, when we went round the camp next morning, we found Hubble's *basha* empty, his cooking-pot and blankets gone; and it made us uneasy to feel that in the gloaming a man had actually crept into our camp undetected, and got away. For the Mishmis were not friendly, and our situation was a lonely one.

During the first fortnight of our stay men sometimes came up from the village bringing us a few eggs, and occasionally a scraggy fowl, which would have been a poor meal for one; we had to make it last the two of us for two meals. As for the eggs, they were always far gone, and Buttercup at last discovered why. The Mishmis did not really want to sell us eggs at all, they preferred to hatch them. Therefore, they left them under the hen. But if nothing happened, when the time was ripe, and we wanted eggs, why not turn an honest penny by selling them to us! So we got the farmyard failures, and I am afraid we usually ate them, though we were saved from sudden death once when an egg detonated out loud while being lifted gingerly from a Mishmi's bag! It was a well-hatched plot!

With only Luso in camp, he had to be on his guard when the Mishmis paid us a visit, for they prowled about, and it was impossible to keep an eye on them all at once. We learnt to take reasonable precautions after Buttercup had had a good knife he left lying about stolen by these pick-pockets, and one or two cooking-pots had gone the same way. On the other hand the Mishmis were not above begging for empty tins, and were profuse in their thanks if we gave them a bottle!

At this season Kaso slept so soundly under the snow that it did not seem much use to tackle the Alps yet; nevertheless, I was keen to climb to the top, if only to see how long it took, and what it was like.

By the end of May we had explored the ridge as far as the point reached by Buttercup on his reconnaissance; and we found that though we were still some way from the alps, the ridge descending again, quite a number of alpine plants had thoroughly established themselves on the cliffs all the way along here.

Beyond the Look Out—a flat bare crest hedged with *Rhododendron cinnabarinum*—the ridge was open, and the view across the valleys on either side to a world of mountains was grand; though we rarely enjoyed a view from here on account of the dense cloud. The cliffs culminated in Primula Rock, and an awkward step down, with precipices flanking a narrow saddle. On the wet rocks grew tough cushions of crisp leaves, tightly com-pressed and bearing flush with the surface large sulphur-yellow flowers. This was a Diapensia. The little flycatching Butterwort, *Pinguicula alpina*, was common, and bunches of *Paraquilegium grandiflorum* shivered on the cliff, its long tap root probing far into the rock. But *Primula Clutterbuckii*, which gave its name to the cliff, was rarer. It has purple flowers on twin stalks, which scarcely protrude from a packet of toothed spoon-shaped leaves whose under-surface is snowy white. *P. Clutterbuckii* grew on this one cliff wedged into crevices, and I found a few plants under the Rhododendron bushes, in the alpine region; but it was not a common plant. It is a near relative of *P. yunnanensis*. On the grass slopes, facing the midday sun, *Primula alta* flowered in May, and an Onosma in July. While peering over one of the cliffs, I spied, just out of reach, a dwarf Rhododendron—the first—unlike anything known to me. As we could not reach it from above, we continued along the ridge, and descended an easier gulley, forcing our way through Bamboo and Rhododendron. The black mould was pierced with red-tipped sheaves of *Omphalogramma Souliei*, which showed never a leaf yet amongst its gaping violet flowers. Tight clumps of it produced a dozen flowers, or more. And then we came to a slanting rock, over which spread a drift of the *Rhododendron patulum*, promptly christened Rock Rose. The threadlike stems crawl over the clammy surface, and bear only

137

a few tiny sharp-pointed leaves. But the solitary prostrate flowers are large, and of so delicate a shade of purple as to be almost pink; within the throat are constellations of darker spots. In the Alps many a rock was closely carpeted with the wide filmy corollas of Rock Rose, and it formed a quiet foil to the brilliant scarlet of *R. repens*. Beyond Primula Rock, the ridge mounted steadily. A dwarf Bamboo grew thickly here, amongst Firs and Rhododendron bushes, and in the moss beneath, *Bryocarpum himalayense* was very common. The stem grows twelve or fifteen inches high and ends in a solitary nodding bright yellow flower, as it might be a Lloydia. The leaves, which develop later, however, remind one of Omphalogramma, and so also does the long thin sausage capsule. But the seeds, instead of being flat, are little restless roly-polies. Now, *Bryocarpum himalayense* is a very rare Sikkim plant, and has never been recorded from anywhere else. Its discovery, therefore, 400 miles east of Sikkim was particularly interesting. In May and June I was able to collect quite a lot of seed of the previous year; for the parchment capsules are persistent, and the seeds are trapped in the bulged base, and can only be shaken out one at a time.

The trail grew steeper, we passed through a dark tunnel where the snow lingered late under the trees—Gloomy Glen we called it, though the gloom was illuminated by the caustic red flowers of *Rhododendron cerasinum*—a small tree with smooth leaves, and presently came out on to another open top. This hillock was purple with a tumbled sea of *Rhododendron riparium*. There were peaty pools of water lying about, and Buttercup told me that when he came here on May 2—this being his farthest north—snow lay in patches. Buttercup's ridge was bare of trees, but there were thick coverts of Bamboo. The sides of the ridge were, as usual, more or less thickly covered with shrubs, such as *Rhododendron trichocladum*, *R. pruniflorum*, and Birch. Later we found *Primula prenantha* on the grass and *P. alta* on the rocks, besides the maroon Nomocharis under the Bamboos. A short ascent through Fir forest, the path thickly edged with low-growing bushes of the silver-leaved *R. didymum*, whose dusky red flowers glowed hotly in the shadow, brought us to a second alpine top, likewise carpeted with *R. riparium*. One side was forested: the other almost bare, but so precipitous that it was impossible to descend. The altitude was fully 12,000 feet and the flora was of the alpine type; yet immediately afterwards the ridge sagged down again into the Fir forest and we could see no end to it from where we stood; and Firs struggled up the flanks, wading through deep seas of scrub Rhododendron. Had the ridge ascended from here, we must very soon have reached the end of the forest.

It is necessary to draw a distinction between relative and absolute height. The summit of a peak 10,000 feet high will always be without forest, covered with shrubs and alpines. If a peak of that height stood amongst the foot-hills, that is to say near the plains, it would have a smaller proportion of alpines than if it was situated in the interior, close to the great mountain chains; its covering would be influenced by the more aggressive vegetation below, which hemmed it in. On the other hand, 10,000 feet is not necessarily the limit of forest on a mountain 15,000 or 20,000 feet high. Protection can be given by the slope and by the snow, which now lies longer. Moreover, the trees protect each other, tier by tier. Thus forest extends probably 2,000 feet higher, though not as a rule continuously. Alpine valleys are wind funnels: and trees persist at higher levels on the flanks of the valley than along the bottom. The crests of the spurs also are wind swept, the flanks more or less sheltered; alpine plants, therefore, establish themselves along the cliffs, while forest covers the flanks.

On June 4 we decided to go for the alpine region, wet or fine. Leaving camp at 7.30, we forged steadily ahead, and did not halt till we reached Buttercup's ridge; we had then been marching for 1¾ hours. So far we had not seen much that was new to us except a small Cherry-tree in flower, and a long-tailed jay! But just here, where the pink-flowered *Rhododendron crinigerum* clustered thickly, we noticed a clump of Rhododendrons with the same olive-green and cinnamon-coloured leaves, but flowers of bright cherry red! There appeared to be six bushes of this species; we never found any more. It is a species closely allied to *R. Smithii*. Six weeks later, farther down the ridge, I found a solitary Rhododendron bush in the midst of a thicket of *R. crinigerum*, which, although out of flower, seemed different in some odd manner; and on examining it more closely, I found that the leaves lacked the cinnamon woolly coat beneath. As the shrub was small for *R. crinigerum*, which usually grows into a tree, I was about to conclude that it was immature; for it is a matter of common observation that the leaves of seedling Rhododendrons do not assume the hairy coat of the adult plant until they are several years old, while on the other hand seedlings may have hairy leaves, although the adult plant is quite hairless. I then noticed, however, that the little bush had borne two trusses of flowers, so it was not so immature after all! The lack of a hairy coat to the leaf was obviously a permanent feature; and it will be interesting to see what is raised from the seed I collected. It was significant to find two plants, closely related to, and growing with, *R. crinigerum*, perhaps the commonest species of Rhododendron in the Mishmi Hills, and yet so distinct from it in important characters! Both the 'Cherry Barbatum' (*R. Smithii*?) and this other plant (K.W. 8431) are quite distinct from one another and from *R. crinigerum*.

Beyond this point the ridge fell away again, and we plunged once more into a forest of Fir, Rhododendron, and Bamboo. The Fir-trees were stunted and bulky, with trappings of moss in which grew large bunches of *Rhododendron megeratum* and another epiphytic species. The bush or tree Rhododendrons included *R. crinigerum*, *R. deleiense*, *R. Hookeri*, and *R. cinnabarinum*. But the most interesting was yet another species of the 'Barbatum' series. This shrub was outstanding in several respects: firstly, for the uncommon size of its leaves; secondly, for the persistence of its leaf-bud scales, several years' growth of which bearded its stems; thirdly, for the deep crimson brick-red of its flowers, which though individually small, formed bulging trusses; fourthly—though this only appeared later—for the beauty of its breaking leaf-buds. In July every bush shot up long jets of curled pink bud scales tipped with an emerald-green plume of leaves, which lasted for weeks; the bud scales were still pink, when the leaves were fully expanded. I was elated to see this Rhododendron in flower, because I had been dogging it for some time without success. I first met with it in the gorge of the Tsangpo in 1924, growing in the most impenetrable scrub on a precipice, but to my chagrin I could not find a fruiting specimen. In 1926 I had better luck, for I met with it again, in fruit, and collected seed of it. Now for the third time I had found it, and in flower too; nor was it disappointing. Indeed in some ways with its big bristly leaves and shaggy stems *R. exasperatum* (as it is called) is one of the most distinct Rhododendrons I have seen. Luckily it was very common on Kaso, replacing *R. crinigerum* on the high exposed cliffs; indeed the latter disappears where the main forest consists entirely of Silver Fir—that is at about 11,000 feet altitude.

The next break in the forest was Iris Cliff, where we found a number of jolly alpines. There were clumps of dwarf Iris, and white bells of Cassiope dangling from Heather-like stems, and *Primula alta* in flower; we found also a yellow-flowered 'Nivales' Primula with strap-shaped wash-leathery leaves, silvered beneath, called *P. mishmiensis*. On the cliff grew colonies of *Cypripedium tibeticum* and another maroon-flowered species.

In July a third Cypripedium with small milk-white flowers (*C. Wardii*) appeared here, with the blotched *Nomocharis aperta* which looks like an escaped Odontoglossum.

After another ascent we came to a hill smothered under a tangle of scrub Rhododendron, which tripped us up at every other step. We took it on a slant, and reached the top, panting and worried. Headless trees, Larch and Fir, straggled on for a hundred yards, then ceased altogether. We had reached the end of the forest; the Alps at last! Clots of snow lay like foam over the coloured crests of dwarf Rhododendrons which washed over our ankles. Ahead the ridge rose sharply in a row of irregular teeth, as though smashed with an axe; beyond, flights of rude steps led to the foot of the final precipice. On the north side, some hundreds of feet below us, lay a wide basin filled with snow, and striped with sulphur seas of *R. telopeum*. On the south side the ridge broke off in a series of precipices separated by chutes, or by belts of Rhododendron scrub.

Cowering under the shelter of the precipice on the south side, a bush Rhododendron like *R. lanatum* was conspicuous. The small leaves were wadded beneath with a reddish fur, and the flowers, though pink in bud, open faintly yellow, speckled purple. The stunted shrubs formed an impenetrable tangle, rising above the general Rhododendron level achieved by *R. sanguineum, R. pruniflorum,* and others.

The smallest Rhododendrons are found on slopes fully exposed to wind and sun. At this altitude plants are very sensitive to the least change of aspect, and immediately the direction of slope changes the plants change; sometimes a change of angle alone is sufficient. It is this sensitiveness to aspect—a sensitiveness almost entirely controlled by water demand and supply—which produces the great diversity in the alps. Shortly, there is more water available, and the supply is better regulated, on north slopes the snow falls earlier, lies later, and melts more gradually than on south slopes; also there is less sunshine. As a result, with the same degree of protection larger plants can exist here. These arguments do not apply to a garden in Britain, however. A north aspect may shade a plant from direct sun in the Summer, but in a normal year it makes no difference to its water supply. Direct sunlight in Summer is the one thing alpine plants on the wet ranges do not suffer from. In this latitude, between 25° and 28° north of the Equator, the sun at midsummer is almost vertically overhead, and in the clean rarefied air of the alps, the naked sun at 13,000 feet is very powerful. On the dry interior ranges, where Summer sunshine is not so rare, the alpine floor is utterly different; and although Rhododendrons still bulk largely, the carpet is of a more uniform pattern. The remarkable thing is that we are able to grow so many of these plants 25° farther north, where the heating and lighting power of the sun are so different, to say nothing of the mere mechanical effect of a difference of pressure double that to which they are accustomed!

We found Scarlet Runner (*R. repens*) clinging to the steep naked rocks. Sometimes it formed carpets, or completely covered a slab, and its vermilion flowers were visible a long way off. Where there is more shelter, the 'Sanguineum' Rhododendrons begin to raise their heads and form low scrub plants, with bigger rounder leaves than those of *R. repens*, and flowers no longer solitary and prone, but borne in trusses of three and four, amongst the foliage. These are perhaps the most beautiful of all the alpine Rhododendrons; the flowers are large, and hang loosely, and are of the most exquisite shades of pink and cerise. Carmelita is a glorious plant with carmine flowers. Rose of Kaso has flowers of pale damask pink; some specimens have at the base of the corolla five circular crimson spots, which are honey glands, but these are often absent, or rather, are not more deeply pigmented than the rest of the corolla. Scarlet Pimpernel has cherry-crimson flowers. They all flower in June, and are buried under the snow by the middle of October, shedding their seeds *under* the snow; thus they have four months in which to flower, ripen their fruits, and shed their seeds. It is perhaps not surprising that they are rare plants!

On the highest escarpments where Rhododendrons grew, we found a dwarf species allied to *R. cephalanthum*, with wiry stems and tight heads of comparatively large flowers of an enchanting shell-pink. So compressed are the half-dozen or more corollas, that at a little distance the whole pompom looks like a single flower. This is made possible by the corolla being salver-shaped, the wide flat limb, its delicate edge crimped by pressure, passing abruptly into a narrow slightly curved tube. The stalks of the individual flowers are so short as to be invisible without dissection; and the throat of the tube is plugged with a tuft of hair to keep out the rain. Rhododendrons of this type, with heads of flowers as described, and aromatic leaves, are usually stout little undershrubs, sometimes small bushes; R. crebreflorum is the first example of an absolutely prostrate species. Moreover, the 'Cephalanthums', as we may call them, together with their allies the 'Anthopogons', are typical of the dry zone, being abundant, for example, in North-West Yunnan, and in Southern Tibet where they grow socially; few of them cross over the passes to mix with the Rhododendron carpet of the wet zone.

About noon, having reached a point some 2,500 feet above our camp, that is to say an altitude of between 12,000 and 13,000 feet, we halted for lunch. It was not raining, but there was a sharp wind, and the dense cloud rolling up from below hid everything; now and again the wind tore the veil aside, giving us tantalising glimpses of Kaso, but all we saw was snow. Somewhere not far beneath us we heard running water. We ate our lunch quickly, because we were being badly bitten by sand-flies which gathered in swarms as soon as we halted. Lunch consisted of a few biscuits, some figs, and raisins, and half a slab of Mexican chocolate. Buttercup had packed these in $\frac{1}{4}$ lb. tobacco tins, and we standardised this form of lunch ration, which served admirably as long as the figs and raisins lasted. In order to conserve supplies, we enacted a statute that you could only draw the lunch benefit if you were out for three hours or more; but as a matter of fact one was often out for longer than that without drawing it, or at any rate, without eating it. Only on deliberate occasions when we were engaged on a serious alpine climb did we bother much about lunch: our resources were too strained to make it a habit.

After lunch we decided to leave the ridge, and explore the valley on our left whence came the murmur of water; and finding a slope between two escarpments we descended towards the snow. The ground was all black and brown with dead vegetation, which had just been relieved from the pressure of snow, and oozed water; but a faint flush of green had begun to kindle in the wake of the melting snow, as thousands of plants broke the surface.

Passing through a belt of Willow bush, its buds tightly closed, we noticed scattered sprouts of Primula vernicosa with flimsy white flowers already open, shrinking amongst the packed etiolated leaves. And then came a surprise: colonies of a Primula with heads of flowers, delicately yellow as a candle flame, springing from a socket of reddened sheaths, not yet developed into leaves. It needed only a glance to see that here was the lost

P. calthifolia, the Marsh Marigold-leafed Primula. I had found about half a dozen specimens of this queer 'Petiolaris' in the Seinghku valley in 1926, and had collected a single specimen, leaving the rest to set seed, and expecting to find more plants later. However, I never did, but on Kaso *P. calthifolia* grew in thousands. It first opens its flowers along the edge of the snow, at the beginning of June, without visible means of support. It was still in flower in July, by which time the leaves really were almost as big as those of the Marsh Marigold. Later, however, its wan yellow was utterly quenched by the orange flood-lighting of the Gamboge Primula, which sprang up in its midst in hundreds of thousands; both plants indeed were astonishingly abundant, sharing the stony slope. *P. calthifolia* when fully grown is a large, rather coarse plant, with ample heads of flowers of a pleasant Primrose colour, lifted well above the big leaves, which become much nibbled by beetles.

Descending to the bottom of Boggy Valley, as we called it, we found a spring of clear water. Deep snow lay all around, but where it had melted the red leaves of a giant Rhubarb were showing amongst the croziers of Ferns, the sappy shoots of Monkshood, and many other unrecognisable things.

The chief source of colour amongst the snow-filled dips and downs were the sea-green waves of *Rhododendron telopeum*, breaking against the cliffs in yellow foam. But scrambling up to the ridge again through a breast-high scrub of Rhododendron we noticed a new species which we named Glow-bell. The leaves, olivine green above, and felted below with a foxy-red fur, supported large trusses of flowers, borne in no niggard fashion, of a sultry scarlet. The breeze twisted the leaves over, and the flutter of red-brown, green, and scarlet was fascinating. This species, *R. cœlicum*, which forms a neat bush, six feet high and as much through, is an even finer thing than *R. chœtomallum*.

On a rock, the white stars of *Androsace geraniifolia* twinkled bleakly. We also saw two woodcock; this on June 4 at an altitude of over 12,000 feet! On the 17th I found a nest with four eggs on the steep face at about 21,000 feet altitude; they were all hard sat. Then on July 3, at 13,000 feet, I found another nest, also with four hard-sat eggs. This lay amongst a patch of dwarf Rhododendron, on a slope of 30° to 40°, and was made of moss, with a few dry Rhododendron leaves at the bottom on which the eggs rested. I found both nests accidentally as it were, walking so close to them that the birds rose. We saw quite a number of woodcock all told, so they must be fairly common here in the Summer. In the Winter, of course, they go down. The Mishmis sometimes trap blood pheasants, besides serow, but do not shoot; indeed few of them possess guns. However one can hardly imagine even the best shot shooting woodcock under these conditions, on a broken slope of 35°, where one has to watch almost every step!

On the way back to camp it poured with rain, and we got home drenched and shivering in time for a cup of tea, while we were changing. We dined at seven o'clock and were in bed by nine o'clock. My diary remarks briefly: "A very fair day, but not as rich in results as I had expected."

Our days in this camp were divided between long trips to the alpine region and the exploration of the forest itself, especially of those cliffs within the forest which were colonised by alpine plants. The cliffs were drained below by long stone shafts, which went down for hundreds of feet, and were often too steep to descend. How well we came to know the sequence of landmarks, as day after day we pushed through the dripping barrage of Bamboo, flooding our pockets, and drenching our clothes till the water squelched in our boots!

We had our troubles in camp too, drying plants, photographic plates took five days to dry, and much of one's time is occupied in preserving the collections already made, rather than in adding to them. Luckily heat did not aggravate the dampness of the atmosphere. I do all my own collecting. The mass production of herbarium material by means of native assistants is all very well in its way, but does not appeal to me, if only because it is such a fruitful source of error and inaccuracy. Of course, mass production is only possible in civilised countries like India and China; though the Lepchas of Sikkim are said to be born botanical collectors.

It was very interesting to observe how much better some plants retain their colour when dry than others. Speed has something, but not everything, to do with it; the more quickly a flower is dried, the more likely it is to retain its original colour. Very deeply pigmented flowers sometimes retain their original colour—the Gamboge Primula, for example, retains to-day the rich orange colour of life. White flowers almost invariably dry brown, as also do pale yellows, and pinks. Some of the deep crimson Rhododendrons keep their colour well, but are apt to turn darker, e.g. *R. didymum*; the original colour may often be seen by holding an opened flower up to the light. *Gentiana sino-ornata* usually keeps its colour perfectly, and anyone who wants to know the colour of *Primula fea* or *P. silaensis* in life has only to look at my dried specimens! The general rule seems to be that if the colour is due to cell sap, it will be lost, but if it is due to chromoplasts, it is usually preserved. Fleshy flowers are much more likely to lose their colour than skinny ones, because it takes longer to dry them. Of course, if any chemical change takes place in the flowers, or even in the leaves, the colouring matter may be oxidised, and disappear. The yellow flowers of *Meconopsis paniculata* dry green; the whole plant is full of a bright yellow latex, which undergoes some change as the plant dries. *Primula sikkimensis*, though without the yellow juice of *Meconopsis paniculata*, often dries green too as does *R. telopeum*; and many Irises stain the drying paper. It is the same with leaves. Many leaves keep their original colour, but some turn quite black.

The collector who saw the plant alive, and who now sees it laid out for a *post mortem* in the herbarium, is apt to feel his heart sink; but if he has collected seed of it, there is at least a chance of a glorious resurrection in the years to come.

So much then for the ridge, a long winding rock lane through the forest, tedious, but the only possible way to the alpine region. Against its walls flowed the tide of forest, sweeping over it in places, but where the ridge cut enormous and misshapen granite teeth, held in check or hurled back; until at last it merged into the great peak called Kaso.

13   Camping in the Alps

AFTER long argument with the Mishmis, we persuaded four of them to carry our loads up the ridge—at a price—and return to bring us down later. Our idea was to pitch a tent on the ridge directly above Boggy Valley, the only place where we could find water, unless, of course, it rained violently the whole time. As we had to take a tent, our bedding, and paper, there was not much man-power left for carrying food; and Buttercup informed me that four days was the utmost he could cater for. Also the Mishmis were mean enough to say that we must come down in four days, or stay there for good, as they intended to leave the valley shortly.

The start was fixed for July 1, and on June 30 the weather cleared up. The Mishmis arrived in camp that evening. Next morning in bright sunshine we started up the familiar ridge, everyone carrying something; in fact both Buttercup and I were carrying about 25 lbs. of gear, including camera, a petrol-can for water, and other impedimenta.

The Mishmis had refused to start unless they were paid in advance, but we had expected that. Luso remained below to look after the main camp. Rhododendron Hill, where the forest ended, was reached in four hours, and here we pitched our small 40-lb. alpine tent on the ridge, where the ground was fairly level and covered with brooms of dwarf Rhododendron. This tent, by the way, was historical, having been with Major Kenneth Mason on his Shaksgam exploration beyond the Karakorum in 1926; he had kindly lent it to us.

The coolies now departed and we were left to shift for ourselves. Meanwhile the sky had become completely overcast, and presently it began to drizzle.

Our first concern was to draw water from Boggy Valley, which lay a quarter of a mile away, and some hundreds of feet below us. The slope was as steep as a house-roof, partly clothed with thick Rhododendron bush, and partly with tall meadow herbs, including Ferns, Aconitum, Strobilanthes, and Rheum. Selecting a route, and cutting a trail through the high growth, we soon reached the stream at the point where it gushed from the base of the ridge. We were in a meadow filled with thousands and thousands of small but brilliantly coloured flowers, chiefly red Nomocharis, yellow Lloydia, a stunning blue Corydalis (like *C. cashmeriana*), *Caltha palustris* and its variety *purpurea*, *Anemone polyanthes*, and sheets of the glorious Gamboge Primula (*P. Agleniana*, var. *atrocrocea*) which made me gasp with astonishment. As the result of a more intensive search we found little Claret Cup (*P. silaensis*), and a small blue Gentian. On the stony slopes above, *P. calthifolia* was still in bloom, its big leaves now fully expanded and almost as large as those of the Marsh Marigold from which it derives its name.

Meanwhile Buttercup had filled the petrol-can with sweet water from the spring, and we turned our attention to lugging the hateful thing up the slope. It was heavier than it looked, and it proved to be particularly irksome carrying it by the handle as though it were a suit-case, but we had made no provision for carrying it any other way, though we did try slinging it on a stick. However, owing to the steepness of the slope, all the weight fell on the man below, so we gave that up, and carried it turn and turn about. We had almost reached the top when disaster overtook us. Being tired after the day's climb, I found the work extraordinarily arduous, and after barging through a belt of Rhododendron not far from the summit, I set the can down, too breathless and bothered to move a step; it slipped and toppled slowly over! For a few seconds I watched it fascinated, but rigid with horror, while trying to regain my breath. Before I could do anything the heavy tin was leaping and rolling down the slope! We caught one flash of the scarlet missel cleaving the air in an immense final bound, and then it became lost to sight and sound. We rushed down the slope, although I felt certain that our only water-can had taken the valley in its stride, and was lost evermore in the main, thousands of feet below; probably it would hit a tree and explode. Imagine my delighted surprise therefore when I found it lying on its side buried in the basin of flowers, not far from the spring! It was battered and bruised, and leaking a little, but it was not hopelessly damaged. So we lugged it up the hill once more, and this time reached camp without accident.

Our next encounter was with the fire. For cooking, we dug a hole in the bank, sheltered from the wind, collected some twigs, and set to work. However, in spite of a reckless use of matches, then kerosene oil, and finally solidified spirit, nothing happened. We blew till we were black in the face, and choking, but after half an hour, by which time everything was thoroughly wet, we gave it up and crept into our tent. Here, what with bedding, paper, and specimens, there was no room to move about. Wet clothes were thrown outside, and left to get wetter; cooking was done near the entrance, as we sat on our bedding rolls. We tried to boil our rice on the spirit stove, but it was too small and the heat was too quickly dissipated; in the end we had either to give it up or exhaust our supply of spirit. So we gave it up, and had a more frugal supper with plenty of hot coffee.

After this unfortunate experience, we made our fire on the open ridge, having propped up a tarpaulin with Bamboos, to keep off some of the rain. For three days Buttercup performed heroic feats, lying on the ground blowing the sulky embers, despite wind and rain. There were no faggots; we had to feed the fire with twigs of Bamboo and brushwood, and apply stimulants such as kerosene and spirit, frequently. The former gave off choking smoke without doing much good, the latter merely helped the fire to retain its ebbing life a little longer. However, we succeeded in cooking our rice each morning, and we always had plenty of hot coffee. But never did we coax a real fire into existence, and if left to itself for five minutes it invariably perished.

July 2 was fine, or rather the morning was, so putting a chocolate and biscuit ration in my pocket, and taking a bag for plants, I started up the ridge. The climb, as I knew from past experience, was tiresome to begin with, the ridge being badly buckled; but after a series of steep ascents, alternating with short sharp descents, it became easier at about 13,500 feet. At first I tramped over a carpet of dwarf Rhododendrons, some of which above 12,000 feet were still in flower. *R. riparium* made a purplish froth on the surface, then the speckled pinky flowers of Rock Rose (*R. patulum*) and the saucier pink flowers of *R. pumilum*. Woven into this carpet were the finer strands of a plant which looked like *R. patulum* × *R. pumilum*. As for the plum-coloured *R. campylogynum*, it was only just opening. It gave one a gorgeous sensation of power to be trampling about amongst these unknown plants, the rarest of which were as common as blackberries. No, that is not quite true. At least one was extremely rare, but it is rather the exception to come across a really rare species, and even then it often turns out to be quite common fifty or a hundred miles away.

The scrub included also Barberry, Willow, Juniper, Cherry, and *Cassiope selaginoides*; but even out of flower the immense preponderance of Rhododendron was obvious. The yellow-flowered Barberries were small spiny bushes, one species being quite dwarf. There were several Willows, from large shrubs growing gregariously, to flat mats; and the Juniper bushes formed dark tanglements of stumpy plants mixed up with Rhododendrons.

Presently the ridge became smoother, and I found myself walking on the brink of a terrific precipice; on the other side the ground sloped down more gently, and was covered with alpine turf, with divots of Rhododendron scattered over it. I retraced my steps a short distance and descended the steep flank in order to get a sidelong look at the cliff. On a part of the slope which was broken up by outcrops of gneiss into low escarpments, separated by grass ledges, I found something; it was a compact rosette of pale-green jagged leaves clothed with long orange hairs which glistened in the sun. No flower bloomed in the heart, but I knew that it was a Meconopsis or Himalayan Poppy; so now to find it in flower! A search up, down, and across the face, where boulders and brushwood replaced the meadow flowers of more lenient slopes, revealed several of these leaf rosettes, some of them very big, but none of them ready to flower. I was in despair. Last year's plants—those which had flowered—had of course completely disappeared, cut down by wind and pressed into pulp by the weight of snow, leaving no trace; yet there must be some two-year-olds flowering somewhere! I came to the conclusion, however, that although the plant was obviously biennial, the biggest rosettes really were two years old, but had put off flowering till the third year. The biennial Poppies die after flowering; but anything that prevents them from flowering, prevents them from dying. Anxious as I now was to discover a flowering plant, nevertheless, there was a familiar look about those sea-green leaves bristling with golden hairs. I pulled off a leaf, and a bright orange juice exuded from the wound. "Hmm!" I said to myself, "you have sulphur-yellow flowers, my friend". Continuing the search, I returned to the ridge *and* presently found a flaw in it. On one side of the gap the plaster had been stripped from the face of the mountain, exposing the hard framework beneath. A file of towers slanted against the sky, and their foundations dropped sheer, without a plant to roughen them, to the dyke far below. On the other side were straight cliffs, not very high. The gap itself was caused by a deep slot which almost cleft the ridge in twain, but was too steep to descend safely. Where the ridge straddled the gap it was fined down to a blunt razor-blade, along which it was necessary to walk like Agag. There were plants lurking amongst these slab-sided cliffs; the crevices were stuffed with flowers, and a bushy brushwood of dark green Juniper striped the ledges. Retracing my steps along the ridge once more, I descended by another route, to find myself on a grassy meadow slope, shining with flowers; then I began to traverse the face towards the grim walls in front. Success was almost instantaneous. Reaching the brink of the chasm, some distance below the crest of the ridge, I was forced to move upwards; but here and there short winding passages led down between the rocks, like rabbit burrows, and ended abruptly on the lip of the precipice: and in one of these passages I found what I sought. From behind a rock rose a pillar of sulphur-yellow flowers, and there was our first, and as it turned out, only Meconopsis from the Mishmi Hills—*M. paniculata*. Subsequently I found a single prickly Poppy in bud on the cliffs—from its appearance almost certainly *M. impedita*. "Bad luck," you say. "After all your trouble, it *might* have been a new species." Yes, it might have been. Yet at sight of that sunny yellow spire, I danced for joy: I would not have lost it for a wilderness of new species. As a plant-hunter this was naughty of me; my job was to discover new plants, and I ought to have turned up my nose at *M. paniculata*, which may be seen growing cheerfully in dozens of English gardens. But as a botanist I was deeply impressed by my find, for there are other things about plants, besides novelty, which appeal to the botanist. *M. paniculata* for example was hitherto known to occur only in Sikkim and Nepal, and its appearance 400 miles further east had a special interest in relation to the spread of Himalayan plants towards China. But if Poppies were rare in this particular valley, they are common enough in this region!

Early in June 1926, in the Seinghku valley, I noticed the buoyant rosettes of a large Poppy bursting vigorously through the snow. The pinnate leaves were sage green, lined with long silken honey-coloured hairs, which glistened in the sunshine, as it might have been *Meconopsis paniculata*. Yet I felt certain it was not, and I watched it jealously as the tall leafy spire rose inch by inch from the deep crown until finally stopped by a flower-bud. Yet July came before it opened. By that time, from the axil of each bract lolled a fat bud, the topmost had thrown back their green hoods, and several silken violet flowers, piled with dark gold in the centre, fluttered out in the breeze. Such was *M. violacea*, a glorious column of bright colour, which flowered throughout July in the ice-worn valleys, being then about three feet high; throughout the rains it continued to grow however, till in September it was over four feet high, and carried two dozen capsules, the topmost being then ripe. *M. violacea*, though not so common as *M. betoni-cifolia* or *M. rubra*, was common enough, occurring in colonies of six or eight plants perhaps, on the steep meadow slopes, and not another anywhere near; nor does it climb much above 12,000 feet, or descend much below 11,000 feet. Although a true biennial, it should be perfectly hardy in Britain, and in beauty it is second only to the peerless *M. betonicifolia*.

Including *M. paniculata* from the Mishmi Hills, and the tiny *M. lyrata* collected from the Seinghku valley no less than seven 'blue poppies' were on these ranges—not all of them 'blue' be it observed! *M. lyrata* looks like an annual. It is a frail, slender creature, six or eight inches high, bearing a solitary wan blue flower, so pale and delicate that it looks unable to defy the rude winds; yet it too grows at 12,000 feet, widely scattered on steep meadow slopes, or on the fringes of the ultimate forest, flowering in June and swamped presently amongst the coarse herbage. Very difficult is it to find the plants for seed later, nor do the slim capsules contain much. Yet if it is truly an annual, it might yield good results in the hands of the cultivator.

It is interesting to note that there is not a single representative of the Grandes alliance—that which contains *M. quintuplinervia* and *M. simplicifolia*—on the wet ranges: they are plants of the dry inner ranges only.

Continuing along the ridge which now eased off, I found a network of *Rhododendron crebreflorum* glued to the rocks.

Presently I stood in a white sea of Anemones. Where the turf was short grew clumps of scented dwarf Iris, their large amethyst flowers almost flush with the ground. Some of the clumps contained eight or ten blooms. On the rocks were scattered plants of *Primula alta*, with soft downy leaves and truncated cones of flowers, like a lavender Grape Hyacinth.

I was now fairly high up, where only stray tufts of Rhododendron remained; more and more rock showed through the threadbare turf carpet, and patches of snow chilled the air. Cloud was blowing up from the valley like thin smoke, and the wind had an edge to it. Rain began to fall. It is the perpetual rain mist which makes exploration on these mountains so difficult; never can you direct your steps as you would wish, because you can never see far enough ahead. Yet despite the lack of sunshine and the dimming effect of the mist, the light is extremely bright throughout the flowering period, owing to reflection from the snow. By the time all the snow has disappeared so also have the flowers, and the alps are indeed gloomy!

When I reached the grey cliffs which tower up to the twin peaks of Kaso the snow was so deep that there was no point in scrambling amongst the boulders any longer. On my right, between the screes and the cliffs, lay a steep but not difficult gulley. Far below was a bright green meadow; and so far as I could see there was nothing to prevent me reaching the meadow, and returning by the same route; although a natural reluctance to descend was strengthened by an even greater reluctance to climb up again. But the meadow looked interesting, and there was no other way of reaching it. So down the gulley I went.

It was safe enough on the snow, but lower down I had to proceed more cautiously, so steep was it. However, after descending a thousand feet, I found myself on stony but not steep ground, where many streams had their sources; these all plunged quickly down towards the beginning of the forest, cutting deeper and deeper troughs for themselves. This rough ground at the foot of the cliffs was covered with alpine flowers such as we were familiar with. There were thousands of white Anemones blowing in the breeze, their finely cut leaves clothed in silver silk, and of red Nomocharis, which had now reached its full stature of about eight inches. But for some time I found nothing new except a solitary Cremanthodium. The Cremanthodiums are a genus of Sino-Himalayan alpine plants closely allied to the Senecios, though many of them recall in outward appearance (but not in colour) the South African Gazanias. They appear to be constitutionally unsuited to the British climate, which is a pity, because several of them are well worth cultivating. Generally speaking, they do not exceed six to nine inches in height, and have solitary nodding flowers, white, yellow, or a pale vinous purple, the disc florets being more or less hidden by the long ray florets which converge modestly inwards. They are plants of high altitudes, which is sufficient excuse for their unadaptability[1].

Continuing the search I was at last rewarded with a fascinating new Primula, which lined the banks of a trickling stream. A clump of small heart-shaped leaves on thin stalks, a straight scape twelve or fifteen inches high, and at the top an umbel of drooping maroon-red flowers, frail, and fragrant. But for the leaves and the narrower corolla, one might almost have taken the plant for a red *P. sikkimensis*. Clearly it was of that alliance; but its nearest relatives are equally clearly *P. reticulata*, *P. firimpes* and the Giant Cowslip, *P. Florindæ*, all of which have the same type of leaf, and yellow

[1] For a full account of the genus Cremanthodium see R. D'O. Good, in Linnæan Society's *Journal*, June, 1929.

flowers; whereas *P. sikkimensis* itself and its red-flowered kin, *P. vittata*, *P. secundiflora*, and Ruby (*P. Waltoni*) have oblong or narrow oval leaves which taper gradually to a hardly distinguishable stalk, as in the English Primrose or Cowslip. Here therefore was a plant with a double claim to honours; botanically speaking, it was of interest as being the first known of the round-leafed 'Sikkimensis' Primulas with red flowers; and it had gracious charm and poise as a bog garden plant. Perhaps its chief merit is however potential. So far, no one has been able to mate a pure red-flowered 'Sikkimensis' Primula with a pure yellow-flowered one; why, it is impossible to say. Certainly in nature they keep each within their own caste. Thus in Szechuan I have seen a yoke of *P. sikkimensis* crimson-veined with *P. vittata*, as though the whole might presently hatch into a fledgling; but there was no sign of a cross; red to red and yellow to yellow. In Tibet, Moonlight, the lambent form of *P. microdonta* var. *alpicola*, did indeed hold aloof, turning the green July fields into sulphur seas; and the white-flowered *P. microdonta* also grew by itself; but the reds, purples, and violets of lower caste, herded together and though tending to segregate, each according to its kind, were no doubt involved in many a *mésalliance*. Yet the red- or purple-flowered *P. vittata* and the yellow *P. sikkimensis* are closely related species—possibly too closely related—and both have the same type of leaf. That is to say the oval-leafed pure reds refuse to cross with the oval-leafed yellows. So perhaps it is too much to expect that an oval-leafed red will cross with a round-leafed yellow. Now we can try whether a round-leafed yellow, such as *P. Florindæ*, will cross with our new round-leafed red, *P. rubra*. This latter is quite a small plant, and *P. Florindæ* is of course the giant of the race; but if extremes mate, we may expect in three or four years to see a race of beautiful creoles comparable to those derived from *P. pulverulenta* and *P. Bulleyana* in the 'Candelabra' group, which also are either yellow or purple flowered.

I strolled about in the meadow for some time without seeing anything more of special interest until, happening to glance towards the screes, a serow rose close beside me and bounded lightly away over the boulders. Though the Mishmis trap them, there seem to be plenty of these animals.

I now returned to the main ridge, and sat down to eat my lunch. Actually, it was long past lunch-time, but as usual when plant hunting, I had forgotten all about it. Late in the afternoon I got back to camp, where I found Buttercup valiantly blowing our comic fire, to cook supper. The tent was becoming more and more congested; wet clothes, wet specimens, damp paper, cooking-pots left little room to sit down even. We had no dry clothes left and not very much dry paper, but so long as we had dry blankets we cared not at all. Our tent, though tiny, was at any rate waterproof.

By this time we had managed to catch a little rain water for the pot. But the mist, though persistent, was thin, and the water did not go very far;

so another fatigue to Boggy Valley was necessary. This time we had no accident with the can, nor did the journey prove such a toil and tribulation as it had done on the evening of our arrival.

For the next two days we wandered about, but now that the Rhododendrons were nearly over we did not find very much that was new. We did however see various remarkably handsome birds, including two Blood Pheasants (*Ithagenes cruentus*). I also found a Woodcock's nest in the Rhododendron scrub at a height of 13,000 feet, as recorded in Chapter 12.

The commonest alpine flowers on Kaso in the first week of July were the following: *Anemone polyanthes*, *Caltha palustris* and *C. palustris*, var. *purpurea*; *Omphalogramma Souliei*, *Primula Agleniana* var. *atrocrocea*, *P. calthifolia* Lloydia, Iris and red Nomocharis. These occurred in countless thousands on the boggy turf slopes. Less abundant, but certainly not rare, were such plants as *Diapensia himalaica*, *Androsace chamœjasme*, purple Morina, the yellow-flowered *Viola biflora* var. *hirsuta*, *Primula silaensis*, *P. alta*, *P. rubra*, *Meconopsis paniculata*, Corydalis, and on the cliffs *Paraquilegium grandiflorum*. Several cushions of this last, bursting from the cliff, were as big as a decent-sized cabbage, and bore dozens of fluttering mauve flowers; they looked like some beautiful Cœlenterate of the deep sea, with its ardent tentacles waving in the current. Much rarer were the following: *Primula crispata*, which was not in bloom; the white-flowered *Androsace geraniifolia*, *Primula Clutterbuckii*, of which I found a few plants beneath a Rhododendron bush, *P. mishimiensis*, scattered amongst the dwarf Rhododendron, a cushion-forming Potentilla, *Meconopsis impedita*, represented by a solitary plant, and Cremanthodium, also represented by a single plant.

Thus even without the barbaric blaze of Rhododendrons of three weeks ago, there was plenty of colour in the alps. No greater contrast to the rain forest can be imagined. In the forest, as we have seen, flowers are rare and quite disproportionate to the development of wood and leaves. Curiously, the ground flora includes a good many Monocotyledonous plants. Except of course for the Rhododendrons, one has a feeling inside the forest that there are no flowers at all, and this is due in part at least to the wonderful development of purely vegetative parts, especially foliage. Flowerless plants too abound—Mosses, Ferns, Lichens, and Fungi; many of the trees have inconspicuous flowers, which adds to the illusion; and the various Bamboos flower only at long intervals. It is quite otherwise in the alps. There foliage is reduced to a minimum, and from May till August there is an endless spate of flowers. Whole hillsides are festive with colour throughout the Summer. Flowerless plants are quite uncommon, though a species of meadow Fern is abundant in places. The influence of light on the flowering of plants, and of darkness on the production of green tissue has already been discussed.

We expected our coolies back on July 5. It was raining steadily when we got up, and having breakfasted and collected a few plants I wanted from Boggy Valley we packed everything except the tent and sat down to wait for the relief party. We still had a light lunch ration, otherwise we were at the end of our resources, so when three o'clock came and still there were no coolies we decided not to wait any longer but to pack what we could on our backs and go down. It was now raining harder than ever and we had a dismal march down the ridge and through the dripping forest. Nevertheless it was pleasant to get back to our summer house, and a fire, and our chairs, and to be able to stand upright and turn round, after being cooped up in a tiny tent; though it was not so jolly that we had no bedding, as of course we had had to leave our blankets behind. However, it was very much warmer here than on the ridge and we slept peacefully in our clothes with canvas sheets for cover.

Luso had fever and did not look well. Our Mishmi coolies were also in camp. They had come up early that morning intending to go on to our camp but the heavy rain had daunted them, so they stayed where they were.

Next day it rained pitilessly, but the coolies went up the ridge and returned half drowned in the evening with our loads. For the first time I saw Mishmi coolies looking utterly fagged out and white with exhaustion. They had earned their pay!

Only three Rhododendrons of note now remained in the forest; but what they lacked in variety they made up in numbers. In the upper Fir forest thickets of the blood-red *R. cerasinum*, with the jet black eyes, glared through the rain. Occasionally a plant, short of pigment, appears with pink flowers, and crimson glands. It forms a large but rather ramshackle bush, or even a small leaning tree, and grows more or less socially with *R. sanguineum* breaking round its feet. In the lower belt, amongst big-leafed Rhododendrons and Conifers, stout bushes of the white-flowered *R. manipurense* are common. The narrow trumpet-shaped flowers, very like those of *R. crassum*, form magnificent bridal knots amongst the heavy dark foliage.

Another bush which was common in the upper rain forest, conspicuous if only because of the general rarity of Rhododendrons, was *R. Keysii*. The individual flowers are narrow red-hot tubes, and they are borne in a peculiar way shared only by half a dozen other species such as *R. spinuliferum*, *R. racemosum*, and *R. oleifolium*. That is to say the flowers are axillary instead of terminal, and *R. Keysii*, in fact, bears axillary bunches each composed of three flowers. This arrangement would lead to diffusion of flowers and much wasted effort but for the fact that the leaves are crowded at the ends of the shoots, so that the flower power is in fact concentrated, till the shoots glow all up their tips like hot iron bars. These two are the very last of the summer Rhododendrons, and outlast July; indeed *R. manipurense* flowered well into August.

But the most interesting plant I collected now from the ridge was

Nomocharis aperta. It is not a beautiful flower, but it is an interesting one, and in its own flamboyant way it possesses attraction, even charm. It was at Iris Cliff that I first noticed a plant growing under the Bamboos bearing two flowers with a large starfish-shaped corolla, heavily blotched with purplish crimson on a white or flushed satin ground. At the base of the cliff, on either side of the ridge, growing amongst meadow plants I found about a dozen specimens, but I forbore to collect more than one for the herbarium, leaving the others to set seed. The discovery of *N. aperta* so far west was of great interest. Apart from being the first Nomocharis recorded from Assam, the nearest locality for the species is the Burma-China frontier, over 130 miles to the south-east. Between these two localities stretches the Irrawaddy-Lohit divide.

Another rock Rhododendron which was just opening its small magenta eyes was *R. lepidotum,* always a late bloomer. It is a dwarf twigulous bush, very like a 'Lapponicum' at first sight, having the same tiny crisp scaly leaves and heads of little round flowers; and it grows on the gneiss cliffs too, more or less socially, like any 'Lapponicum'. But there all resemblance ceases, and in flower colour, the crude horror of *R. lepidotum* cannot compare with the best 'Lapponicums'.

We now decided to return to Peti. Our rations were finished. Luso was ill with fever, and was also suffering from toothache. So bad was he in fact that on two nights I gave him morphia. We ourselves were tired of the wringing wet and gloom of the rain forest. We had the greatest difficulty in drying anything in the saturated air and always had to put on damp clothes. In the *basha,* the fire heated the paper below even while it was absorbing moisture above. My specimens were a constant source of anxiety, although heat was not added to our other troubles; the combination of tropical heat and dampness is the collectors' greatest nightmare.

So on July 9 we called up the coolies and the following day we all trooped back to Peti, where the first person we met was our truant Hubble who was waiting for us with a mail. It appeared that Hubble had returned to Denning, whereupon the Indian Officer in command, finding him without his discharge papers, had telephoned to the Political Officer in Sadiya. The Political Officer replied that he must go back to us at once, or he would skin him; and so our Hubble returned to the fold. We were glad to see him; only Luso had picked up a little Mishmi during our enforced schooling in the tongue.

On the way down the ridge we passed fine bushes of *Rhododendron Keysii* and *R. manipurense* in full bloom. *Magnolia globosa* was still in flower, and on the mossy rocks under the bushes a tiny striped Orchid (Zeuxine) was common. Interesting too was a distinct 'Barbatum' Rhododendron plant, growing amongst thickets of *R. crinigerum, R. megacalyx, R. tephropeplum,* and Larch. Below the Tsuga forest there was nothing of particular interest.

We were surprised to find that, in spite of all the rain, the torrent from Kaso was actually smaller than it had been in May, and we had no trouble in crossing. It is the melting of the snow which swells these torrents so enormously, not the steady Summer rain. On the other hand, in the Winter they must almost cease to flow. At the point where we crossed the Delei by rope bridge in May the river is spanned by a wooden foot-bridge in the Winter! We were informed that it had only just been washed away at the end of April, by the sudden spate, following a spell of fine weather. The reason why the Mishmis had refused to take us to the pass was simply that they could not cross the unbridged torrents; or, having done so, feared they might be cut off from their villages. It would be possible to go to the head of the Delei valley between December and March, if the snow were not too soft, but of course no Mishmi would go at that season. The Mishmis cross the pass, if at all, during the summer break, that is in July or August; and probably that is the most favourable time. But few of them go even then. In early Winter a few Tibetans cross; but probably the pass is little used.

14   Rhododendrons and Primulas

LET us however return to our forest camp for a short while, and say something more about the flowers there. The wealth of the forest flora was astounding, and the alpine region was not a whit behind. Pride of place must naturally be given to the Rhododendrons, which between 9,000 and 12,000 feet probably form half the woody vegetation. During our sojourn of seven months in the Delei valley, we collected altogether forty-five species, not a great number, but very fair considering how immobilised we were.

In 1926 however I collected about seventy-two species, of which fifty-four came from the Seinghku valley alone. But though the Delei and Seinghku valleys, separated by the gorge of the Lohit, are less than seventy-five miles apart in an air line, yet not more than twenty-five species are common to the two localities; which, at a conservative estimate, gives a total of eighty-five species for the three valleys explored[1]. Add to these some eighty species collected farther west in Tibet in 1924, half of them not known from either of the other localities, and one can begin to realise the wealth of Rhododendrons in this region. At the present moment over 400 species are in cultivation in this country. But it is not the number of species which is so impressive a feature of Sino-Himalaya; it is rather the *number* of Rhododendrons. In the alps, hundreds of square miles are a seething mass of them; fifty per cent. of the upper forest belt consists of Rhododendrons. Thus although really fine specimen plants are comparatively rare, and can generally be more than matched by cultivated plants in this country, the whole effect in Summer, when the majority are in bloom, has no parallel anywhere else in the world, and never will have.

Spring is the season of the great Rhododendron feast. The frivolous might say that there are only two seasons; eight months wet and four months damned wet. Actually the seasons vary a good deal with the altitude. In the valleys there are three, the hot weather, the rainy season, and the cold weather; in the temperate rain forest the seasons are Spring, rainy season, Autumn, and Winter; in the alpine region, just Summer and Winter.

Is it not therefore a tribute to our English weather that we have hardy plants from Sino-Himalaya collected as low as 7,000 feet and as high as 14,000 feet?

[1] i.e. the Seinghku, Di Chu, and Delei.

In the sub-tropical jungle, where a monsoon climate prevails, the few Rhododendrons met with flower in the Winter, or dry weather. They are shrubs, like *R. Nuttallii* and the very similar *R. sino-Nuttallii* which occur scattered in the forest, or small epiphytic bushes like *R. notatum*. Where sub-tropical jungle is passing into lower temperate rain forest, the first tree Rhododendrons are met with at about 6,000 feet altitude. The best known is the blood-red *R. arboreum* which may be in bloom any time between December and March. When *R. stenaulum* is a cumulus of faintly-pink blossom, and the yellow catkins of Corylopsis are swinging in the breeze, when the long sharp buds of *Magnolia rostrata* are beginning to blunt their tips and the ground Orchids are throwing up long spikes of bloom, you know that spring has come in the temperate rain forest. It is April. Other Rhododendrons just coming into bloom now include the amethyst-flowered *R. tanastylum*, stamped with a Prince of Wales plumes worked out in dark commas, *R. Griffithianum* with coral-red buds fading as they open to snow-white flowers nodding amongst enormous leaves, and the glorious shining scarlet *R. sperabile*. They are scattered trees and shrubs, not of the largest size, though they may crowd on to a windy ridge.

May, the last month before the rains break, sees practically all the forest Rhododendrons in full bloom. At 7,000–8,000 feet, mixed forest begins, and with it the first of the big-leafed tree Rhododendrons which grow gregariously and higher up form at least half the forest.

R. sino-grande, *R. sidereum* with the yellowest flowers of any of the 'Grandes', *R. arizelum*, and *R. crinigerum* all flower in May. This last has remarkably variable flowers, white or pink or white *and* pink in broad bands, always with a dusky blotch at the base of the corolla, and a peppering of dots and dashes. The trusses are not large, but being very floriferous and furnished with handsome cinnamon-coated leaves, it is what nurserymen call a desirable plant. Although it was already over at 9,000 feet by the end of May, at higher levels it was in flower right through June; and at 11,000 feet, where in the Fir forest it is reduced to a small shrub, there were plants in flower in July.

There are not many small Rhododendrons in this belt, except epiphytes. In the tanglewood however one is sure to see *R. megacalyx*, a leggy shrub with pale squat buds and neat oval leaves whose veins are deeply impressed above, giving an almost rugose appearance. The white trumpet-shaped flowers are borne loosely on long stalks in bunches of four or six, and are deliciously fragrant, with a suggestion of nutmeg (it might be called *R. nutmegacalyx*), and the large leafy calyx stands up round the base of the trumpet like a pink or green collar, eventually almost enclosing the globular capsule. When first discovered on the Burma-China frontier, *R. megacalyx* was, naturally, perhaps, assumed to be confined to that particular locality. Since then its range has been extended over the hills and far away to the west, even to the Himalaya. It has the supreme advantage of flowering all over at once, and a bush in full bloom is a fine sight.

Other notable May flowering shrubs of the tanglewood thickets are *Rhododendron aureum*, the sticky purple-flowered *R. vesiculiferum*, and the orange *R. mishmiense*.

Nevertheless it is the tree Rhododendrons which are the chief glory of the mountains. *R. sino-grande* sometimes forms forests single-handed. We passed through whole glades of its gnarled and twisted branches, when its pale yellow globes were alight and shining brightly under the dark canopy of leaves. Some of the trunks were twenty-four inches round, though the tree rarely stands more than thirty-five or forty feet high. One advantage about *R. sino-grande* is the lateness of its new growth. The great spear-headed buds burst in July, and even in August one can pick out the trees a mile away by the plumes of silver foliage shooting up from ruby-red tubes. The trees grow very slowly, and the queer hard angles at which they branch adds to the picturesqueness of the forest. All the Rhododendrons seem to do that: possibly it is connected with a sudden change of direction by the growing shoot in its quest for light. The leaves of these tree Rhododendrons plunge the forest in gloom, those of *R. sino-grande* reaching a length of eighteen inches, by nine broad, the upper surface dark green with a bright yellow midrib, the lower surface burnished as though it had just been dipped in silver amalgam. The corolla is pale yellow with a small crimson flash at the base, ten-lobed, and almost regular.

In the higher forest, where the Conifers are usually all of one species, either Silver Fir or Spruce (*Tsuga Brunoniana*) with scattered Larch, *R. arizelum* is often the gregarious Rhododendron. Though not so big a tree as *R. sino-grande*, growing only about twenty-five feet high, it is even more handsome. The flowers, which are in large trusses, are at first pink, or in some varieties cream, or even white; at the base of the corolla is a crimson-purple flash. The leaves, dark green above, are felted below with a thick coat of tawny fur. In August the young leaves project like silver spears powdered with bronze-dust from amongst the tawny red and bottle green of the old leaves.

After the Conifer forest is left behind, the Rhododendrons again dwindle in size, though they become ever more gregarious. In the upper Fir forest, practically all the undergrowth consists of Rhododendron species, small trees, shrubs, and bushes, which grow as they can crowded along the draughty ridges in dense thickets.

The climax of the Rhododendron fête is in mid-June, when the alpine species flower. Not till the warm rain blows up from the plains does the snow begin to melt rapidly, though a few species flower earlier, in the snow. Now the blood-red 'Sanguineums' flower, the flame-coloured 'Nerii-florums', the purple 'Lapponicums' and 'Saluenenses', and many more. Some of these continue well into July. But returning to the forest now, we find the glory departed; the cherry-red *R. cerasinum*, remarkable for its ring of five coal-black pit-glands at the base of the corolla, is passing over, and there are none to take its place. Lower down amongst Spruce, however, we come on two or three very late-flowering species—*R. manipurense* for example which does not begin to flower till July, and often lasts well into August; the aromatic-leafed *R. brevistylum* and the crimson-flowered *R. Keysii*. By the end of July however even these—except *R. manipurense*—are finished, and the forest is dark and dreary. The flowering of the Rhododendrons thus sweeps up the mountain in a steady tide which rises and swells with the northward march of the sun; beginning in April at 5,000 feet and finishing in June at 12,000 feet.

The timber of the tree Rhododendrons is very hard and close grained. It makes excellent fire-wood; for cabinet and inlay work, and for turning, it would probably prove first rate; though the largest trunks are of no great thickness. A curious feature is the way the trunks have of growing out horizontally from a steep face, only the upper half eventually turning upwards; obviously on a precipitous face, covered with forest, this is the shortest cut to the light. These horizontal trunks are always oval in cross section, being laterally compressed.

Such magnificent flowering trees cannot fail to attract a large share of attention from the botanist, and he soon begins to ask himself, why are they so overwhelmingly successful? That is not an easy question to answer, but certain facts are obvious enough. In the first place hardly any moss attaches itself to their trunks, and hence they support none of that crowd of perching plants which gradually smother far bigger trees in the rain forest. Nor has lichen much better luck. In the second place, they are astonishingly free from disease. I noticed Blister Blight, which attacks the Tea-bush in Assam and elsewhere, on certain species; *R. dendricola*, *R. Keysii*, *R. megacalyx*, and *R. lanigerum* all suffered in greater or lesser degree. It was conspicuous in the Spring, and again in the Autumn; individual plants were badly attacked, but the disease was far from general. The leaves of *Pieris ovalifolia* also suffered from this unsightly disease.

In Tibet in 1924 I had seen the leaves of *R. triflorum* covered with the hard black crust of a Capnodium which however was parasitic on honeydew, derived probably from scale insects and not directly on the leaves. Again, the capsules of one of the 'Lapponicums' (*R. microphyllum*), already described from the Seinghku valley, were badly attacked by a fungus which completely destroyed the tissues, though so far as one could see the mycelium confined its attentions to the capsule, which of course involved the seeds. But these things are insignificant, and Rhododendrons usually look, and in fact are, supremely healthy.

As for their powers of reproduction, these are prodigious, and the future is thoroughly provided for. Their large brightly coloured flowers are greatly sought after, firstly by insects in search of honey, and secondly by birds in search of insects. They set an enormous amount of seed, which is nearly all wasted, for in such close confinement, what chance of survival has even one more seedling, until something dies to make room for it! Yet these seeds, though tiny, are amongst the most reliable of all seeds as regards their keeping qualities, and afford a certain means of introducing the plants into other countries. When one stops to consider that many of these Rhododendrons have never been seen by man, it is no small thing that they should have been rescued from utter obscurity, and shown to thousands who will enjoy them for an indefinite period. For what, one asks, is the good of them there, in remote and hostile places where even the surly Mishmi never sees them! After Rhododendrons, species of Ilex and Euonymus, amongst the smaller shrubs and trees, were most prominent.

On June 14, three Mishmi hunters passed through our camp on their way up Kaso to set traps for serow and pheasant. Eleven days later they returned saying they had got nothing, except a little wild honey. We bought some, but it had been boiled down to a hard sticky lump, and was not very palatable. The Mishmi hunters must have had a dismal time, for it had rained incessantly and the so-called caves on the upper ridge—all those we had discovered, at any rate—were miserable leaky rock shelters, affording little protection from wind or rain. Probably they knew of some we did not. Their trails were easy to find. In the forest we often came across a series of pheasant nooses, along a ridge; in the alpine region long bamboos were stuck in the ground all along the main ridge to mark traps. The serow traps were set where the animals were in the habit of crossing the ridge, or climbing to a convenient look-out point. We saw no pheasants, but several serow. On June 26 we went for a long climb on Kaso. From high up on the ridge, Buttercup descended one side while I descended the other, wading through thick Rhododendron scrub. In the course of a traverse, I happened to look up the glen just in time to see a serow (Nemorhaedus) leap nimbly up and disappear over the rise. Ten minutes later I topped the next spur, and almost trod on a female serow! She sprang up, gave one bound, and stood staring at me scarcely ten yards away. I could not understand why she did not go off immediately, though I myself stood stock still, watching her. Her lips trembled, and she wagged her stump of a tail violently, but did not move until I did; I noticed that she was foxy red all over except for a sharp black line all down the backbone. When I moved, she went off through the shrub in huge bounds, and finally disappeared. She made no sound. Seeing a movement at my feet, I looked down; and then I knew why the serow had held her ground so long. I was almost standing on a tiny baby serow! I picked up the little creature which neither showed any sign of fear nor tried to get away. Indeed it could hardly stand on its feeble little legs. I carried it back to camp in my arms. In a day it was tame, sucking at my fingers and lapping up condensed milk. It was the same colour as its mother, but had grey ears. One might judge of its age from the fact that it could not quite stand upright on its feeble little legs, and that the umbilical cord had not yet withered. The ends of its hoofs were soft like butter, and of course it had no teeth. For two days we fed it on milk. Sometimes it bleated, but on the whole seemed happy. But on the fourth day poor little William Rufus suddenly became very ill and died in a few hours. The new diet had upset him, I suppose. We had not the heart to eat him, and in the evening I buried him under a great Rhododendron tree below our camp, and planted some Ferns on his grave.

On July 4 at 13,000 feet, I saw another animal which I took to be also a serow, though possibly it was a goral; anyhow it was all grey, instead of foxy red. These animals were always solitary, though on occasions there appeared to be two in the neighbourhood. June–July is evidently the breeding season. In the upper Seinghku valley also I had frequently seen serow, or goral, in fact almost every time I climbed the cliffs above 14,000 feet in the Summer. There they were always either solitary or two together, one standing sentinel on a rock, the other browsing below. The colour was yellowish red with a black stripe down the back, conspicuously large ears, a bob tail, and short straight horns, deeply ringed. It is thus obvious that, whatever this animal may be, it is not particularly rare in these remote regions; for if they can be seen without fail where the Mishmis hunt them, it may be supposed that they are even more common a little further back where even the Mishmis do not go. It is hard to realise what an enormous area of lofty land in this region is absolutely uninhabited and unexplored. It is a great body—of rock, intersected with veins of water, along the banks of which men live. The Mishmis are not great hunters, far from it. Some villages in the Delei valley did not hunt at all. The hunting rights appeared to be strictly preserved, and belonged to those villages which happened to be placed at the foot of a convenient spur; not all the spurs which buttress the horseshoe range provide a route to the Alps. As for the Tibetans of Haita, in the Seinghku valley, they did not hunt either; farming took up all their time. The fact is that unless hunting is going to furnish a sure and steady livelihood, no one can afford to indulge in it; and if many do indulge in it, it can afford neither a certain nor a steady livelihood. All these mountains are full of game—one sees that clearly enough in the Summer when the crops are ripe and families sit up every night scaring the animals from the fields. But what chance have the ignorant Mishmis, with their feeble little traps! They have no arms, so their hunting is of a purely passive variety. At the headwaters of the Irrawaddy the Nungs, Lisus, and others at least have crossbows, and know how to use them. The Tibetans have a few gaspipe guns. But Nature is always on top in this terrific country, and it is only at certain places, such as the hot springs already referred to, that hunters have much chance.

To return to our climb of June 26. When Buttercup and I met again on the ridge, I was carrying William Rufus, while he held in his hand a superb

Primula. Here is a short description of it. From a small bulb composed of overlapping scale leaves, rimmed ruby red, rises a short stem, bearing two or three large bell-shaped flowers of a brilliant orange colour. The inside base of the bell, which forms a sort of crater, is coated with cream-white meal. The plant rarely exceeds nine inches in height, or carries more than two or three flowers, though Buttercup found one with five; but this was obviously exceptional. The Gamboge Primula, as we called it—*P. Agleniana*, var. *atrocrocea*, to give its full title—is a fitting companion for the Tea Rose Primula, *P. Agleniana*, var. *thearosa*. They are the Gracchi, and their mother is just plain *P. Agleniana*, a white-flowered plant of the eastern Burmese Alps.

When I climbed Kaso on June 17 I had actually looked down from the ridge into Boggy Valley, over a field of the cloth of gold, and remarked that *P. calthifolia*—which it will be remembered we collected there on June 4— was very abundant and a fine colour. Actually of course I had been gazing at nothing less than the Gamboge Primula, which Buttercup had now collected. *P. calthifolia*, which had looked pale when first it pushed its leafless flower-stems though the black mud, was still there in quantity; but it was utterly eclipsed by this daring newcomer, of which there had been no visible sign at the beginning of June. The bulb of the Gamboge Primula rests under the snow for seven months instead of under the earth; like any other bulb, it consists of scale leaves tightly wrapped round each other and enclosing the embryo flowers, leaves, and stem for next year; from its base radiate a few strong fibrous roots. Only thus is it enabled to go through the entire process of flowering and fruiting in four months.

In October I dug up some of these hard acorn-shaped bulbs, cut off the current year's leaves, gave them a surface drying in the shade, and raced back to Sadiya with them. They were packed in dry moss in an open bamboo basket, sewn up in cloth, and posted to London. They were actually planted in pots within five weeks of their being exhumed in the Mishmi Hills! Seed was also sent; but the seed of these 'Nivales' Primulas does not long retain the power of germination, or else is killed passing through the tropics. The plants too are perishable in England. If brought to the flowering stage under glass and planted out hopefully in the rock-garden, they generally fail to reappear the following year. The English Winter kills them by kindness. They do not want soft treatment. Cold they can understand, but damp no! Besides, detached portions of the English Spring have a bad habit of appearing in the Winter, with a further instalment of cold weather hot on their heels; and that is fatal to many other plants besides 'Nivales' Primulas. In the Sino-Himalayan Alps there is no looking back, once Summer has begun. The temperature rises slowly, but steadily, and as the snow retreats, the plants come up out of the ground.

Primula Agleniana, the mother of the Gracchi, grows in the Burmese Oberland along the Yunnan frontier, where several collectors have gathered it and sung its praises. The large, white flowers are borne in loose heads of six or eight (sometimes as many as ten or twelve). In general it resembles Tea Rose Primula, except in the important matter of colour, but it is a distinctly taller plant, and the flowers are carried more loosely. *P. Agleniana*, if it grows with anything like the freedom of the Gamboge Primula, must be a fine sight, yet it lacks the vivid colouring of its twin offspring. At the moment it is in cultivation, and has even flowered in England; but it will probably be lost before long.

The layman will naturally ask, what is a 'Nivales' Primula? For although over fifty species are known to botanists, very few have found their way into horticulture, none are finally established in our gardens, and several have done no more than flower and pass away. Definitions are notoriously risky; nevertheless, I will endeavour to answer the question.

Primula nivalis itself is found throughout northern Asia. It has fleshy, strap leaves, mealy below, and heads of handsome drooping lilac-coloured flowers. The calyx is coated inside with meal, which gleams between the acute teeth. The sausage-shaped capsule projects well beyond the calyx, and opens by teeth at the apex, the brown angular seeds lying at the base.

Many species of Primula found in the Sino-Himalayan mountains having showy flowers, occasionally white or yellow, but much more commonly purple or violet, conform more or less to the above description, and belong to the section 'Nivales'. They seem however to fall into three well-marked groups: (i) tall alpine meadow plants mostly with several whorls of flowers, (ii) dwarf high alpines with violet or purple flowers and very long capsules, from which the seeds are shaken by the wind, (iii) medium-sized plants with large flowers of various colours, and more or less globular capsules which crumble to let the seeds be washed out by rain. Groups (i) and (ii) are confined to the dry inner ranges of Tibet, Yunnan, and Szechuan. Group (iii), with which we are here concerned, is confined to the wet outer rim of mountains, from the eastern Himalaya through Assam to Burma. Only two species are known, *P. Agleniana*, with its two beautiful children already described, and *P. falcifolia*, a remarkable yellow-flowered plant from Tibet.

During the six weeks we were in this camp our meals were as follows: 6. a.m., tea or coffee and a chuppatty, with butter and jam; 10 a.m., breakfast, consisting of a teacup full of porridge, some curried rice, and two chuppatties, with tea; 3 p.m., tea—the same as *chota hazri*, with potted meat; 7 p.m., dinner; soup, curried army ration (one tin had to last us three days!), and a sardine. At 9.30 p.m. we had a tot of rum and hot water, and a biscuit. I think we enjoyed that quiet half-hour before bedtime more than any other part of the day, and always looked forward to it when things were going badly for us. There was also a daily ration of half a slab of chocolate; everything was rationed! There was little variation in the diet, and never enough to eat! Sometimes our mail runners got through to us, and then there were sausages and bacon and other good things from Calcutta by post; but those occasions were few and far between after the rains began. The routine was only varied when we went out for the day, as we frequently did. That meant early breakfast and late tea. Since April, local supplies had been practically nil; and Luso's efforts to shoot something for the pot—once it was a green pigeon in the valley, another time a deer—were ludicrous. We collected a few bamboo-shoots in the forest, but for all its wealth, that was the only vegetable it offered us to eat.

We might indeed have eaten the voles which abound in the forest, and which are easily trapped; but we were never driven to quite such desperate straits—though I *have* eaten, and enjoyed, roast vole! These creatures live amongst the rocks and tree-roots beneath which there is always a maze of tunnels. There were rats also, and shrews, the latter particularly in the Rhododendron scrub at higher levels. The voles and rats of course are vegetarian, and nibble down the young trees which spring up everywhere, and gnaw the roots; the shrews live on insects. Both must play an important part in the life of the forest. On the rocks I also trapped a pica hare (Ochotona).

Small birds were legion. The forest was also full of insects. Where there are flowers, there are insects, and where insects, birds. On fine mornings, we could hear the steady hum of insect life plainly; and on wet nights great numbers of beetles and moths, attracted by the lamp and fire-light, would flit out of the darkness into the circle of light. This invasion always ceased abruptly at about 10 p.m., as though it were bedtime.

After our return to Peti in July, the Mishmis began to give trouble again. They flatly refused to take us anywhere except down the valley; and gave us to understand that they were not only willing, but anxious, to lead our footsteps in that direction. I did not take them very seriously, believing that we should have no difficulty in returning to our forest camp in September. But what should we do in the meantime? It seemed silly to stay where we were for two months.

Eventually I agreed to move down the valley to Meiliang, where our friendly *Gam* was in charge, and attack the next peak to the south of Kaso. This peak, called Polon, is about 14,000 feet high, and overlooks the valley of Meiliang. There was one very cogent argument in favour of this step— we had barely a month's rations left. We must send to Denning for more food immediately; the matter was urgent. No Mishmi from Peti would carry letters to Denning for us and our only hope was to persuade the *Gam* of Meiliang to send a man.

Shortly after our return to Peti there came a break in the rains, and we had a succession of bright sunny days, often interrupted by thunder-storms at night. The heat was intense, and in that highly saturated atmosphere one felt it with crushing effect. I made excursions into the temperate rain forest, on one occasion ascending to 9,000 feet; but I found few temperate flowers, though any number of leeches. Amongst several species of Begonia was one with large leaves and bright yellow flowers. An orange-flowered Globba grew in small colonies, and on the trees a rather scraggy-looking Æschynanthus, with blood-orange flowers, was sometimes seen. *Viola serpens* was in fruit, but proved a troublesome plant to collect ripe seed of. What had been conspicuous enough in May was now completely smothered under larger vegetation. Again, one could only be certain that the seed was ripe when the capsule had opened; but when a Violet capsule opens it does so with explosive violence. Click! and the seeds are shot into the undergrowth and lost. But the worst trouble was with grubs. Capsule after capsule opened tamely to expose rows of empty white shells, like rows of grinning teeth; the contents had been neatly cleaned out, and the robber had gone. Nevertheless I did manage to collect ripe seed of this pretty Violet, and it has flowered in England.

There are at least a dozen species of Violet in these mountains. They occur everywhere from as low as 3,000 feet in the forest, to as high as 12,000 feet in the Alps. Perhaps the most curious thing about them is that their flowers are almost any colour except violet, as bright yellow, purple, blue, mauve, or white!

Down in the valley I found a Creeping Jenny (Lysimachia) in golden flower, a handsome Saurauja festooned with pink silken flowers, and a waxy-flowered Lysionotus.

It was impossible to keep the Mishmis out of our camp, planted as we were in the midst of their cultivation; and moreover since we had no means of enforcing our demands, it seemed better to fraternise with them in the hope of allaying their suspicions. Nevertheless, the result of this was a series of petty thefts, mostly from the cook-house; and it was partly from a desire to escape this persecution of publicity, prying and pilfering, that we decided to return to Meiliang.

There was a lull in agricultural activity at the moment, though a good deal of hand weeding still went on. The Beans were ripe, and we bought some. The crops were always mixed: for instance, Beans, Maize, and Colocasia were all planted together, also Maize and Eleusine. The Mishmis however said that there was not nearly enough food raised to feed the whole population; hence the annual exodus. The fact that cultivation is never carried above 6,000 feet of course strictly limits supplies, and the whole head of the valley necessarily remains uninhabited. The 6,000 feet contour in not an arbitrary choice, and has probably little to do with climate; it is simply that, above 6,000 feet the mountains become so steep and the solid rock comes so near the surface, that agriculture is impossible. The result of felling the forest is merely to have the soil stripped from the rock in the first rains.

Although the Mishmis regarded us as fair game, and robbed us covertly when they could, they molested each other with as little concern. One

THE *Gam* OF PETI VILLAGE, DELEI VALLEY, MISHMI HILLS.

Rhododendron bullatum, GROWING IN THE TREE TOPS,
MISHMI HILLS, 9,000 FEET.   FLOWERS SNOWY WHITE.   JUNE.

affair threatened to develop into village warfare. Two Mishmis had stolen a mithun from Meiliang, and eaten it. Meiliang demanded compensation from Peti; Peti denied complicity, and told Meiliang to go elsewhere. Here were all the elements of a fracas. However, in the end the matter was talked out, and settled amicably; perhaps our presence had a soporific effect!

The next rumour was that the dreaded Chulikata clan were coming over from the Dibang valley to raid the Digaru and Miju clans; and as some of our worthies were reported to have crossed the pass and stolen three head of cattle and a goat from someone on the other side, retribution in some form or other might well be anticipated. Whether these things came to pass or not, I cannot say, for on July 22 we packed up our traps and marched back to Meiliang. It was a gruelling hot day and we arrived completely exhausted. The prospect of camping a thousand feet lower, and more shut in was not alluring; but at least we were now quite free of the gadfly of Mishmi curiosity.

August came, and with it the rain began again. We had sent a man to Denning with a letter asking for food; meanwhile our supply dwindled steadily, though we were able to buy beans, pumpkin, and a few potatoes. Our friend the *Gam* was frankly puzzled about us. Of course no Mishmi could for one moment believe that we had come here just to collect plants; but if not, we disguised our real object too well for him to discern it, and continued to collect plants. Local excursions yielded, amongst other things, *Saurauja subspinosa*, a Chinese plant not previously recorded from India, *Clerodendron Wallichii*, and a fine Hedychium with a bottle brush of orange and crimson flowers. We opened negotiations with the *Gam* for coolies to take us up Polon ridge, but a fortnight elapsed before any definite arrangement could be framed. Meanwhile, Peti had put a veto on our return, saying that we had spoilt the hunting! The Peti Mishmis threatened reprisals on Meiliang if they brought us back, and Meiliang promised not to! So it was Polon or nothing for us.

At last, after endless procrastination, the Mishmis promised to move our camp up the mountain. On the 15th we explored the ridge, chose a camping-ground, and fixed up a reservoir to catch rain-water. On an exposed grass cliff, a hundred yards long, covered with bushes, I found a dozen species of Rhododendron, including *R. Lindleyi*, though the only one now in flower was *R. manipurense*. *R. Lindleyi* is usually a small rather leggy shrub, but sometimes the thin purple-barked stems get drawn up in the dense bush to six feet or more. The very narrow oval leaves are characteristic, and the big blunt capsule projects far beyond the calyx, requiring about nine months to ripen. The magnificent white scented flowers of this and several allied species, such as *R. megacalyx* (which also grew on the ridge), seem out of all proportion to the size of the plant. First discovered in Bhutan fifty years ago, I rediscovered it again here.

The day chosen for this excursion was fine, and we had an opportunity to observe how dry and waterless the ridge really was. About half a mile beyond where we proposed to camp, however, we found a water-hole amidst a grove of Bamboos. The water looked foul, as being stagnant it might well be; but at any rate it was water. The tent cover we had brought with us was set up close to the camping-ground, in the hope that it would soon be filled with water.

There were many butterflies abroad in the forest, and it was very interesting to observe how they differed from those commonly met with in the open valley, in colour, in shape, and in their powers of flight. They are marked in such a way that when settled on the ground, covered as it is with dead leaves, they assimilate with their surroundings; they do not become visible, till they take to flight, and one may almost tread on them before they will give themselves away. One suspects that their chief enemies are birds, certainly not men. The edge of the hind-wing is sometimes curiously jagged, as though pieces had been pecked out by birds. The flight is generally slow and jerky; larger species have an undulating motion. A common species had black wings with a bar of bright yellow like a streak of sunlight across it. Others had spots and rings, like the spots of light which filter through the foliage and smatter the earth; the under-wing is generally speckled and spotted on a dull ash-grey background.

The hills were now teeming with life and we had a fair sample of it in camp, where lizards, snakes, shrews, blisterflies, horseflies, butterflies, praying mantises, and many other creatures came into our tents.

There was still no news of our supply, although our messenger had departed three weeks ago, and we were all on short rations. It seemed madness to go up the mountain with only a few days' food in hand; yet now was the time to go, before the Mishmis had time to change their minds again. Also another spell of fine weather had begun, so we fixed the start for August 17, come what might. It rained on the night of the 16th, so we expected to find water in our bath, but the 17th was fine and hot. We reached our camping-ground late in the afternoon, having slaked our thirst at a hollow tree, which we found to contain a certain quantity of liquid; but our reservoir was empty, the water having leaked away or evaporated. We had, however, brought up one petrol-can full of water, sufficient for our immediate needs.

15   Flowers of the Alps

REVIEWING the sequence of vegetation, from the lowest valleys to the alpine tops, one is immediately struck by the fact that, where conditions are most favourable to tree growth the forest is as diverse as it can be; but that as the conditions grow sterner, uniformity increases, until finally the forest is composed only of two or three, or even of one species. In fact we find an epitome of what takes place in the course of a journey from the Equator to the North Pole.

The valleys are filled with sub-tropical jungle, where no two trees in contact are alike, and the number of species, genera, and even families represented is considerable. A wealth of creepers, epiphytes, and under-growth apparently fills all available space, so that the jungle presents an impenetrable front to the outside world. That the interior is really hollow, is due to the fact that the roof *is* impenetrable, even to light. So deep is the gloom within, that green leaves can hardly perform their function, and the interior is mainly occupied by the scaffolding which supports the overhead canopy.

The standard being set by the tallest trees, every tree measures itself by that standard, and tries to push its way to the top. Many plants have achieved the same end by climbing; others, by perching themselves on the shoulders of the big fellows. The number of plants which have adopted none of these wiles, but have meekly contented themselves with the best position they could get, is comparatively small, and comprises chiefly the more ancient and less highly organised plants, especially Ferns.

The next higher zone, where snow falls in Winter, is the temperate rain forest, which may be compared with the temperate forests of Europe. We even find many genera common to both, as Maple, Birch, Oak, Holly, and Hornbeam. In the temperate rain forest also there is great variety, though not so great as in the jungle. Epiphytes still abound; but climbing plants are rare—in a partly deciduous forest there is less need for them.

What was an advantage in the temperate belt becomes a menace 2,000 feet higher up, where it is in excess; namely snow. Now the Winters lengthen out and the conditions are altogether more severe. The forest is composed almost exclusively of Fir or Spruce, with scattered Larch, and an undergrowth of Rhododendron, or stunted Birch, or Willow. This we may compare with the Coniferous forests of Northern Europe, Siberia, and Canada. At last forest ceases altogether, and we step from darkness into light; we have reached the alpine region.

Here, although there is ample water at certain seasons, it is not always available. Owing to their size and surface exposure, trees, in spite of severe restriction, lose much water by transpiration; and in the high winds and rarefied air of the Alps, transpiration is excessive. Unless this loss of water is made good by the roots, trees cannot exist. Sooner or later a point is reached where, owing to the coldness of the soil for six months in the year, the loss of water cannot be made good by the roots, which are reduced to inactivity; and tree growth ceases, to be replaced by shrubs. Shrubs require less water and expose less surface, therefore they are able to survive where trees cannot; and this is the true beginnings of the alpine region. Immediately the type of vegetation changes from the less to the better adapted, its diversity increases again.

Finally the conditions become so severe that no woody plants at all survive, though there are meadows of alpine flowers, with scattered flowers still higher; these gradually become more and more rare, until they too cease.

We have now reached the equivalent of the Artic region with its brief Summer and its long Winter sleep under the snow. Thus the first protest of the forest is to become deciduous, or partly deciduous; the second, to become evergreen again, but more uniform.

In the alpine region life starts afresh with the utmost diversity, as in the jungle; but as we ascend the same change comes over the scrub and herbaceous flora as we have already noticed in the forest; it becomes more uniform, dwindles in size, and finally ceases altogether.

Most alpine species occur in prodigious numbers; but the number of genera is comparatively small. Primulas, Anemones, Nomocharis, Iris, Rhododendron, are all gregarious. Whole slopes are flame-coloured with Primula, or blue with Iris. It is an unforgettable experience to wade through softly fragrant moonlight seas of *Primula microdonta alpicola*, or to squelch over meads violet with Irises. Yet despite the enormous numbers in which they occur, alpine plants do not take up so much room, and there is plenty of scope for variety. The number of species represented, however, is excessive as compared with the number of genera or families.

Though altitude does correspond roughly to latitude, and the zones of vegetation from the Equator to the Pole can be traced in a condensed form on the face of the mountain between 3,000 feet and 15,000 feet, these comparisons must not, of course, be pushed too far.

I have said that temperate rain forest, 6,000 to 9,000 feet, has its counterpart in the north temperate forests, between the parallels of 40° and 50°. But it must be remembered that the north temperate forest is almost entirely deciduous, the rain forest not more than half deciduous. A few genera are common to both; but most genera and all the species are peculiar to each. As for the undergrowth, that is entirely different. In the rain forest Spring really belongs to the trees, and especially to the Rhododendrons, and to the epiphytic Ericaceæ, the glassy-flowered Pentapterygiums and

Agapetes. For it is in early Spring before the leaves are on the trees, or the catkins off them, that the yellow 'Grande' and pink 'Barbatum' and 'Falconeri' tree Rhododendrons are smothered in blossom.

Comparing the Fir forest of the mountain zone between 10,000 and 12,000 feet, with its extension in latitude between the parallels of 50° and 70°, we find a greater similarity. But whereas in the northern zone there are forests of Larch, in the corresponding mountain zone *Larix Griffithii* never forms forests by itself, but occurs scattered in Abies forest. In the eastern Himalaya in fact, the topmost forest zone is always composed of Abies, with species of Rhododendron for undergrowth. In the corresponding northern zone the ultimate forests may be composed of Abies, or of Larix, or Pinus, or even of deciduous trees, such as Birch; and there is no Rhododendron.

Finally, the alpine region as a whole has been compared to the Arctic region, and it is this comparison in particular which, apt as it looks at first sight, must not be stressed. One is the more tempted to draw a comparison because it happens that in Europe, a number of Arctic plants *are* found in the alpine regions of Scotland, Norway, and Switzerland. But no such facile relationship exists in the eastern Himalaya. There are many genera common to the Arctic and to the Himalaya, but not a single species. There are also a great many genera in the Himalaya which are not represented in the Arctic.

But leaving aside the composition of the flora, and dealing only with plants found growing together, one may say that the alpine meadow has its counterpart in the meadowlands and steppes of the Eurasian continent; the alpine scrub in the Heath associations of the north, and in the *Rhododendron lapponicum* scrub of the Arctic; and the alpine turf and scree flora of the mountains in the tundra, although the characteristic plants of the last are Lichens.

Generally, the nearer the mountains are to the Equator, the more exaggerated are the differences between their alpine flora and the Arctic flora.

The Burmese Alps are wonderfully rich in flowers of all kinds. Ascending the Seinghku valley, one emerged from the forest at an altitude of about 9,000 feet, into high meadow with scattered thickets of Rhododendron. This was not the end of the forest, but it was the begininng of the alpine region. It was the same in the Mishmi Hills, where we ascended, not by a valley, but astride a ridge. Long before we reached the end of the Fir forest, the ridge rose up in rugged cliffs, and was split in twain, and the rocks were covered with alpine flowers. The transition from forest to alpine meadow is through scrub, composed almost entirely of Rhododendron. Meadow lines the streams and fills the hollows where the snow lingers; it creeps down the gullies far into the forest and up the cold northern slopes to the foot of the screes. Rhododendron bush and scrub, which forms so much of the undergrowth in the Fir forest, extends by itself up the mountain-side far beyond the tree-line. It covers the warm south slopes with generous growth and stripes the north slopes wherever it can find shelter from the stormy blast. At still higher elevations it forms a flat carpet, until finally it dwindles into hassocks and tuffets, and disappears altogether. But though forest and meadow meet and mingle, though alpine flowers grow on cliffs buried in the forest, and trees grow on moraines away up in the alps, yet there is no mistaking when the alpine region is reached at last. Whether one approaches the white peaks by hill or dale, one emerges abruptly from the dim padded forest into the snowlit alpine meadow, one's ears filled with the loud clatter of torrents, and the shuddering roar of the avalanche. Whether the change takes place at 9,000–10,000 feet, as in the high shining valleys of the Burmese Oberland, or at 11,000–12,000 feet, as on the warped rock girders of the Assam frontier, it is equally welcome. The sense of freedom, after being cooped up in the forest, is almost overwhelming. At last one can *see* the shape of the hills; also one can go anywhere—or so one fondly imagines, though this illusion quickly vanishes when one comes to realise the scale on which everything is built.

But what of the astonishing wealth and beauty of the flowers which surge round us! There are flowers everywhere, daring the snow, and their colours are indescribable. A tongue of scarlet Rhododendron licks the foot of a cliff, changes to carmine, and to flame colour, and runs like molten lava down a gulley. A sheaf of tall powdered stems, from which is hung a carillon of sulphur bells, lines the stream, clogged with clumps of the fragrant lavender-purple flowered *Primula involucrata Wardii*, or *P. sikkimensis*, giant Senecio, Irises, Cremanthodiums, and Buttercups.

Primula melanodonta, one of the new 'Candelabras,' occurs in countless thousands. In July whole hillsides are sunshine-yellow with it, and it spreads over the valley floor in wide drifts, ascending to over 12,000 feet. It is a near relation of *P. serratifolia*, producing as a rule only one, sometimes two, whorls of bi-coloured flowers. In *P. melanodonta*, however, the colours are arranged concentrically, as in the English Primrose, instead of radially as in *P. serratifolia*, a darker 'bull's-eye,' with a pale 'outer.' In the Seinghku valley both *P. serratifolia* and *P. melanodonta* occur, though the latter is far the commoner of the two: but so jealous are they of each other that they will not share the same ground, *P. serratifolia* generally growing at a considerably higher level than *P. melanodonta*.

On grassy windswept lawns there are sure to be large colonies of that strange and beautiful flower, *Omphalogramma Souliei*. Unlike other species of this remarkable genus, *O. Souliei* bursts out of the sodden earth in consolidated clumps, and no sooner does the first red spearpoint push through the soil, than it unfolds an enormous flower, of an intense violet colour, white-banded inside the furry throat, whose heavy chin almost rests on the ground. The portly shape and size, and audacious colour of the flower suggest some tropical Bignonia rather than a lady of the snow! At this time the plant is about three inches high, and the whole slope is hackled over with its sheaves, all the flowers gaping in the same direction. After the flowers are over, the heart-shaped leaves unfold, and stem and leaves continue to grow for weeks, the acorn-shaped capsule, which finally opens like a Grecian urn, being hoisted up to a height of two feet. Most Omphalogrammas grow widely scattered in meadow or turf, and are not particularly abundant, though *O. Delavayi* sometimes occurs in great numbers. But for stark reckless profusion, *O. Souliei* in the Seinghku valley beats them all.

In the next patch of meadow several tall Poppies are opening sky-blue flowers to display a shower of golden anthers in the centre. This Poppy is a lovely slender sea-green thing with dangling blue bubbles which swing to and fro in the breeze. It grows in great drifts and clumps all up the open valley, streaking the jade meadows with turquoise shadows. Most people now know *M. betonicifolia Baileyi*, the famous blue Poppy of Tibet. This plant is very like it, only it grows in the open instead of in the woodland, coming out in hundreds and thousands in July, and ascending to 12,000 feet, though never growing in such serried ranks as do Primulas.

Blue Poppies have been known to gardening enthusiasts for a generation, and to botanists much longer. But it was only last year that their real existence was grought home to the general public, a magnificent bed of *M. betonicifolia Baileyi* having been staged in Hyde Park, London, and another in Ibrox Park, Glasgow. This indeed is the first and only species, of the many that have been tried, to grow like a weed in Britain. Amongst the hundreds of plants I saw in Tibet and in the Burmese Oberland I never saw one with anything but azure blue flowers or with more than four petals. In Britain, on the other hand, there is sometimes a tendency for the flowers to come purple—a ruinous colour—due possibly to the presence of lime in the soil or to too rich feeding. There is also a strong tendency towards doubling. But, since *M. betonicifolia* is perennial, and seeds itself freely, there should be no difficulty in keeping up the highest standard.

Another wonderful little alpine Poppy is *M. rubra*, which grows scattered up and down the long screes, being very abundant between 11,000 and 12,000 feet. *M. rubra* is very like *M. Morsheadii*, a plant common on the high mountains of Kongbo, in Tibet, except for its deep ruby-red petals—they are violet in *M. Morsheadii*. It is still more like *M. impedita* from the mountains of North-West Yunnan, but that too has violet petals. The first time I saw *M. rubra* peeping from a crack in the bare gneiss cliff, with a solitary red flower glaring balefully at me, I thought it was a freak: for the colour of these alpine Poppies is not always fixed. But it was not a freak, for no flower of the hundreds seen ever opened any other colour; in the Seinghku valley *M. rubra* has definitely replaced *M. Morsheadii* and *M. impedita*[1].

---

[1] For the distinction between these three species, see 'Burmese Species of Meconopsis,' *Annals of Botany*, October 1928.

Another Poppy of the Seinghku valley is *M. calciphila*, found only above 12,000 feet, and almost confined to limestone screes. It is a prim and prickly creature with flowers of a taciturn blue, not to be compared with the glorious sky-blue prickly Poppy, *M. latifolia*, but no doubt quite as hard to grow! *M. calciphila* made so slight an impression on the alpine flora, that I shall say no more about it here.

But despite the gorgeous carpet of colour in the Alps, how rare a thing is scent! Of all these vivid flowers, how many are fragrant? Almost none! So uncommon is it to find a scented flower in the alpine region, that any exception is made a fuss of in the field notes!

Quite a number of dwarf Rhododendrons, belonging chiefly to the 'Lapponicums,' 'Cephalanthums,' and 'Anthopogons,' have aromatic foliage; but these are just the groups which are lacking on the rainswept mountains. On the drier ranges, where they grow by the million, they tint the crisp air with a faint clean perfume when the sun comes out. The 'Glaucums,' on the other hand, which abound on the wet ranges, distil an oil from their leaves, which is almost fœtid in its beastliness. But scarcely one of the scores of alpine Rhododendrons has fragrant flowers: I only know of *R. suaveolens*, with its delicate hint of green plums, and *R. fragariflorum*. None of the Poppies is scented—except *Meconopsis speciosa*. None *of* the Irises—except the dwarf purple Iris. None of the Saxifrages, Gentians, Androsaces, Lloydias, Anemones, Violas, Cassiopes, Omphalogrammas, Campanulas, Incarvilleas, Geraniums, Nomaocharis, Pedicularis, or Paraquilegium. It may be objected that none of these genera are scented anywhere else. Very well; none of the Roses, Barberries, Honeysuckles, Cotoneasters, Asters, or Gaultherias are fragrant in the Alps! On the other hand, the alpine species of Codonopsis are at least harmless, while their relatives from below just stink.

But there are a few notable exceptions to this wholesale alpine inertia; and the most notable of all are the meadow Primulas. The rock Primulas are indeed nearly all scentless; but fragrance is universal amongst the 'Sikkimensis' and 'Muscarioides' groups, and some of these occur in such prodigious numbers as to scent whole valleys. Large streams, held back by clumps of *Primula Florindæ*, scent the coppices in Southern Tibet; meads of the Moonlight Sikkimensis, *P. microdonta alpicola*, perfume the vales. Even the little Maroon Meadow Primula, *P. rubra*, which has a delicate fragrance, and never forms drifts, sweetens the air. As for the 'Muscarioides' Primulas, though usually scattered, they are often powerfully scented.

Lastly some species of Cremanthodium are delicately fragrant, but, although they may occur in considerable numbers, the scent is hardly perceptible except at close quarters, though no doubt they add to the general sweetness of the alpine air, which has a faint suggestion of honey about it.

It may be that fragrance needs not only a drier atmosphere but a warmer one, for its production, or at least its perception. The minor ranges of

Tibet and Western China are more fragrant than the soggy Alps of the Burmese Oberland, or the Mishmi Hills; but the temperate rain forest is more fragrant than either, and the still drier and warmer Coniferous forests of the interior, more fragrant still. There is of course an odour of incense in the air on a warm day, a pleasant aromatic scent distilled from the leaves of Conifers and dwarf 'Cephalanthum' Rhododendrons. Many of the bush Rhododendrons too are fragrant—*R. decorum* in the Pine forests, and the 'Maddenis' in the temperate rain forest. In the sub-tropical jungle too are many powerfully scented trees, shrubs and climbing plants. But it is worth noting that these, like the scented 'Maddeni' and 'Fortunei' Rhododendrons, nearly always have white flowers; whereas white-flowered Rhododendrons are quite exceptional in the Alps.

On a slope which rises at an angle of 45 degrees for a thousand feet to the chimney-stacks on the roof of the world, amongst Primulas, Irises, and Delphiniums, are clumps of baggy red Cypripedium, so large and heavy that their stems can hardly lift them from the ground, and their bulging fat chins sag on their broad leaves. This is *Cypripedium tibeticum*, a montrous alpine Orchid, rarely seen in Britain, though it is common over a wide area in the Himalaya. Here also grows the morocco-red *Nomocharis Souliei*, a dwarf Lily, whose solitary nodding flowers, though not so delicate and refined as the dazzling watered-silk blooms of *N. pardanthina*, have a sort of semi-precious beauty, as of polished porphyry. In the Mishmi Hills this red Nomocharis is incredibly abundant on alpine turf slopes, growing no more than six inches high; it also grows scattered amongst dwarf Rhododendron, and, at lower elevations, on grassy slopes in dense Bamboo brake.

Where *N. pardanthina* grows tall and stately, its innocent-looking flushed flowers floating on the ruffled surface of the meadow, *N. Souliei* is brisk and matter-of-fact. In the Mishmi Hills, on the other hand, *N. pardanthina* is unknown, its place being taken by the similar, though swarthier, *N. aperta*. This last is rare, and indeed in the Mishmi Hills only *N. Souliei* is abundant. *N. pardanthina* seems to have reached its western limit in the Seinghku valley.

The Seinghku valley boasted at least three species of Nomocharis. Besides *N. pardanthina* and *N. Souliei*—the latter always higher up the valley—there grew on the most forbidding gneiss cliffs, though rarely, the dwarfish *N. nana*, with solitary nodding flowers of a reddened purple colour—not the port-wine red of *N. Souliei*, but a duller red—and smaller. This plant is much more common, however, in the Tibetan Himalaya and farther north-west.

N. nana has a curious dual personality. At the head of the valley, the high belt of limestone already referred to reappears, crowned by some of the loftiest peaks in the neighbourhood; and on this limestone there grows yet another Nomocharis. Anyone seeing this plant for the first time would say it bore no relation to *N. nana*, at any rate, since it is distinctly taller and has fragrant flowers, finely peppered with purple spots on a pale yellow ground. Typical *N. nana*, as found in Tibet, and also in the Seinghku valley, grows on igneous rocks, and has purple or dull red-brown flowers, without a suspicion of fragrance. Nevertheless, in spite of these obvious differences, the structure of the flower is the same in both plants, and so both are included under the one name, *Nomocharis nana*; even varietal rank is unfortunately refused the taller yellow-flowered plant, although the mere addition of the name *flavida* would serve to remind us that it was once very logically considered by Rendle to be a distinct species under the name *Fritillaria flavida*. Many a plant has been named with less justification[1].

The dwarf form and the taller yellow form may be kith and kin: at any rate they disliked each other as kith and kin frequently do. In fact they would have nothing whatever to do with one another. The dwarf form grew only on the Burma or south-east side of the range. The yellow form, though found on both sides, was far more abundant on the Tibetan (north-west) side, and occurred at distinctly higher levels, though not so high as typical *N. nana* is found in Tibet. The two never grew in company, and the yellow form, growing at a higher elevation, opened its flowers about a fortnight later than the other. The small bulbs of Nomocharis are usually rather deep down about six inches below the surface. The soil is a black tenacious mould, with plenty of clay in it derived from the disintegration of felspar; for most species are found on schistose rocks. The only exception I can recall is *N. Mairei*, which grows in a rather sandy soil.

The cliffs are the home of many delicious things. From crevices hang the dream flowers of *Paraquilegia grandiflorum*, their lilac cups fluttering amidst tuffets of sea-green Maidenhair foliage as large as a man can hold in his hand. It is a glorious plant, but the flowers are fugitive. In cracks and crannies amongst soft beds of moss, minute Primulas such as *P. rhodochroa* have established themselves, together with yellow or white-flowered Lloydias, which have grass-like foliage. On the long smooth screes which slant steeply up from trough to crest of the hills are scattered violet and red Poppies, woolly cones of Saussurea, tufts of golden Saxifrages, and crimson Pedicularis.

Before saying anything more about the alpine flora it will be convenient to hark back to a comparison and a warning. I have previously compared the alpine flora of Sino-Himalaya with the Arctic flora. This comparison serves its purpose, so long as it is not carried too far. The conditions in the two

[1] For a full account of the genus Nomocharis, see W. E. Evans, in Notes R.B.G., Edinburgh, June 1925, and August 1926.

It is worth noting that *N. Souliei* grew on the sloping scree just below the cliffs, where I found the half-dozen plants of *N. nana*. *N. pardanthina* grew in the same meadow, all three species being therefore within a few hundred yards of each other. The yellow *N. nana*, however, grew by itself a couple of miles away.

regions differ widely; indeed there is little in common between them except the abundant snow and intense cold of Winter, and the short Summer. The result of this is reflected in the flora, which, though of different composition, is of the same general type in both regions.

The more obvious differences in the conditions for plant life in Sino-Himalaya may be shortly stated. In the first place there is no midnight sun: day and night succeed each other in the familiar way, all the year round. The sun, far from circling round the horizon, low down, so that the light and heat rays strike the plants at a low angle, and on all sides, moves right over them at so steep an angle as at one season to strike them almost vertically. For Sino-Himalaya lies entirely within the parallels of 25° and 29° N. latidude, so that at midsummer the sun crosses the sky near the zenith. The latitude of London is 52° N., a difference of 25° of latitude, and it is quite remarkable how so many plants from low latitudes and high altitudes adapt themselves to high latitudes and low altitudes.

When the sun does come out in June, as in the drier country behind the rain screen it frequently does, it is extremely powerful, in the rarefied atmosphere of the high alps. Thus even at 14,000 feet it may be quite hot in the middle of the day. There is no shade anywhere. The surface soil becomes heated, and for this reason alone the roots of alpine plants must strike deep into the soil to find water.

There is another obvious difference between the mountains and the Arctic, namely altitude. What direct effect, if any, altitude has on plants is not known, but at 15,000 feet the atmospheric pressure is only half what it is at sea level. This must affect the breathing of plants, as it does that of animals: it may even affect all the chemical processes which take place in plants: and it certainly increases transpiration. The indirect effects of high altitude are, of course, chiefly climatic.

Finally, the immense distortion of Sino-Himalaya, which is everywhere uplifted into great mountain chains, furrowed by deep gorges, its endless variety of feature, and its wide range of temperature, compressed within a narrow belt of country, have no parallel in the Arctic. There the physical features of the country are often uniform over wide areas; and most Arctic plants are circumpolar.

The alpine plants so far described exhibit no unusual features. Most of the Poppies, Primulas, Anemones, Lilies, Slipper Orchids, Irises, Louseworts, Larkspurs, Gentians, and many other alpine flowers are such as one might expect to find in the woods and meadows of England. But growing at still higher levels are a certain number of plants which seem to be especially adapted to harsher conditions of life. These are scattered about, growing on the cliffs or amongst the boulders on screes and moraines, and by the cold trickling streams and old glacier lakes. They are not gregarious, like the meadow flowers and Rhododendrons; at these extreme heights nothing is gregarious.

The most curious of these adaptations is the cushion habit. The individual plant, if one can distinguish the individual from the colony, is small; the leaves are very small, often needle-like, or if flattened, then closely overlapping. Even the flowers are small, though being closely crowded the effect is to make them conspicuous. The plant grows as a whole in the form of a hard and compact rounded cushion, the short, erect stems branching repeatedly, each branch keeping close to the parent stem, the two interlocking by means of their leaves. Thus a cushion is formed, sometimes reaching a great size, and persisting for a long time. There is commonly one thick and immensely long root, arising from the centre of the cushion, composed of several roots plaited like the strands of a rope. This long root has a twofold object: to get water from a stone, as it seems—though actually the scree is moist at no very great depth—and to anchor the plant to its shifting foundation, leaving some free play.

Quite a number of plants have taken to the cushion habit. The most beautiful of all is *Myosotis Hookeri*, whose closely overlapping leaves are clothed with long glistening silken hairs, thus further checking transpiration. One of the commonest is *Arenaria polytrichoides*, whose big smooth hassocks are in July starred all over with tiny white flowers. This plant may be found so high as 18,000 feet. There is a small cushion Potentilla also, besides several species of Draba, *D. involucrata*. A small rock Primula found in the Seinghku valley, and also in Sikkim, *P. muscoides*, also forms a cushion.

At a height of about 17,000 feet in July I found that, on plunging the bulb of the thermometer in amongst the stems and leaves of various cushions the average temperature recorded was almost 7° F. higher than the corresponding soil temperature.

Then there are the rosette plants, mostly belonging to the family Compositæ. These simply telescope the stem until it is reduced almost to vanishing point, and the plant consists of little more than an immense tap-root, crowned, apparently, by a large disc of flowers set in a circlet of leaves; the whole being drawn down flush with the surface by the powerful pull of the foot. They are nearly all scree plants. The purple-flowered *Lactuca Souliei*, and several yellow-flowered species of Crepis, including *C. rosularis*, are of this type; they are found on the drier ranges. A few small Primulas such as *P. rhodochroa* may also be regarded as rosette plants, though the flowers are reduced to one or two. This habit, of course, depends upon the almost complete suppression of the stem, which is reduced to a collar bearing leaves, and, at the summit, flowers. It has the twofold effect of reducing wind surface, and concentrating the flowers in such a way as to focus the insect visitors' attention.

The mat-forming plants also hug the ground as closely as possible, but they are spread thinner than rosette plants. The stems creep over the surface, or fall in tresses over a cliff, and are nearly all shrubs. Plants like *Diapensia himalaica*, *Gaultheria nummularioides*, *Diplarche multiflora*, and some of the Gentians are also mat weavers; indeed it is one of the commonest habits assumed by alpine plants.

Other plants, particularly Sedums and Saxifrages, grow in close clumps, the crowded stems and leaves affording each other some protection.

Many alpines, as we have seen, apparently take no thought for the morrow, and are as other plants; but these are not as a rule found at the highest altitudes, nor are the conditions under which they live so very terrible. Some high alpines, for instance species of Meconopsis, although they appear to be normal, really conform to the rosette habit: for being biennials, they need only to survive one winter, which they do as a leafy rosette, from which the tall flowering stem develops in the following Summer.

Thus different plants choose different means of coping with the extremely hostile and unpleasant conditions met with at great heights. No one method is entirely successful: if it were, it would eventually prevail at the expense of other methods. One plant holds its own with one danger, but falls a victim to others, which in turn hold no terrors for a plant differently equipped.

The ultimate object of each is, of course, to survive and reproduce its like; that is, to survive as a race rather than as an individual, and, if possible, to increase. Much energy and ingenuity must therefore be expended on the reproductive organs, in view of two serious difficulties. The first is the shortness of the Summer, and the second, the perpetual mist and rain which prevails at these altitudes, at least on the outer ranges.

Many alpine plants have to flower and ripen their seeds within four months. Quite a number are allowed no more than three; while some of the 'Ornata' Gentians flower and fruit within six or seven weeks, and even then they are often compelled to ripen their seeds in the snow! One result seems to be that alpine plants must produce great numbers of seeds, and therefore the seeds have to be small, and no special care is bestowed on them in the making. There are plenty of them, and they have just to take their chance.

Alpine plants usually have bright and showy flowers; or if small, they are massed in heads. There is no lack of insect life in the mountains, and birds, too, are common. Humble bees, butterflies, and small flies abound; there are also beetles, and spiders. In fact, wherever there are plants there is animal life, though it is not always useful, and may be harmful; plants have to make the best terms they can with such as exist.

The next problem is to protect the material parts of the flower—stamens and pistil—from the rain; and this is usually done by making the corolla tubular, or bellshaped, and inverting it. When the corolla is all in one piece this is a fairly simple matter; most Rhododendrons and Primulas have flowers of this type. Another method is to stand the flower upright, but to plug the throat with hairs, as is done in *Primula bella* and *Rhododendron cephalanthum.* Some of the Gentians have pleated throats and are able to close the tube almost completely when clouds obscure the sun.

The more primitive types, whose flowers are made up of separate petals, have a more difficult task. The Poppies, Anemones, Saxifrages, and many other flowers have poorer security, but they too usually protect themselves by hanging their heads; some indeed take no notice of the rain beyond turning their backs on it!

Perhaps the most carefully protected are those which, like many species of Pedicularis, have closed tubular flowers: but this device, far from being universal, is rather exceptional. But in spite of the wealth of meadow flowers both on the drier and colder mountains behind the rain-screen of the Himalaya, and on the drenched outer hills overlooking the plains, it is the dwarf Rhododendrons which always and everywhere are the chief glory of the Alps.

There are two distinct alpine Rhododendron communities, differing rather in composition than in appearance. On the very wet mountain ranges which lie to the south of the great snow peaks and close to the plains, are found most of the creeping Rhododendrons and their allies, such as Scarlet Runner (*R. repens*), Carmelita, Rose of Kaso, Scarlet Pimpernel, and others; the mat-forming Rhododendrons, such as Limestone Rose (*R. calciphila*), *R. keleticum*, *R. calostrotum*, *R. riparium*, and *R. saluenense*; another group of pigmies, Rock Rose (*R. patulum*), Purple Emperor (*R. imperator*), and *R. uniflorum*; species of the Heavenly Twins group, as we may call them, from the fact that their beautiful little petulant flowers are usually born in pairs—*R. campylogynum, R. myrtilloides,* and *R. pumilum*; and finally the blood-red and blood-orange 'Sanguineums' and 'Neriiflorums' which are tanglesome undershrubs.

The presence of a mixed Rhododendron community containing a fair proportion of the above—and such an association would not begin below 10,000 feet—is certain proof that the mountains are shrouded in mist for five months of the year, and under deep snow for the remaining seven; for it is under these depressing conditions that the Rhododendrons of Sino-Himalaya flourish most furiously, and vary most recklessly. As most of them flower in June, the scene on the hill-tops is one of bewildering beauty, a ruffled sea of colour, wine-purple, flowing to amber, amber flowing to blood-red, and blood-red flowing to amethyst, all breaking and sparkling amongst the white foam of snow.

At the head of the Seinghku valley in the space of three miles, there grew fifteen different species of dwarf Rhododendron, all mixed up together, as thickly as Heather on a Scotch moor. Along the mile of open rock ridge which ran up to the base of Kaso peak on the Assam frontier, I collected ten different species, excluding large shrubs. Even richer was the Doshong La which crosses the loop of the Tsangpo gorge, in Tibet. Taking a mile of valley on either side of the pass, there were found here not less than twenty species, growing so thickly that one trampled over them like flowers in a meadow. The chiming and clashing of colour in the dream dawn of a Summer's day, before the mist quenched everything, was the most unforgettable sight in this high roof-garden of Asia.

Most of the dwarf species are themselves gregarious, large tracts being covered with a few common kinds through which the rarer kinds are scattered; but as higher and higher levels are reached, other species become dominant. So close knit is the Rhododendron scrub that where it attains a height of two or three feet it is utterly impenetrable; indeed, one can sometimes walk on its surface! But to get any idea of the scene when the snow is melting on the high passes, one must first understand the scale of the country. Only thus can one fathom those uncharted seas of colour, and realise the countless millions of flowers seen in one sweeping look!

Turning now to the drier ranges behind the rampart of great peaks, all over 20,000 feet high, we find the mountain slopes still covered with the same close growth of Rhododendron. But here there is less variety. Enormous areas of hill and dale on the roof of the world are covered with two or three species, in habit much more like Heather than those of the misty hills. This is the home of the tiny-leafed 'Lapponicum'[1], Rhododendrons which are broomy shrublets, with heads of small lavender, purple, lilac, or saffron flowers and leaves with glistening scales. Most of the 'Cephalanthum' and 'Anthopogon' Rhododendrons, which bear tight spherical heads of snow-white, pink, brick-red, or yellow flowers of unusual shape also belong here; but there are few other dwarf species. Vast tracts of mountain are covered with a larger scrub, generally a single species, such as *R. agglutinatum*.

Wherever the mountains are covered with the little Heather-like 'Lapponicums' to the exclusion of the more exotic-looking types, one may be quite certain that, though there is abundant rain in the Summer, and the Alps are often covered for days on end with a blanket of mist, yet there are breaks of fine weather, expecially in June and September. The rainy season in fact begins later and ends earlier than on the outer ranges; nor are the moorlands buried under snow for so many months, though the Winters are actually colder. The 'Lapponicum' type is perhaps more zerophytic, better able to withstand intense cold, without the protection afforded by snow, than any other Rhododendron. For this reason alone the type is likely to be one of the most hardy and popular in Britain. In the course of the next twenty years, while the many Rhododendrons recently introduced are being tried and sorted, we may expect these small shrubs, handy alike for the rock garden or for the border, or even massed in beds, to take a high place. In Britain they flower in April and May.

On the southern face of the eastern Himalaya and on the outer ranges of

---

[1] So named from their general resemblance to *R. lapponicum*, a circumpolar species.

Assam, which stretch away to the Burmese Oberland and to China, the number of Rhododendron species seems endless. They form fully three-quarters of the alpine vegetation.

Between the flaming whirlpools of colour, the high gullies are filled with a larger scrub, which surges round the base of the cliffs, and washes in blue-green seas of eager foliage, stained with rose and cadmium, far up the slope. And though the mist which presently comes rolling up may dim, it cannot put out the fires. Indeed, rain is so inseparably connected with the alpine regions, that without its cool friendly presence one feels there is something lacking; and the Rhododendron carpet smoulders redly beneath the smoking mist like lava seen through a veil of steam.

Nor are Rhododendrons the only shrubs found in the alpine region; though they certainly form the bulk of the thickets. Mixed up with them are species of Barberry and Honeysuckle, Juniper, several Willows, Sorbus, Cherry, *Cassiope selaginoides*, *Ilex Pernyi*, and *I. intricata*, *Rosa sericea*, *Potentilla fruticosa*, species of Gaultheria, Vaccinium, and so forth. Although the Rhododendrons far outnumber all these put together, and outmatch them, still they are by no means inconspicuous. Species of Vaccinium in fact sometimes cover whole hillsides by themselves. The dwarf Barberries are particularly fine in the Autumn, when their leaves and larger pear-shaped dangling fruits turn scarlet. The dwarf Hollies are, of course, evergreen, and when crusted with scarlet berries peeping from amongst their hard spiky leaves, they are very striking objects. The alpine Honey-suckles are not like our English Honeysuckle, but small trees, or bushes, or even creeping plants, with regular flowers, yellow, white, pink, or purple. *Lonicera hispida*, var. *setosa*, has large pale yellow flowers, enclosed in pale papery collars (bracts), and succeeded by orange fruits. *L. tsarongensis*, which is a bushy shrub in the valley, in the alps forms mats composed of thread-like stems covered with tiny leaves. It drapes the rocks with long streamers, and is particularly attractive when covered with its smooth blue-black berries. *L. cyanocarpa*, var. *porphyrantha* is an angular twiggy shrub, with flowers of a wounderful wine purple, followed by fruits as big as sloes, painted over with a plum-coloured bloom. The alpine Willows are all dwarf mat-forming plants which sprawl over the rocks, and bear flowers in erect spikes. In the Autumn these spikes, which are sometimes six inches high, become pillars of white down, and the leaves turn champagne yellow. *Ilex Pernyi* in its ordinary garb is a small bush growing in the Abies forest. In its alpine form it is a much compressed prostrate plant, the squat stems bearing crinkly leaves which closely overlap one another. It hugs the cliff, and when fully charged with scarlet berries, is very distinguished-looking.

Another delightful alpine Holly is *I. intricata*, which has rounded, rather glossy leaves, with deeply impressed veins. It forms a larger, more spreading undershrub than *I. Pernyi*, though rising little, if any, higher above the ground. The berries are pillar-box red, sharply contrasting with

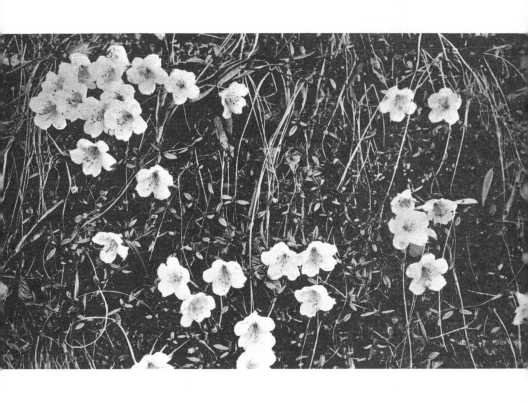

Rhododendron patulum (" ROCK ROSE ") ON THE CLIFFS AT 11,000 FEET, MISHMI HILLS, ASSAM FRONTIER. FLOWERS ROSY PURPLE. JUNE-JULY.

the olive green of the leaves. This plant seeks shelter, often growing deep within the bosom of the bushy Vacciniums and Rhododendrons, or even on rocks in the heart of the Fir forest. But never does it, like *I. Pernyi*, grow into an erect bush.

There is no altitude at which aspect does not to some extent control the type of vegetation, and nowhere perhaps is this more conspicuous than in the alpine region. Owing to the fact that snow lies longer on north and east slopes than it does on south and west slopes, the forest straggles further up the former than up the latter: and when only Rhododendron is left, it forms high scrub on the sheltered, and low scrub on the exposed slopes. At higher levels, where wind and sun rip the snow quilt more quickly from the mountain, the crouching Rhododendrons form mats and carpets over which one may walk easily: but in the hollows where the snow lingers, other species form hassocks and brooms and dense tangles. The alpine vegetation is also very sensitive to wind. Even to the uttermost limit of plant life, shelter from wind plays a part; and here only those plants which snuggle down into some crevice of the cliff, or lurk under a stone, can survive at all.

Smaller variations in the alpine flora are due to differences of soil. Broadly speaking, three kinds of rock are met with: limestone, igneous, and metamorphic; the last being schist or occasionally slate. If, as happens in the Seinghku valley, a limestone range cuts across igneous rock, or, as happens near Muli in S.W. Szechuan, a slate range cuts across limestone rock, the contrast in the flora is easily observed. Certain species of plants are confined to one or other rock, although there is no difference in the general type of flora. This is a remarkable fact. In Britain Rhododendrons are intolerant of lime, or at any rate of chalk. In the mountains of Yunnan and Szechuan, they hardly ever grow on anything but limestone! In the Seinghku valley the limestone range was as prolific in Rhododendrons as the igneous range; and at least one species, Limestone Rose (*R. calciphila*), was confined to it!

16   The Conquest of Polon

AND now to return to our second forest camp above Meiliang, where we arrived on August 17. Polon camp was situated in the forest, at the end of a long spur which ran almost due east to the main ridge forming the divide between the Delei and Dou rivers. Astride this ridge was Polon. Our altitude did not exceed 9,000 feet. The north flank of the ridge was covered with dense forest; the south flank was at this end covered partly with meadow, partly with dense scrub; but both higher up and lower down it was covered with forest similar to that on the other face. Here we spent ten long weeks.

Three problems now faced us: (i) the problem of food, (ii) the problem of water, and (iii) the problem of how to reach Polon. Luckily for us it rained the first night, and we caught some water off the tents; but during the next fortnight the drought below was severe (though it rained higher up) and we were often short of water. Had it not been for the water-hole already mentioned, we must have abandoned the ridge before the rains came on again. Meanwhile, we were searching for other sources of supply, and by the time the water-hole was empty I had discovered a spring of clear water about a mile up the ridge and a few hundred feet down on the north side. This was lucky, because the muddy water from the hole was beginning to upset us.

Just as the discovery of the spring at Rhododendron Camp had led to the finding of *Primula Normaniana* so the discovery of this new spring led to the finding of an interesting Androsace, though it was only in fruit. It appeared however to be identical with *A. Henryi*, a white-flowered plant (K.W. 3171) I had collected in Upper Burma some years ago, found also in Yunnan. It flourishes best in deep shade, and requires a rich soil with abundant moisture; the rock garden is the last place for it! Another interesting forest plant which grew here was *Viola Hookeri*. At the beginning of September the rains began again, and we had no more trouble over water.

The food problem was serious. On August 18, we had four days' supply of rice and flour left, on short rations. By still further reducing the ration we might spin this out a day or two longer. We drew in our belts and clung on, but the rations dwindled steadily, and by the 23rd things looked grim. We ourselves had long since given up eating rice, as we had our stores; but Luso had religious scruples, so he could not touch these when the rice was finished, as it was now. There was still a little flour left, but it was full of maggots and quite sour; Luso refused that also, though we did not! For three days Luso said he ate nothing, except four eggs which the Mishmis brought us, and which we insisted on his taking, together with some condensed milk Buttercup persuaded him to believe was 'made in India'[1]. We were not much better off ourselves, for when the last sour chupatty and the last army ration were finished, we had nothing but medical comforts left. Rum and chocolate, biscuits and O.K. sauce, although excellent things in themselves, are not a diet on which to climb mountains, still less move them. We sent Hubble down to raid the villages, but he returned to the ark empty. We sent him down again to get news of the long-expected supply, if possible, and he returned without even the olive-branch of rumour. This was a heavy blow. Generally, if coolies are plodding up the valley with loads, one hears of them several days in advance, and our camp was not more than four days' march from the Lohit.

It was now nearly five weeks since our messenger had started for Denning. The journey ought not to have taken him more than five days; a week would be a generous allowance. On the return trip, nine days was ample, even for heavily laden coolies, sixteen days in all. What then could have happened? There were two possible explanations: either the messenger had not taken the note—and as we had paid him in advance, we had no means of knowing this, or, the Indian Officer at Denning who was arranging for our supply, had been unable to engage coolies.

We found a few Bamboo shoots, and Luso prowled about with a gun, but shot nothing. And then, on the 27th, we returned to camp from a climb, and found that four coolies had arrived bringing three bags of rice and a bag of flour! Yes, sir, yes, sir, three bags full! We were saved. That night we went back on to full rations and had a good dinner, especially as more coolies were reported on the road, bringing stores and mails. These, however, did not arrive till a week later.

As for the third problem, the solution of that depended more on our own direct efforts than did either of the others. But to reach Polon was not nearly so simple as it sounds; for although there was a trail along the ridge, it was frequently interrupted, and always difficult to follow. The peak on which we had to march was plainly visible from our camp on a fine day; but once inside the forest, we naturally lost sight of it. By the time we had completed a path as far as the main ridge, the rains had broken again, and we did not see Polon for five weeks.

However, from the very beginning we set to work to cut a path along the crest of the spur. Where the forest was open, and the spur was fairly level, we could easily follow the trail, or make one for ourselves. But on the steeper slopes, and in the dense Rhododendron thickets we encountered higher up, there was no trace of a path and we had laboriously to cut a way through

[1] As an orthodox Mussulman, Luso would not eat tinned food from abroad.

for ourselves. Several times we strayed off the ridge on to some minor spur, and wasted both time and energy. Nevertheless, by September 2, when the fine weather ended, we had cut a path as far as the main divide, about four miles from camp; and our worst troubles seemed to be over, when in truth they were only beginning!

Meanwhile, we were looking for all those plants which had been so familiar to us on Kaso, but were now doubly hard to find, firstly because we were on the lower mountain, secondly because they were no longer in flower. All the same, we were finding them gradually, and when one day in a gully not so very far from camp I found both *Primula Normaniana* and *P. deleiensis*, my spirits rose. Another cheerful plant in these north gullies, was a Lysimachia (*L. ramosa*), with tall ascending stems, and nodding flowers leaning singly out of the leaf axils on wiry stalks. It was bright and perky, buttering the rocks above the glen with its wintry sunshine yellow. It grew with *Primula Normaniana* above, not with *P. deleiensis* below. More remarkable was a Buddleia, almost herbaceous, its weak stems flopping wearily down the steep face, as though too tired to stand upright. And well might so reedy a stem be, clothed for its full length of about five feet with immense leaves and ending in heavy clots of orange-eyed fragrant flowers! There was another much more conventional looking Buddleia with spikes of purple flowers, in the thickets lower down the ridge near our camp.

Most of the Rhododendrons had also been found, except the alpine species, and of course the unique species that is to say, those of which a solitary specimen or a small group of specimens occurred in one spot. These, which included the glabrous-leafed 'Barbatum' (K.W. 8431) and the 'Cherry Barbatum' allied to *R. Smithii* (K.W. 8255), I believed to be the only specimens in existence. The only new Rhododendron I discovered on the ridge was a bush like *R. oleifolium*, but with longer, narrower leaves, growing on the sunny side in dense thickets of scrub. The flowers of course were over. In these almost impenetrable thickets, *R. aureum* was also abundant, while *R. Lindleyi* and *R. mishmiense* occurred more rarely. On rocky outcrops *R. bullatum* was common, and tree species included *R. hylaeum* with huge fists of fruits, and *R. manipurense*, which was in flower up to the end of August.

But the plant I most wanted was the Maroon Meadow Primula (*P. rubra*), and the possibility of not finding it cost me many an uneasy night. I descended a number of likely gullies, starting at higher and higher levels as we worked our way along the ridge, but all to no purpose. There were plenty of other alpine meadow plants, which had overflowed from the teeming Alps, into the steep gravel chute whence even the aggressive temperate forest could not drive them; but not a sign of the one I wanted.

What I had to remember was that Polon, being not only lower than Kaso, but closer to the great reservoir of Indo-Malayan plants, its temperate and alpine flora would be more restricted. Thus the Maroon Meadow Primula, which occurred as low as 11,000 feet on Kaso, was not likely to occur below 12,000 feet on Polon, if at all. I could not therefore expect to find it until I reached the alpine zone.

On September 2 we launched our fifth big attack on Polon. Before this, on August 28, we had reached what we called the first alpine top, a treeless hump covered with scrub Rhododendron, where we had again lost the trail. We had tried to continue along the ridge, only to find that it descended into such a tangle of forest that it would have taken days to chop our way through. Why there should be a path along the ridge at all, however intermittent, unless it went as far as Polon, we could not imagine; but a long search failed to discover the continuation, and once more we retired baffled. However, we made one important discovery, namely that the first alpine top was the hinge by which our spur was attached to the main ridge.

Now the time had come to try again. We reached the first alpine top in about three hours, and presently Buttercup discovered the path which dived through a thick screen of bush Rhododendron. After descending a short distance, and traversing round a shoulder, we ascended diagonally to the ridge again and found ourselves on another bare top. We were now quite close to Polon and could plainly hear water crashing over the cliffs; but we could see nothing on account of the dense volumes of cloud rolling up from the Dou valley. The only certain thing was that the ridge plunged down into the forest again. We followed it hopefully, along an obvious trail; indeed the ridge became a knife-edge and the flanking gullies were so steep that it would have been impossible to descend them. Between the gullies, stunted Fir-trees poked their heads up through dense tanglements of *Rhododendron arizelum* and *R. exasperatum,* and these often surged over the razor ridge. It was the more tantalising because we knew that a steady ascent of less than a thousand feet must bring us into the alpine region; and all the time we continued to descend, though we were getting closer and closer to Polon. At last we reached the bottom of the saddle; the ridge began to rise again, but the trail came to an end, and we found ourselves hemmed in on all sides by impenetrable thickets of Rhododendron, and what was even worse, dwarf Bamboo. Once more we retired beaten. Yet we had accomplished something.

While all this had been going on, other things had been happening nearer home. One day two Mishmi hunters came up the ridge from Mitonma, and when they saw where our camp was pitched, they instantly began to make trouble. They complained that we were tramping all over their garden and spoiling hundreds of rupees worth of Teeta[1]. This plant grows wild in the forest, but small clearings are made between 7,000 and 9,000 feet, to promote its growth on a larger scale in accessible spots. It is dug up in the Winter, and the yellow roots are sold in the Sadiya bazaar, where

---

[1] *Coptis Teeta,* a small plant belonging to the family Ranunculaceæ the root of which is used as a medicine in China.

it fetches about seven shillings a pound. The Mishmis put in a claim for compensation on a large scale; but as on inspection we found that we had done little or no damage, and still more, because by this time we were thoroughly sick of Mishmi complaints, we refused to listen to them. The aggrieved village promptly declared war by non-cooperation and refused to sell us bad eggs, or supply coolies, or help us in any way. But as Meiliang was friendly and Minutang, the next big village down the valley, had no quarrel with us, we felt ourselves strong enough to ignore Mitonma, which anyway was a small village sandwiched between our allies.

No less ridiculous was the complaint that we interfered with the hunting. Meiliang did not hunt, so our being on the ridge did not affect them; nor was it their forest reserve. But Mitonma felt bitter, and tried to suborn Meiliang with dark threats. Meiliang however had been well paid by us, and with the certainty of further revenue, was not disposed to quarrel with us over nothing. True, Meiliang had been cowed by the truculence of Peti, which was the more powerful village; but Mitonma was smaller than Meiliang, and the proposed coalition fell through. Thus we stayed where we were in our clearing. I noticed here two or three specimens of *Magnolia Campbellii*, which had been amputated close to the ground and had sent up several strong suckers. Further along the ridge in the boggy hollows occupied chiefly by Bamboo, there were several fine trees of *M. Campbellii*, though I had not seen it on Kaso ridge. *M. rostrata* also grew here, within a stone's throw of *M. Campbellii*, but actually on the ridge, not in the hollows, which in September were temporarily converted into ponds. *M. globosa* did not grow here at all.

Another fine tree was *Acer Campbellii* with handsome leaves and masses of straw-yellow fruits streaked with purple, the wings widely divergent. One particularly splendid specimen grew in the hollow with *Magnolia Campbellii* and a big-leafed Cinnamon. Further up the ridge a Whitebeam (Pyrus) was conspicuous and *Acer Forrestii* was not rare, sometimes growing amongst the rocks and scrub on the south face, where, however, it was stunted.

Two big climbing plants—Schizandra—also deserve notice. One bore short fat branches of purple fruits, like small grapes, the other long interrupted spikes of scarlet fruits, which reached a length of six inches. This latter must have been a fine sight when covered with these tails, but I never saw it; I only picked up the fruits, and, later, leaves to match; the latter are compound. Another climber of which I picked up fruit was an Actinidia, and a species of Akebia grew in the thickets on the south face.

As Autumn approached, several herbaceous twining plants appeared in flower, notably two or three species of Crawfurdia, on the stems of Bamboos and the voluminous *Dactylicapnos scandens* with sea-green leaves and dangling bunches of acid yellow flowers, followed by cherry-red peardrop fruits; flowers and ripe fruit hovered amongst the threadlike stems and pale leaves at the same time, giving a very pretty effect.

Throughout September the rain came down in sheets as though it never would stop. The steeper parts of the ridge were almost unclimbable, and it seemed hopeless to seek the way to the Alps until it cleared up sufficiently to allow us a glimpse of Polon. After the middle of the month I was kept busy collecting seed of the woodland plants. I also explored the south face of the ridge, where on outcrops of rock I found a small Impatiens with lurid magenta flowers—a typical garden annual beloved of those who like striking colours. The hoary-leafed Begonia also grew here.

The temperate rain forest, so poor in Spring flowers, is no richer in the Autumn, and such colour as began to creep over it now came from the changing foliage. Two or three species of Arisæma sprang up, and the large dangling scarlet balloons of *Podophyllum versipelle* were conspicuous, though this Chinese plant was not common. Another plant to flower was the little epiphytic *Rhododendron concinnoides*, whose purplish-pink corollas lay all up the ridge under the Fir-trees. A change was coming, and that swiftly. We heard the cries of unfamiliar birds, as the approach of Winter drove them down from the heights or the ripening fruits drew them up from the valley. A gaudy woodpecker was not rare, and there were many long-tailed magpies about. The only thing which did not change was the weather.

A welcome diversion was caused by the arrival of fresh stores and a mail. Alas! the magazines and weekly papers were in a sorry state, and half our letters were missing. The natives who brought them had slept one night under a rock just off the path where mithun from a neighbouring village were accustomed to wander in search of food. While they slept, their loads, with bundles of mail tied on top, beside them, a herd of mithun had come along, and finding the paper on which our superior journals are printed good fodder, had pulled them out, chewed them, trampled what remained in the mud, and gone on to browse fresh pastures.

Amongst the stores were 30 lbs of pemmican in sealed tins which Buttercup had ordered from England. Arctic experience had taught him its value, and he had long ago decided that this was the stuff to solve our food problem. And so it proved. It came by the last mail, just in time to tide us over the most difficult period. A pound tin of pemmican, which could easily be slipped into a jacket pocket, would feed a man for a week if necesssary. We at once stopped our rice ration, which was making serious inroads on our limited supply, and substituted a bowl of pemmican, in the form of a thick soup, for breakfast and dinner. Thus we now lived almost entirely on pemmican, chuppatties, and chocolate, with of course, the usual extras and medical comforts; for we had plenty of butter and jam, rum, biscuits, tea and coffee left, besides a few tins of sausages and bacon, which had been sent up by post. When we first left Sadiya, we had with us a cooked ham, which stood us in noble stead for weeks. We therefore wrote to Calcutta for another. Two months later we received news to the effect that it was on its way; but when the next mail, which should have brought it, arrived, it brought only the intimation that the tin had reached Sadiya in such a battered condition that the ham had to be buried at once. It was then too late to write for another, even if it had been any use trusting it to the Indian post.

Almost every evening we scrambled up from our camp in the dell on to the lookout, a bare rock on the ridge whence we had a fine view to the south and west. At sunset there was often a reshuffle of the clouds, and a deceptive promise of fine weather, never fulfilled. Often we saw, not only all the high peaks sticking up out of the asbestos whiteness, but far down the Delei valley as well; sometimes we could trace the course of the Lohit valley almost to the plains. Then, as night came on, the blinds would be drawn over the pale-green windows in the sky, and the clouds turn slate grey, tinged with an angry violet.

Every night a large owl visited us, and sat, like the raven, on a branch just above our chamber door. It was not till we discovered that our camp was a hot-bed of jungle rats, we understood the reason for his visit. We trapped eight rats in two days. The rats ate the food stored in the cooking *basha*; the owl ate the rats; nothing ate the owl, at least, not while we were there. The owl was more amusing than amused when we turned the electric spotlight on him. Craning his head forward, he revolved it in circles, trying to get outside the beam or to pierce it with his powerful vision. Obviously he was puzzled. The extraordinary thing was that he sat still under this ordeal. Sometimes his wife came, and we would hear them hissing to and kissing each other and sometimes hooting gently. Then when we had gone to bed, and the camp was in darkness, we would hear the soft swish of wings, a squawk, a dying gasp, and—silence. Sometimes at night we heard a despairing wail from the depth of the forest, but we never discovered what it was, whether bird or mammal.

The days dragged on till Autumn had laid a heavy hand on the forest. At last, on September 27, tired of waiting for fine weather which mocked us, we decided to attack Polon once more, wet or fine.

We made an early start, having breakfasted by candlelight.

In less than three hours we stood on the alpine top, where the ridge began to descend to the saddle; and here we dumped some tins of pemmican as a supply for the proposed trip from Polon to Kaso. Continuing along the razor back in a smother of cloud which hid every landmark, we soon reached our furthest point, and set about our task. We were surrounded by a dense tangle of *Rhododendron arizelum*, whose thick ascending stems, interlacing breast high, formed a serious obstacle. Buttercup noticed a faint trail down a spur; and while he explored in that direction, I started on the apparently hopeless task of hacking my way along the ridge. Presently I reached a cliff: it was certain that there never had been a path here. The left flank seemed equally hopeless; probably Buttercup had hit on the right trail after all.

190

Half an hour later we were calling to one another in the mist and eventually I made my way down the face, through high herbage, to Buttercup. He was a few hundred feet below, and on a real path! He told me how he had descended the spur for 500 feet along the faintest of trails, noticing where the Moss had been worn off the rocks, until at last, just when he was about to give it up in despair, he found a genuine path traversing across the face again parallel to the ridge above! A little further along was quite a good cave, and from here the trail went straight up the face, through a dense grove of Bamboos. The riddle was solved; the way to the alps was open at last!

However, we decided to return to camp now and complete the exploration another day. Back on the ridge we marvelled at our success. Who would ever have suspected that the path plunged down into the forest like that! Of course, had we been able to see Polon, and the ridge, and the whole face, it might have been obvious that the only possible route from the saddle was on a long traverse, and *not* straight up the ridge. But as usual we could see nothing except cloud, and we had to *guess* the way, or find it by trial and error. Once more Buttercup's uncanny instinct had proved invaluable.

Along the razor back there grew a dwarf Ilex (*I. intricata*) with small matt-green Box-like leaves, and abundant tiny scarlet berries. It formed a massive undershrub, here spreadeagled on the rocks, there scrambling up into a sitting posture; an ideal covering plant for the rock garden. At lower altitudes amongst the big-leafed Rhododendrons it was replaced by a larger bushy species with shiny leaves and scarlet berries on stiff stalks like crabs' eyes. This looked as though it would make a good hedge. Unfortunately, the Hollies, especially the dwarf ones, grow very slowly.

There was plenty of colour along the razor back now. A small Viburnum had claret-red leaves, those of *Rhododendron deleiense* had turned flame-coloured, with flashes of orange, while the odious little yellow epiphytic species had justified itself by turning vivid scarlet, with vermilion fruits!

To the stout trunks of Larch- and Fir-trees, stunted and mutilated by the rage of the wind, clung immense cushions of Moss: and firmly fixed in these were large bunches of the silver-plated *Rhododendron megeratum*, with pale green fairies' scarves of Lichen (*Usnea barbata*) fluttering from it.

We got back to camp much pleased with ourselves, after ten hours climbing. Three days later I determined to carry out the final exploration and reach the alpine region. It was a terrible day, pouring with rain before dawn, and breakfast by candlelight was a cold and dreary affair. Once away, and quickly wet through, I made good progress up the familiar trail, reaching the cave in three and a half hours. Here I dumped the pemmican brought on from the alpine top, and also a tin of biscuits. The day was still young, and I started up the steep face, through the Bamboo screen, full of confidence. Then came a sprawling undergrowth of *Rhododendron arizelum* beneath the last fringe of wind-clipped Firs; thickets of scrub *R. cinnabarinum* fledged with verdigris green, *R. saguineum* and *R. cerasinum*, with Rose bushes, and Pyrus, bearing panicles of snow-white berries: next minute I was climbing a rock scupper which spouted water as the rain descended in sheets! The banks were lined with Rhododendron bushes, and all along the edge grew hundreds of plants of the Gamboge Primula in ripe fruit! I had to go slowly here, collecting seeds as I went, but always climbing up and up towards the invisible summit. Now the trail turned across the face again, converging on the ridge, amongst rocks and crouching bushes, and quite suddenly I came out into the open. There were no more trees, no bushes even, only steep alpine meadow, with rocky outcrops and low escarpments beneath which clumps of Rhododendron huddled, and dwarf shrubs of Rose, Spiræa, and Honeysuckle pressed themselves into crevices. On the very first slope I found the yellow-flowered *Primula mishmiensis* in fruit; and then pushing my way up the slope through the dying meadow, at last the Maroon Meadow Primula (*P. rubra*). That was a glorious moment! The meadow plants were dying and rotting all round me, the flying rain stung my face and froze my hands, and the mountains with the clouds smoking over them looked utterly forlorn. But for a moment that scene was blotted out and what I saw lay in the womb of the future. It was an English garden steeped in June sunshine; with waving clumps of golden and violet Primulas, and outcrops of white Candytuft, and Oriental Poppies bouncing like scarlet balls on a sage-green sea; and in the foreground a drift of scented Primula with neat rounded leaves and slender wands, shaking out clusters of maroon flowers, brought by someone from the Mishmi Hills years ago!

After that I roved about and climbed to the top of the ridge; collected the fat translucent blood-red berries which dangled from the dwarf Honeysuckle (it had once borne fragrant white starry flowers like a Daphne); noticed a number of flowers, especially clumps of bright yellow Saxifrages, an Aster, a pink Polygonum, and a tiny pale-blue Gentian; and speculated as to where the highest peak was, and which ridge connected up with Kaso. I could see nothing beyond fifty yards.

The leaves of a small Euphorbia formed brilliant scarlet patches on the turf, and I saw lots of familiar plants in fruit, including the red Nomocharis, Anemones, the tall yellow Gentian, Geranium, Phlomis, and *Cassiope seloginoides*. But the only dwarf Rhododendron was *R. riparium*; just over the ridge were bushes of *R. lanatum*. All the time I was gathering seeds, and when I started back for camp I had a good bagful, and all my pockets bulged. I reached camp half an hour after dark, the climb having taken eleven and a half hours; four hours to the alp, three and a half hours coming back, and three and a half hours wandering in the wet paradise. So ended October 1, another memorable day.

17 Ordeal by Storm

OCTOBER came at last. It was the critical month. On the 2nd, rain fell steadily till the evening, when the clouds opened, letting out a sword of sunlight which cleft the forest. At dusk Buttercup and I sat up on the lookout rock near our camp. Six thousand feet below lay the tilted fields. The valley zigzagged between bulging spurs to the sugar-loaf mountain, just across the Lohit, which stood out a hard indigo blue; and because we could nowhere see into the bottom of the valley, where the river was drilling its way under forced draught, everything looked absurdly near. We measured all distances in the air, or along high contours, neglecting the innumerable ups and downs and re-entrants below. It was only a few miles down the Delei to the Lohit; only a few miles down the Lohit to where the mountains flared out to the plains. And we might hope to march the distance in eight days! Down the Lohit valley we could recognise a big scar on the hillside, caused by a slip; we had camped opposite to it in March. It was only ten miles distant, yet we had picked our way through this labyrinth of gutters and spurs for five days!

During the next two days the weather continued to improve. By the evening of the 3rd the clouds had stretched themselves out into strips; towards the plain the sky was apple green. It was the night of full moon, and our pet owl had as usual perched itself above Buttercup's tent. After dinner, we strolled up to the lookout again, and sat down in the cold vivid moonlight, a thing we had not been able to do for many months. The mountains looked like a pen and ink drawing, and from invisible depths came the muffled song of the river. From time to time an owl hooted in the black forest, and was answered far away. It was a wonderful night, warm and still; in the glow of the moon, now high above the sharp curve of the mountains, everything looked strange and glorious. Except for one small thing, fine weather seemed certain; but chancing to look up, I saw a distinct veil pass over the face of the moon, followed by a brilliant bow—a complete halo of rainbow hue set round the disc. At first I thought this was an illusion, and I rubbed my eyes; but when I looked up again, the moon was perfectly clear! No longer could I deceive myself; the halo was caused by a thin mist flying up from the valley. It was the first time I had seen such a thing happen at night. I returned to my tent thinking hard; I did not like the look of things at all. At midnight, when the camp was wrapped in slumber and profound darkness, without warning, the storm burst. The din was terrific; a violent wind came sweeping over the ridge, clutching at the trees and driving before it rain which stung. But the wind was from the south. "It always does this at the change of the Monsoon," I said confidently to Buttercup next day; "in fact, it's a good sign. The rain will be over in a day or two." Meanwhile it poured; and the air was too warm. "Wait till the temperature drops," I said, "then we shall have crisp Autumn weather, with cold nights and sunny days."

That night the wind changed right over and blew with increasing fury from the north. The temperature dropped eight degrees, and we found ourselves shivering in our tents. But the rain kept on, a colder, more pitiless rain.

"This is the end of the Monsoon," I said, my heart sinking. "Now that the wind has backed to the north, we shall have fine weather. As soon as these dregs have been drawn off, the wind from the plateau will be dry, and we shall have bright sunshine."

We were cold and miserable. Day after day, we awoke in the bleak dawn to hear the rain drumming on the canvas, and the wind soughing through the wet foliage. Most days I went up the ridge, gathering seed of the forest Primulas and other plants; and at sunset, when the fury of the storm died down, while the cloud broth was settling itself, we went to the lookout and turned our eyes anxiously towards Polon. The days dragged on. The start of the journey to Kaso was put off to the second week in October; no Mishmis would even visit our camp while the storm lasted, let alone climb the mountain. Then came a morning when I went early to the lookout. The mountain-tops were visible above the seething cauldron of cloud; and peering through the trees, I caught a glimpse of Kaso, white with snow. Polon was the same. A day or two later, there was a sprinkling of snow on the bump called Atsin; though Atsin was only 12,000 feet high and almost overhung the Lohit valley!

Later the sky cleared for an hour, and I followed the ridge down with my eye to where the sulphur Poppy and Rose of Kaso grew, and tried to make myself believe that the snow had not yet crept down so low as that. But I knew I lied. It will melt, I assured myself without conviction. It was useless to try and climb Polon in such weather. I should only lose myself. But on October 9th we went up the ridge to collect Rhododendron seed, and got as far as the first alpine top. A gusty wind drove the rain in salvos, and it was wretchedly cold. But it was rain, not snow, even at 11,000 feet! However, looking across to the cliffs of Polon, visible through the torn shreds of mist, one could see snow along the ridge, and I reflected that it would descend to lower levels on a mountain 15,000 feet high than on a mountain 13,000 feet high. The outlook in fact was not encouraging. At last, on October 13 the storm blew itself out. The next day was really fine and I went up the ridge to collect Rhododendron seed and to find out what damage had been done. When I returned to camp, I found twenty-five

Mishmi coolies assembled. That night Buttercup and I laid our plans. I was to go up to the cave with two men, and from there try to reach Kaso in three days, returning by the old ridge to Peti, and so down the valley to Meiliang. Meanwhile, Buttercup, who was still lame, would return to Meiliang camp and wait for me there. If it proved impossible to reach Kaso, I would spend two days on Polon, collecting everything I could find, and return the same way; the matter of then climbing Kaso by number one route, in order to get seed of the June flowers not found on Polon, could be discussed later.

I awoke late on October 15, having been taken ill during the night; Buttercup twice visited me and sat up to do everything possible for my comfort. It was raining hard and blowing a gale from the north. The coolies, who had had no sleep since midnight, were soaked to the skin and shivering with cold, for the driving rain had inundated their flimsy bamboo and leaf shelters. What should we do? Once more the clock had been put back, and now we were in a fix. The coolies, thoroughly miserable, said that if we did not return to the valley at once, they would go without us and never come back. The threat was obviously the outcome of present discomfort, and yet I could hardly ignore it. Buttercup, brave soul, was for sitting tight and risking the transport problem; no one was more sick of Polon camp than he was, but in his heart of hearts he thought I was not fit to march, so he suggested that we let the coolies go and trust to luck! But I thought otherwise, and as Kaso was much the more difficult, as it was also the more important peak, I decided to tackle it from below, and gave the order to retire; Kaso from Polon was, I knew, impossible now; there remained only the direct line of attack.

We packed up our sodden tents and scrambled down the steep path, collecting seeds as we went; on the lower ridge there were many flowers, including Orchids—species of Pleione, Cirrhopetalum, Cymbidium, and Cœlogyne. Next day the weather mended again, and in the evening Polon became visible; but it was bitter white with snow.

On October 17, accompanied by Hubble and the *Gam* of Meiliang, I started up the valley for Peti. We carried blankets and food for five days, light loads which enabled us to march fast. It was roasting hot, and the rough track, now completely overgrown, proved more exasperating than ever. However, we reached Peti early, and crossed the ravine to the opposite village, at the foot of Kaso ridge. At the first two huts we approached with a request for a night's lodging, we were refused admission. At the third, I told my allies not to sue but to command; so in we went.

The hot day drew to a close, and after sundown I was glad to stretch myself out on the bamboo floor by a good fire. Down the gorge of the Delei the sky looked hazy, but I had no premonition of disaster.

I awoke early to hear the rain dripping off the thatch! The whole valley was filled with mist, which came rolling on steadily up the gorge. Even the tops of the cliffs were wreathed in cloud; the high peaks totally immersed. No good climbing Kaso to-day, I thought! I went along the path through the gorge, and after a hunt amongst the wet bushes, found the Golden Leycesteria. It had fruited as generously as it had flowered, and I collected all the seed there was.

By this time the news of my presence was all over the village, and many people had gathered together to watch my return; but they were more curious than hostile, and did not molest me.

On the following day I knew we must climb Kaso, be the weather what it might; the local situation demanded it. It drizzled all night, and when morning came, there was no change. The last hope that the early snowfall on Kaso ridge would melt vanished.

We were not destined to leave our hut scatheless. At a very early hour, three young bucks burst noisily into my room, talking at the tops of their voices. They were fashionably dressed; naked almost to the waist, with long scarves thrown carelessly over their shoulders, and the small square sporan like a remnant of cheap red carpet. Each carried a big knife in an open sheath. It irritates me to have strangers wrangling in my dressing-room before I have had my morning tea, so I told Hubble to turn them out. He replied that they were abusing the householder for letting me in, and would be very angry if he told them to go.

"I will be very angry if you don't," I said. Hubble smiled sourly, but did nothing; so as I could not order the men out myself, I went up to them, spoke them fair, and taking an arm of each, pushed two of them into the next compartment. The third I left, as he looked fierce. They went quietly, but never stopped talking. My heart was beating rather fast, I noticed, but I carried the thing off. One of them might easily have drawn his knife and cut me down; and the last thing in the world I wanted was a fracas when I was so near the end of my task. Whatever the outcome of a scrimmage—and as I was unarmed, a real row could have only one end—it could be of no possible advantage to me. At the worst I might be killed; at the best I should have to leave the Delei valley quicker than I had come into it. At all costs, therefore, I must keep the peace.

On the other hand these youths looked mischievous. I had been warned not to return to Peti, and here I was; every Mishmi in the three villages knew it by this time. Suppose these men followed me up the ridge—well, it might be awkward. Better to assert myself, and hope for the best. Hence the action taken to checkmate the gang at the outset.

It was drizzling when we started at eight o'clock, and I was not reassured to observe that a party of Mishmis were following us; afterwards they went ahead. We made poor progress at the beginning, the path being like a butter-slide; but once on the forested ridge, we got along well enough. At our old camp we halted, lit a fire, and dried some of our clothes before going on to the Rocks for lunch. The Mishmis thought I meant to camp here, but of course I had no such intention; it was much too far from the alpine region. The ideal place would have been the ridge above Boggy Valley where we camped in July; but without tents and bedding, and without water or firewood, and the ridge under snow, it was out of the question. The next best place seemed to be Buttercup's Ridge, or if that too was snowed up, Primula Rock.

It was raining harder than ever now, and forcing our way through the drenched bushes, we were soon wet to the skin; water streamed off us and my feet were perishing cold. Nothing was visible except that broth of cloud hanging mournful and motionless over the weeping mountains. Hubble kept on repeating: "There will be snow, sahib! We shall die! We shall die!" and though I did my best to reassure him, I felt I could not rely on him. How I hated the whole business! The discomfort was bad enough, without the discouraging attitude of the Mishmis. But—but there were seeds I *must* get, or perish in the effort. It was simply unthinkable to return without them. Besides, we were there. I told Hubble that we would not go any higher, that there was a comfortable cave to sleep in (would that it were true!), and that he had nothing to fear; and he struggled on in silence. At last we reached Primula Rock, and the cave which was below the ridge on the south face; and leaving the men to light a fire I started on my errand.

Scrambling round the north face of the fang, I first looked up *Primula deleiensis*. This grew on an almost vertical rock face to which a veneer of mud and turf gave a false sense of security; but it was not so high that a fall even from the top need entail serious consequences. The rain of course had turned the face into a butter-slide—and icy cold butter at that. I slipped and fell, not once, but half a dozen times before I had searched out every capsule of a Primula which, after all, yielded only a few dozen seeds. Many a capsule had aborted; nor are the few seeds I did secure likely to produce a plant which will increase and multiply, or one which will gladden the hearts of my horticultural friends if it does! I hope I may be wrong!

Going on to the cave, I began collecting seed of *P. Clutterbuckii*, but finding very little of that either, I pulled out whole plants to send home alive. Finally, I went up the ridge a short distance and descended the gulley to where in June I had found a sheet of Rock Rose (*Rhododendron patulum*) sprawling over the face and flowering profusely. I soon discovered however that it had not fruited equally profusely, and set to work to search out every capsule. Had capsules been as plentiful as flowers, I must have got plenty of seed. But they were not, by a long way. While reaching out for a capsule, spread-eagled on the wet and shiny face, the better to hold on, both my feet slipped at the same moment, and I slid thirty or forty yards down the rock at great speed, before being stopped by the bushes below. I had been expecting this to happen at any moment, and though my face and hands were lacerated, I was not badly hurt. What with this shaking up, however, and the meagre results of my effort, I was bitterly disappointed with Rock Rose. I ought really to have been grateful. Certainly it grew in a perfect beast of a place; but the wonder was that it did grow here at all! More legitimately it sheeted the high alpine ridge at 13,000 feet, where there had been immense numbers of flowers in June; but immense numbers were all in vain now, as I was to learn next day. At any rate, Rock Rose was safe, and is now in cultivation. I can hardly look at it without a shiver of fright!

It was now growing dark, so I returned to the so-called cave. 'Cave' was an euphemism, though it had once looked more attractive than it did now. Primula Rock overhung a ledge at this point; below the ledge, on which there was hardly room for one man to lie down, the slope dropped at an angle of 60° into the Rhododendron bushes. It was on this ledge that the three of us spent a hideous night.

The roof was neither flat enough to keep off the rain, nor steep enough to draw off the water, which consequently gathered and dropped on to us from a dozen points. The front was of course wide open and the recess being very shallow, we had to press ourselves against the cliff behind so as not to roll off the ledge. On a clear day, the view out over the heads of the trees at our feet, with Kaso towering up behind, was doubtless very fine. But now everything was smudged in mist, and the cold rain fell remorselessly.

With some difficulty we lit a fire, cooked our supper, and drew our blankets round us for the night. We dozed at times; but the cold and wet, and nightmares of the morrow troubled me. After midnight the last of the wood was used up and the exhausted Mishmis let the fire go out. Towards dawn the rain changed to snow, which the wind blew straight in our faces; and before it grew light I arose, and with numbed fingers put on my boots. The vigil was over. As quickly as possible we lit the fire again and I made some hot pemmican. Outside the cave the bushes were white with snow, and the ghost of Kaso loomed up fitfully through the mist. The moment had now arrived to dare to put it to the touch to gain or lose it all! I told the men to go down to the Rocks and wait there for me; they were to make the place comfortable, and might expect me at dusk.

I had made a list of the plants of which seed was required, where to find them, and by what marks, if any. But of course any plants buried under the snow must be written off as lost. What, I asked myself, was not buried under the snow, which now reached Primula Rock?

No sooner had I started up the ridge than I found myself shaking wads of soft snow from my shoulders as I pushed through the frozen bushes; nevertheless below 11,000 feet the snow was soon melting again.

Buttercup's Ridge was well covered. I collected seed of the dwarf *Rhododendron riparium*, and of the red Nomocharis here, without difficulty. The next landmark was the clump of *Rhododendron Smithii* with cherry-carmine flowers, and the securing of a dozen capsules from that put new life into me. Iris Cliff was too exposed for the snow to lie, but here I received a shock; on the easier side, not a single plant of *Nomocharis aperta* could I discover! Yet there had been half a dozen flowering specimens here—what had happened to them? I searched high and low, but without result. There remained only to scramble down the cliff on the other side and search there, which I did; but though I found several marked plants, they yielded only two capsules between them. It was not much consolation to me to remember at this crisis that the flowers of *N. aperta*, and other species, often have a rudimentary pistil, and therefore set no seed; it merely explained things without remedying them. Several headless plants mocked me, looking as though a collector had been here before me, so I gave up the quest and rested content with my two capsules. I had lost a good half-hour over that Nomocharis, and there was still a 'Sanguineum' Rhododendron to collect here. But in all the dense tangle of scrub which surged over the cliff, I could find only a paltry half-dozen capsules, and in the haste and confusion, either capsules or seeds were subsequently mixed with some other Rhododendron; which just shows what pitfalls beset the plant-collector when hard pressed!

Primula alta had set no seed, and as for the dwarf Iris, I could not find a single capsule, nor was there time to search more closely; I must make for the Alps at once, and strain every nerve to find seed of the good things which remained. So I pushed on as hard as I could go, snatched a handful of capsules from the yellow *Primula mishmiensis*, and reached Rhododendron Hill, where I bagged good seed from Glowbell; it did not look very glowing just then!

What a sight met my gaze, as twenty minutes later I topped the hill and the last plucked Fir-trees dropped behind me! I looked on a world which lay sleeping beneath a mantle of snow, not to be lifted for seven months! Hardly a rock or a shrub showed through. Not in one swift disaster, indeed, had this befallen; the signs were clear that snow had been falling, layer on layer, ever since the beginning of the storm a fortnight ago! Smooth waves of glistening whiteness rolled in bent curves over hillock and hollow; long sugary banks swept without a ripple for a thousand feet to the precipices below. Only the crest of the ridge had been whipped clean by the wind. Boggy Valley was a snowfield, and the Gamboge Primula was lost!

I trudged up the ridge with one object in life: to find Rose of Kaso and the dwarf pink *Rhododendron crebreflorum. Meconopsis paniculata, Primula apoclita*, and the rest, could go; I was resigned to their betrayal. But the two pink Rhododendrons I must have. Thank heaven I had collected Rock Rose the previous evening; there was not the faintest hope of getting it here, or *R. pumilum* either!

Rose of Kaso lay at the root of a great ugly sabre tooth, the last on the ridge until you reached the peak itself. It seemed doubtful whether it was possible to reach the sabre, much less the precipice under the crown. But there was one plant in a gap on the ridge itself. The creepy 'Cephalanthum' grew much farther along, but there were a few plants on the cracked crown. As I went along the ridge I plucked the furry capsules of *R. lanatum*, which had been brusque enough to shake the snow from itself. Its dejected leaves, twisted into squills, hung down by its side.

Arrived opposite the dent in which Rose of Kaso lay buried in a thicket of *Rhododendron sanguineum*, I picked up my marks easily enough; they had withstood the storm. When the Rose was incarnate in a bloody sea, you could not miss it ten yards off; out of flower, on the other hand, you could not recognise it a yard off. Imagine the difficulty now, when the whole confused tanglement was buried beneath the snow! Yet, thanks to my marks, a quick and ready measurement by cross bearings brought me right on top of it at the first attempt. I scraped away the snow, and revealed the familiar foliage; next minute I was digging like a badger, until the whole plant was exposed. And not one single capsule did it bear! There was nothing for it then but to try the cliff, perilous though it might be. So I climbed the first fang on the ridge and slipped down into the next hollow, at the base of the sabre tooth, beneath whose contumelious lip slept Rose of Kaso.

Although the whole face was snowbound, I knew exactly where to take off for the traverse. A deep groove or chute was cut diagonally across the face, from the root of the sabre tooth, at a steady angle; a thousand feet below, it was broken across by an escarpment, where the snow ceased. The dark rock showed up harshly.

It was impossible to descend into the chute from above because at its head it was lined with tilted paving-stones. But the far side, though steep, was well covered with scrub Rhododendron, and therefore both safe and easy; it was this bank which I had ascended in June to the foot of the cliff, working my way along to the ridge again above the sabre. This was tricky, but not dangerous—in June; even the chute itself, once you were in it, offered no obstacle to a cautious climber.

Now everything was changed. Every pitfall hidden under that dread mantle of snow, which lay at a dangerous angle, was doubly accentuated; and the task had suddenly assumed a fearful aspect. What was the condition of that snow? Was it soft and cloying, ready to slip with increasing momentum down the long chute to where the precipice gaped? Or was it frozen so hard that, without an axe, I could not cut steps by which to cross? The more I looked at it, the less I liked it; to make matters worse, it was blowing hard from the north again, and the air was once more filled with whirling flakes. If I hesitated any longer I was lost from sheer terror; so I took the plunge, thankful that the whole ghastly business would soon be over, anyhow.

To reach the lip of the chute, I had first of all to cross a belt of scrub Rhododendron; and if that had been difficult in the summer, it was infinitely more so now. Before I had progressed ten yards, my mits had been torn to shreds, the cold chisel-like branches had lacerated hands and face, and more than one wad of snow had found its way down my neck. However, I got through the tangle at last, and stood shivering on the brink of the chute, not with cold, but with fear. That sleek white slant filled me with an indefinable dread; but when at last I dropped on to it I found a firm crust of refrozen snow overlying puffy snow in which my heavy nailed boots could kick deep holes

Immediately confidence returned. I had only to cross twelve or fifteen yards. The cairn I had so laboriously built over the Rose was not visible, but I reckoned I must be almost opposite it; and I directed my steps slightly upwards and across the chute, kicking deep holes for each foot before venturing on another step. Now I felt the want of an ice-axe to steady me. Glancing down the slope, I shuddered; there was no comfort to be got out of that view, so I kept my gaze firmly fixed on the opposite bank.

Half-way across I had to dig my hands into the snow above to increase my grip, and lean back against the slope with the whole weight of my body, so steep was it. Even then I was standing almost upright. Probably it was this which caused the next incident. Or perhaps my foot slipped. I have no certain recollection of what happened. Anyhow, I slipped. Then things happened swiftly. I gave one squawk of fright, and the next second was flying down the slope at a horrible speed, enveloped in a cloud of snow. I shot down for twenty or thirty yards, and then came to rest, mercifully. It seemed a miracle; but I was hardly in the mood to appreciate miracles just then. In fact I was badly shaken. Besides, I was still in the gulley. To go back was as bad as to go on; worse perhaps. So, having rested a minute, and recovered my morale, I continued across the chute, and reaching the far bank, thankfully plunged my arms elbow deep into the snow and grasped the firm branches of Rhododendron which I knew lay beneath.

Meanwhile I had lost my bearings, and search as I would, not a sign of my cairn could I see; it was in fact completely buried under the snow. To find the Rose under these conditions was well-nigh hopeless—three or four plants amongst thousands, and all invisible. I soon gave up the search and started for the ridge; for indeed I was unnerved, and anxious to reach the safety of the ridge, now almost a thousand feet above me. As I kicked my way up towards the ridge, sinking knee deep at each step, what should I do but tread right on and thereby expose a solitary bush! This was sheer good luck, and moreover I found two good capsules. But although I spent half an hour dredging round this spot for more treasure, not another capsule could I find. The cold then compelled me to abandon the search; indeed my fingers were beginning to show signs of possible frostbite, and all feeling had left my toes. The climb up to the ridge, above the sabre tooth, was arduous; and if any question yet remained of climbing higher, here was the complete answer to it. Even on the windswept ridge, the snow was two feet deep, and on the flank I was sinking in up to my knees. No bushes were visible. A flock of Tibetan sand grouse were whistling not far from me; apart from that a grim and awful silence reigned here, 13,000 feet above sea level; even the wind had ceased, and the pearl-grey mist hung motionless round the peaks. Below lay a heap of torn and ragged cloud.

The descent of the sabre tooth, never easy, was made more difficult by the deep snow. On the rock ledges of the northern face I found several frozen plants of the creepy 'Cephalanthum' (*Rhododendron crebreflorum*), but all the capsules had aborted, and I got no seed. I reached the bottom of the sabre, went on down the ridge and over the next fang to where the snow had been spun off, and stopped to consider the position. It was late, and I must start back for the cave, or I should be benighted in the forest. My hands were torn and bleeding; I was dreadfully thirsty, but neither hungry, nor particularly cold now; only rather tired, and terribly disappointed. *Rhododendron crebreflorum* had been lost, and so had *R. pumilum*; Rose of Kaso, Rock Rose, and *Nomocharis aperta* had been barely secured, and the same probably applied to *P. Clutterbuckii* and *P. deleiensis*, which anyway were rare plants.

On the other hand, I had got the carmine *R. Smithii*—all there was of it, and Glowbell and *R. lanatum*, besides other things. Yet I felt that nothing would compensate for the loss of the creepy 'Cephalanthum.' It was no good claiming that I had got this and got that if I went away from the Mishmi Hills without it. Why, the plant was growing within half a mile of me at that moment! In the years to come, I would never be able to look a Mishmi plant in the face, all spick and span in an English garden, without hating myself for a deserter if I abandoned it. But what was to be done? Nothing —now! I turned my tired eyes towards the valley, and as I did so I saw a wonderful vision. Beyond the nearest ridges, the whole horizon was slowly turning porcelain blue, and on this faint sea floated the dark keels of ships with all canvas spread. Even as I looked, the ghostly scene changed. An ethereal milk-white mist was gradually dissolving like silver from a photographic plate, and the picture was coming into strong relief-mountains, glazed on the deepending blue of the sky! It was God's sign that the storm was over. Weary days were ahead; hours of toil and effort, of rage and despair, moments of triumph; but always my thoughts came back to that vision, which comforted me a lot. Who could ever forget it, up there on that bitter storm-swept ridge, during the lull, when at long last the veil was torn aside and all the mountains appeared in white apparel beneath the turquoise dome of heaven!

I went on down the ridge slowly, collecting seeds. One by one I reached the familiar places—Iris Cliff, Primula Rock, and at last the Lookout. Dusk had fallen; but the view of Kaso on the one side, and the row of mountains across the Delei on the other, was superb. At each familiar place I stopped, and looked around me a little sadly. Never would I see them again! Wreathed in flowers, swamped in mist, dripping and chilling, they were yet dear. I tramped on, climbed down under the Water Cliff and up to Buttercup's Well—and at nightfall reached the Rocks. Here I found my men, sitting beside a good fire; a bed of leaves had been prepared for me and there was room to stretch myself out, well protected from the rain. But there was no rain; the mist had gone, and the gunmetal sky was riddled with diamond splinters. So I made myself some pemmican and sorted my collections before lying down.

As the dawn brightened, the mountains across the valley sharpened into black and white teeth set against the luminous blue of the sky. We made an early start, and by the time we emerged from the forest—going slowly, for I had to collect many seeds—the sun was up and was warming us. The whole valley, with Kaso enthroned above, was steeped in sunshine; and by the time we reached the village it was hot. A Mishmi met us, and invited me to his hut. He was quite friendly, because he wanted to sell me a chicken, which I was eager to buy. Then we hurried on down the valley, marching all day, and at nightfall we reached a village only a few miles from Meiliang Camp, and halted again. Early next morning I rejoined Buttercup in time for breakfast. His news was good. Friendlies from Minutang had arrived two days ago to take us right through to Denning without fuss; but as they had waited two days for us, Buttercup thought we ought to start at once, or they might disperse to their villages again. I heartily agreed, and we arranged to start next day, October 23. Immediately we began sorting and packing seeds, and drying sodden bundles of capsules in the warm sunshine. By evening camp was dismantled and everything was ready for the journey home.

18   The Last Round

IT was a gorgeous day, the deep-blue sky almost cloudless; so warm was it in the sunshine that the thinnest summer clothing—shorts and a cotton shirt—sufficed. Polon was perfectly clear, and seemed to have little snow on it, but of course, we were looking at the south-west face, which moreover is sheer. How I wished I was up there. And then in an instant I had formed a resolution. One more round! Why not? By Jove, I would go; silly of me not to have thought of that before! The weather was set fair for ten days at least, surely! I told Buttercup my plan at tea-time, and he agreed. We would start together next day, he going down the valley with the loads, stage by stage, I with my two Mishmis going up to the cave on Polon. After my dash to the top I would descend the other side to Minutang, and on to the Lohit. Polon would need four days; on the fifth or sixth day I would reach the bridge and probably meet Buttercup there. He had to do four marches to the bridge, and I expected him to be held up a day at Minutang, and perhaps a day at the bridge. So that was settled.

On October 22 we struck camp and started together up the mountain. It was hot, and we were glad to reach shade on the ridge. There were seeds to collect and Calanthes to dig up here, and then we parted, Buttercup to traverse round the shoulder of the mountain, me to continue up the spur to our lately abandoned camp, which we reached about three. The Mishmis made one of the shelters comfortable for me, and we lit fires: but there was no water except a little from a pool, the colour of coffee. After collecting some seeds, I sat up on the lookout rock as we had so often sat there before, looking across the mountains. It was a radiant evening. Every ridge and peak showed up clearly, receding into the distance till the last range ducked below the curve of the world. Puffs of cloud floated lightly in the southwest, reddening as the sun went down, and you felt that you could actually see the plains, though all you could really see was the last hill range between us and the plains. The air was so still that the rumble of the shrunken river, 7,000 feet below, could be heard distinctly.

The air was quite sharp even in the forest, after dark, and I was glad of a fire to sleep by. But I was warm and dry. The stars shone brightly, and I lay on my back watching them hide and peep amongst the leaves of the trees as they marched majestically across the meridian and slid swiftly down into the west.

It was barely light when we were astir. After breakfast we started up the ridge; for the last time, I thought to myself. We passed the old familiar landmarks, and our own handiwork—the path we had cut—and halted on the alpine top where I had cached the water-bottle. To my surprise, the top of Polon was swathed in mist, and above the Dou valley, clouds clung to the range; but the hard rim they had possessed yesterday was blurred. Before ever we reached the cave, the sun was hidden, and all the country below us was enveloped in a greasy whiteness. Even then I was not seriously alarmed.

The steep glens which scar the flank of Polon are filled with a thick scrub of Rhododendron; and scrambling up a sort of stone stairway, now dry, I shook seed from the gaping capsules. Higher up I found a rare pool of water under the shadow of a rock, and on the bald granite, staring into the south, lay mats of the dazzling blue *Gentiana setulosa*. I ascended to where the Gamboge Primula grew beneath the Rhododendron bushes, and dug up some plants, besides collecting seed.

The short harsh dusk was falling as I turned back to camp. Peering down the steep rockway which cleft a passage through the forest, I noticed that a thin mist had separated out, completely obscuring the valley. The ghostly masts of derelict trees rose above the waves, and I shivered. The sharp edge of the Winter air had been turned; it no longer cut the flesh cleanly; it scratched.

The cave, though small, was comfortable and warm. I found the biscuits and pemmican which I had cached here, had supper, and went to bed—that is to say, I took my boots and coat off, changed my socks, and lay down under my blanket. But I did not go to sleep. From the ledge on which we lay the mountain-side dropped so steeply that we could see over the heads of the near trees far down into the Dou valley. As the night advanced the mist thickened. In the rising wind the dead plants on the ledge chaffered together and the creaking Bamboos made ghostly sounds. Not a star was visible. Hour after hour I watched. If I dozed it was only to dream horribly, and I would come to with a start, to see the dead white mist all round me; it gave me a choking sensation. Towards morning I dozed for the last time. When I came to again, the stars were shining in a clear sky, and almost immediately I fell into a dreamless sleep.

At seven o'clock Hubble and I were climbing the steep path which slanted up towards the ridge. Traversing across the wooded face, amongst the stiffened Rhododendrons, we reached the open, where in Spring the snow-water splashes down the rock into its appointed glen. A steeper climb across the slotheads brought us to the crest, and the first snow; and the view opened out.

A heavy mist lay in the Dou valley; but already it had begun to heave; in an hour or two it would be upon us. Kaso was completely hidden; so also was the ridge. As for Polon, though it was so close, I could not tell in which direction to look for it. Rounding a shoulder, we found ourselves on crisp snow and a few minutes later, the top of Polon stood revealed. Huddled together on the cliffs were Rhododendrons of several species, and on the sheltered flank they formed the usual impenetrable thickets. The talus slopes below were covered with thousands of plants of the Gamboge Primula, its jagged leaves now limp and yellow. There were also scattered plants of *P. apoclita*, of which I secured a little seed. Ascending a steep snowy glen, we reached the summit of the lower peak, a wilderness of loose rocks under a foot of snow. Searching amongst the dwarf Rhododendrons which stuck out here and there, I found a colony of the pink 'Cephalanthum', *R. crebreflorum*, and devoted an hour to collecting seed of it; but the cliffs were so steep and slippery that I was glad when this hazardous work was done. I had found perhaps twenty capsules, nor could I discover any more, search as I would. Rose of Kaso, too, though it must grow here, eluded me. When the alpine Rhododendrons are in flower, one can pick them out a hundred yards off, even on a dull day; especially a plant like Rose of Kaso, with flowers of so rare a colour. But sweep away the flowers, and what chance is there of picking out any but the commonest species from amongst that mob! Add to that snow, covering perhaps four-fifths of the alpine region, and the task becomes almost hopeless; and mist to that, and everything, including life itself becomes a gamble. Mist, on an unknown mountain, is the climber's worst foe; and all the time I was searching for these dwarf Rhododendrons, the mist was slowly but surely creeping upon us.

When we first reached this summit, I could see the curving ridge by which we had ascended, across the wide valley. We had come round on the outside; I proposed to retire along internal lines, that is to say, straight across the valley, in order to vary our hunting-ground. Now I could no longer see the ridge, but my sense of direction, which is luckily acute, told me where it lay. Mist was pouring into the valley over several gaps as we withdrew; but we found a way down, and collected the dangling coral-red peardrops of dwarf Barberry, and the rosy-cheeked yellow flasks of dwarf Rose as we went. One hardly expected to see flowers here: and yet the piercing blue of *Gentiana setulifolia* gleamed bleakly from many a dull stone!

Delayed by our search for seeds, the mist was on us long before we reached the crest of the ridge: and unable to see where we were going we had to guess the best route and soon found ourselves trapped amongst the frozen Rhododendron bushes. At last, after a struggle, we reached the crest of the ridge. On the far side lay a meadow, which I recognised as the Maroon Primula meadow—or thought I did; but a violent snowstorm was now raging, which further hampered us. Visibility was reduced to twenty or thirty yards; and on an unknown mountain that is not much use. We hurried down the open slope, and though I could not find a single recognisable landmark I thought this might possibly be due to the snow. Efforts to discover our exact whereabouts proving fruitless, we plunged down a rock gulley, hoping to strike the path obliquely lower down; the alternative being to sit still and do nothing. In this crisis Hubble was useless, as he had never been here before; but he bore up well. After descending the gulley for a thousand feet, not without difficulty, and finding that it grew steeper and steeper as it plunged into the forest, I realised that we must be right off the track. Indeed we were making straight for the Dou valley! So we scrambled up again, finding the snow-covered rocks painfully cold and slippery. Just as we regained the top, the snowstorm ceased, and the loaded sky having discharged its first missile, the air cleared somewhat. But the mountains were now all white again, and the clouds so low, that it seemed doubtful at first whether we should derive much advantage from the improved visibility. However, the lynx-eyed Hubble, who was in the lead, now shouted to me that he could see the end of the path; and when I reached his side, he pointed away to our left, over the next rise and across the next meadow. We had indeed struck the ridge a little too high up, beyond the end of the path, which we thus never could have crossed, since parallel straight lines never meet! It was cold comfort to reflect that had it not begun to snow at that minute, we would never have wandered and strayed like lost sheep.

It was one thing to see the path in the distance, another to get there across a steep scrub-and-snow-covered mountainside. Sliding down the slippery rocks, pushing through the wiry scrub, ducking amongst wet bushes, we reached it at last; not before I had collected more seed of *Primula mishmiensis* and the red 'Sikkimensis'. Half an hour later we were back in the cave, glad to sit round a good fire.

It was my intention to climb Polon again the following day if the weather were fine and to search once more for Rose of Kaso, Meconopsis, and anything else which might turn up. But a fine day was essential; it would be not only futile, but dangerous to climb Polon in thick weather. It was no use tramping about the snow-field looking hopefully for dwarf Rhododendrons which were under the snow, more especially since I had not been on the mountain in June, and therefore did not know where anything grew. In fine weather, I could direct my search towards likely-looking places, where there was not much snow, and would be sure to find something; but in thick weather I would merely lose myself, as we had already done once, and in all probability fall over a cliff.

During the night, the mist thickened, and spread. We awoke at an early hour, to hear a steady drip, drip from the Fir-trees, and to see the Bamboos glistening with raindrops. The woolly sky wept softly, the peaks were veiled, and snow was falling on Polon. The game was up. The last round had been fought.

The storm lasted a week. When it was over snow lay deep on the Mishmi Hills, and all alpines were buried for seven months!

The descent of the ridge to our old camp took nearly four hours, as I was collecting seeds the whole way. I collected especially ample seed of the big-leafed *Rhododendron exasperatum*; for though I had previously collected it in 1926, now that I had seen it in flower a second gathering seemed desirable. Even in the Winter it looked a magnificent shrub; nor had it closed its handsome leaves.

We reached the old camp soaked through, and halted for a quick meal. I noticed that the grove of *Magnolia Campbellii* here was in full green leaf (October 24th), the flower-buds exactly the same as a month ago. Instead of descending the north ridge towards Meiliang Camp we now went down the south ridge towards Minutang. How often we had looked over this side from the crest of the ridge! I had even descended it a thousand feet. One slope was forested to the very top. Then the forest ceased abruptly, and the other slope was clothed with Bracken, and scattered bushes, but the forest began again, even on this slope, a little lower down. On the edge of the forest *Rhododendron megacalyx* and *R. Lindleyi* were both conspicuous, and a species of some Araliaceous plant, with tall spikes of cream-coloured flowers, followed by black berries. Farther down I noticed a magnificent tree of *Magnolia rostrata*, in full foliage, bristling with bright red pineapples. It might have been some giant Tritoma, so fiery and erect were they amongst the still green leaves; also several old and gnarled trees of *Rhododendron sidereum*. There were big clearings for Teeta here. On the grass slope, fat bushes of *Gaultheria Hookeri*, their stems bulging with bluish-white berries, were common, and so also was *Gaultheria Wardii* with black berries. Lower down, *Rhododendron arboreum* and *R. stenaulum* appeared, in the bottom stratum of temperate forest. Spruce died out: we reached more grassy slopes, and cultivation began. At last we came to the hostile village of Mitonma, where I supposed we were going to halt. But my Mishmis thought it would be tactless to halt here, so we pushed on. A deep ravine, drawing its waters from Polon and from Atsin, still separated us from Minutang. It was farther than it looked, and the steep rough climb up the far side proved almost too much for me. In the end we had to halt at a village two miles short of Minutang, because it was pitch dark. We had been marching ten hours, and I for one had had enough.

Continuing our march early next morning, we reached Minutang in half an hour. Here I was given a note from Buttercup saying that he had gone on two days ago with all hands. He had secured coolies right through to Denning, and had not wasted a day. He was forging steadily ahead, march by march, with the thirty-five coolies under his command, making all necessary arrangements, and being entirely responsible for everything. What an immense comfort he was, I reflected! Not only the most delightful and uncomplaining companion, but absolutely reliable. I had only to ask him to do a thing, and he carried it out straightway, without fuss or words; and I knew that it would be well done, too. Yet perhaps his most valuable services, as quartermaster, had been those due to his own initiative and suggestions.

With the note Buttercup had left some stores, of which I was greatly in need—nothing elaborate, because on a forced march there is not much time for cooking, but just what was required, viz. a tin of pemmican, a tin of biscuits, a tin of *café-au-lait*.

We now bent our minds and legs to speed, in the hope of catching Buttercup at the bridge; though his arrangements were evidently working so smoothly that there seemed little likelihood of his being held up there either, and he was two marches ahead.

We dropped quickly down into the river-bed, and began the long weary trudge over the boulders, up and down the cliffs by the monkey-path, swinging and clawing and climbing along. The morning was fine and hot, and when we got into the full flood of sunshine on the shingle bank, I would dearly have liked to bask for an hour and laze about. For the first time for months I felt comfortable and warm. We were back in the subtropical zone, amidst trees and birds and flowers! No more cold! But this feeling of comfort and well-being was short-lived! For as the sun rose higher, it grew unbearably hot in the gorge, and in my warm clothing, with a considerable weight on my back, I began to loathe the heat and bother of it all! "Very well," said the Gods on Olympus. "You asked for it, and we gave it to you. If you don't like it, you need not have it." Slowly the clouds rolled up. The sun was obscured; and just as we reached our old half-way camping-ground on the sandbank, it began to rain steadily.

We halted here for a meal. Over the rocks from the direction of the bridge came a file of coolies, who presently joined us. They were some of Buttercup's men returning to Minutang from the Lohit, where they had been replaced by the local riff-raff. They brought me another note, written that morning just as Buttercup was leaving the bridge, saying that all was well and that he would camp on the sandbank by the fishing-pool in the Lohit that night.

All that afternoon we slogged over the wet rocks in steady rain. I was beginning to feel the strain of the last fortnight, and derived no pleasure from the scenery. The light had gone out of the sky. The jungle was just a wet beastliness; the mountains represented an endless penance; the thundering river was nothing but an obstacle—though I did not forget that it was also the one kinetic thing, trying to divest itself of the tyranny of imprisonment, and that it led to the plains and freedom. In this grey mood I tramped on hour after hour, till I was ready to drop. Whether we could reach the bridge or not that night all depended on whether we could traverse a dangerous section of cliff before dark. Unless we reached the cliff with at least half an hour of daylight to spare we might as well camp now. However, by the time I reached the foot of the cliff, the others had gone on, and though it appeared to me that dusk was imminent, I had perforce to follow. Dusk did indeed descend upon us while we were scrambling desperately along the ledge, high up on the rock face, but the only hope of salvation lay in going on as fast as possible. I was terrified. The rain made the rock dangerously slippery, and in one place had completely washed away the earth sill on which we relied for foothold, exposing the naked rock. Down below the river skidded violently on a corner, and the noise coming up out of the gloom filled us with alarm. Here we had to swing and jump, holding on to such roots and branches as we could find, all slippery with rain. A long stride round a wicked-looking rock, a scramble and drop over a fallen tree, and the worst was over. It was dark by the time the last danger lay behind us, and we slid exhausted down the cliff on to the boulder-strewn beach once more. From here to the bridge was not far, but in pouring rain and utter darkness it proved a tough business to tired men. We had half a mind to camp, and certainly would have done so had the night been fine. As it was we decided to go to the village. If the last half-mile in the river-bed had been difficult, the climb up the steep bank to the village on the terrace was worse. What glimmer of light we had obtained from the foam on the river was utterly lacking in the forest, and the path seemed to be made of butter. However, at 8 p.m. we reached the village, and entering the first hut, tore off our soaked clothing, and sagged down on the floor. Buttercup and I had often agreed that from Minutang to the bridge was a decent day's march for a Mishmi not carrying a load; but I had never contemplated doing it in the rain. Besides we had actually started the other side of Minutang; nor am I a Mishmi.

Next morning we awoke to the most familiar scene the North-East Frontier of India has to offer. Clouds muffled the tops of the hills, and a pearl haze of rain filled the Lohit valley! I decided to rest a day, and spent a couple of hours sorting a miscellaneous collection of soggy fruits and seeds, gathered during this hurried retreat, and stuffed into every jacket pocket and bag available. Half-way through the morning I changed my mind and decided to push on by forced marches again. The sooner this sort of discomfort was over the better. Wet through all day, lying on the hard floor or harder ground at night, shivering under a blanket and more than a little anxious about the condition of my collections, I felt that the wisest course was to go all out for Theronliang bungalow and administered territory.

It was too late to do a double march, but I had gained one march on Buttercup, and he might decide to halt a day at the fishing-pool. Had it been fine, he certainly would have. But except that he had Luso to cook his meals he was really no better off than I was, and no less anxious to reach Theronliang.

Marching hard all that day, in spite of swollen torrents which had to be crossed by rope, and a slippery path, we reached the sandbank at dusk. There were any number of Bamboo shelters here, and from the fresh

Banana leaves on the roof and the embers of several fires it was plain that Buttercup's party had only quitted the place that morning; he was still a day's march ahead. Buttercup then would reach Theronliang the following day: could we? He would be camping on the path at the turn of the river even now; on the morrow he would cross the spur into the Tidding valley, and reach Theronliang the same afternoon.

I slept better that night, though the sand was hard, but we were up early on October 29 for the last march, as it proved. The sky was still leaden, and it drizzled, weakly but wetly. Six hours' hard marching brought us to the Tidding river in the afternoon, and we saw the clouds smoking on the last range which separated us from the plain of Assam. It was not a day to halt, so we struggled on over the boulders, and when we came to the big slip we lost the path entirely. There was no remedy but to scramble up the cliff, and this we proceeded to do; but it proved more difficult and dangerous than it looked. There seemed to be neither safe handhold nor foothold, and high up on the peeled face, with a terrible drop into the violent river below, while reaching out to grasp a root with both hands, and with only one foot in place, I suddenly became dizzy. For a minute, which stretched into eternity and back again, I hung there, unable either to advance or retreat, and not at all sure that I could hold on. Hubble was above me, seeking a way, and the *Gam* of Meiliang was below. I called out miserably and desperately to Hubble to fix a rope on the face for me, and acting promptly, he cut a creeper, tied one end to a tree and dropped the other to me. With an effort I collected my wits, and laying hold of the rope with both hands hauled myself up to find that I had reached the top; then I suddenly felt very sick.

After that episode, we found the path and descended to the river again. Then came mile after mile through the jungle, mostly ankle deep in water, for the whole valley was flooded. At last, tired, soaked to the skin again, and caked with mud we reached the suspension bridge on the edge of administered territory; and a mile post informed me that we were seventy-six miles from Sadiya. What was more important at the moment, Theronliang bungalow was only a mile away. History was repeating itself almost word for word; this might have been 1926 over again. It was dark now, and the whole thing seemed to be a reproduction of my experience two years before, when we had sat down exhausted at the bridge, having come from the Delei river in two days!

We went on, and presently the lights of Theronliang twinkled through the trees. I shouted, but the river made so much noise it was impossible for anyone to hear. We crossed the last torrent, scrambled up the far bank, and I stamped into the bungalow with a "Come aboard, sir!" Buttercup, who had arrived two hours ago, was as delighted to see me as I was to see him; but he was hardly as surprised as I had hoped. He admitted he had not quite expected me that night, but he felt that there was always a chance of my turning up. As for me, I regarded the forced marches which had brought us from the cave on Polon to Theronliang in four days as pretty good going! When I walked in upon Buttercup, he was unwrapping and spreading out the packets of Rhododendron capsules. We exchanged news, opened our mail, and made final plans for a quick march to Sadiya. We both voted to rest next day, partly because we wanted to dry the fruit and seed collection, and partly because we were both tired; at least I was. To make up for this, we would do a double march straight through to Denning on the 31st.

We purchased a chicken, and Luso gave us a good dinner that night— better than anything we had had for some time at any rate; but we could nor really indulge ourselves until we reached Denning.

Next morning we telephoned through to Sadiya and heard the voice of the Political Officer faintly telling us what he could do to help us. The Digaru river was so swollen as to be impassable for caro which in the dry weather plough through it. Until the rains definitely ceased it could not be bridged. Therefore, we must march from Denning to the Digaru, cross by canoe, and the Political Officer would meet us on the other side.

The day dragged, but we had a good deal to do. In the afternoon the sun shone for an hour, but the Mishmi Hills were always swaddled in cloud. The twenty-four mile march to Denning with the long pull up to the Tidding saddle, and a halt at the windy bungalow of Drei to dry our clothes and have lunch proved boring. It was our last meal off nothing, so to speak. Then down, down, down, like Alice, until when we had but five more miles to do, the clouds rolled back, the bright afternoon sun shone out, and the green forest looked sweet and clean once more.

We reached Denning with all our coolies late in the afternoon, and went straight to the canteen. Then followed a general clean up, and next morning we looked more presentable. There came a great paying off of coolies and giving of rewards to headmen who had stood by us, not forgetting special presents to the *Gam* of Meiliang who had accompanied me on the last two climbs. Nearly all the Mishmis were walking to Sadiya to spend their earnings and see life; and we parted good friends.

At what point can a travel book most conveniently end ? More precisely, at what point should this one end ? Some may say at Theronliang, where we crossed the 'inner line' into administered territory! Others, at Denning Post, where we found ourselves under the protection of sepoy bayonets, and on the cart-road. Others again, at Sadiya, where we dined and played tennis with our fellow-countrymen after eight months' absence! One seeks above all things to avoid an anticlimax. Let us, therefore, end as soon as we have exchanged a tramp's life for the trappings of Western civilisation; and that was at Sadiya. The Political Officer drove out to the Digaru river on November 1, and brought us in the same afternoon; and that evening we put on the solemn garb of British respectability, 'short coat and black tie' as your hostess informs you, leniently.

The time has come to say good-bye to the Mishmi Hills, and to plant hunting. I had only one more duty to perform, a sad one; and I cannot end this book on a more final note than that which struck a few days later, when I went across the Lohit with Buttercup to see him into the train for Calcutta and Home. As I wished him God-speed, I realised that the expedition was indeed over. Staunch, brave, patient, and competent, no man ever had a better companion. Throughout all those months of discomfort, anxiety, and stress, no harsh word, no reproach had passed his lips. It seemed right that, as I returned to Sadiya alone, the Mishmi Hills should be veiled in deep mourning too.

Appendix

THE following hardy plants are known to be in cultivation; others may be. Seed of these numbers was collected mainly on the two expeditions here described; but for the convenience of those who are interested in growing my plants, I have added the names of some, recently identified, collected in Tibet in 1924 within the same general area (see Map 2.). So numerous are the species of Rhododendron and Primula that only new or rare plants have been included. With few exceptions, plants not yet named, even though in cultivation, have been omitted. For the identifications I am indebted chiefly to Mr C. B. V. Marquand, Mr C. E. C. Fischer, and Mr H. K. A. Shaw, of the Royal Botanic Gardens, Kew, and to Professor W. Wright Smith, M.A., and Mr H. F. Tagg, of the Royal Botanic Gardens, Edinburgh. Royal Horticultural Society awards are indicated thus: F.C.C.= First Class Certificate; A.M.= Award of Merit. It must however be understood that the majority of plants here listed have not yet flowered in this country. New species discoverd by the writer (when named) are in heavy type.

F.K.W.

K.W. Number	Name
7634	Abies sp.
5832	Acer caudatum, Wall. var. ukurunduense.
7265	„ sikkimense, Miq.
8215	„ Wardii, W. W. Sm.
8647	„ Forrestii, Diels.
8722	„ Campbellii, Hook. f. et Thomas.
8724	Aconitum sp.
8690	Actinidia sp.
6370	Aeschynanthus bracteata, Wall. } Not hardy.
6377	„ levipes, C. B. Clarke. }
8334	Anemone polyanthes, Don.
8565	Androsace Henryi, Oliv.
6365	Arisaema sp.
6768	Begonia sp. nov. [Also No. 7432.]
5773	Berberis sp. nov.
5936	„ Silva-Taroucana, Schn.

K.W.　　　　　　　　　　　*Name*
Number

5962　Berberis aristata, (?) D.C.
6308　　,,　　pruinrosa, (?) Franch.
6326　　,,　　concinna, Hook. f.
6787　　,,　　**hypokerina**, Shaw. ('Silver Barberry.')
8350　　,,　　sp. nov.
7637　Betula sp. (Red Birch.)
6372　Buddleia candida, Dunn.
8559　　,,　　sp. nov.

6267　Caragana jubata, Poir.
5663　Cassiope selaginoides, Hook. f. et Thomas, A.M. 1928.
8462　Chirita sp. nov.
7761　Chloranthus brachystachyus, Bl.
6290 ⎱
7607 ⎰ Clematis urophylla, Franch.
6803　　,,　　napaulensis, D.C.
6883　　,,　　vitifolia, Wall.
7615　　,,　　**biternifolia**, Shaw.
6371　Codonopsis cordifolia, Kom.
6299　Cotoneaster sp.
6400　　　,,　　　,,
5949　Cyananthus lobatus, Wall.
6082　　,,　　**Wardii**, Marquand.
6382　Cydonia sp. (Quince.)

8649　Dactylicapnos scandens, Hutch.
6393　Deutzia sp.

8024　Gaultheria sp. nov.
8725　　,,　　**Wardii**, Marquand et Shaw.
8562　　,,　　sp.
6221　Gentiana Waltonii.
　　　Geranium sp.

8483　Hedychium sp.
7224　Hypericum sp.
8444　　,,　　patulum, Thunb. (variety).

5623　Incarvillea sp.
5719　Iris sp. nov.
5783　　,,　　Clarkei, Baker.
6289　　,,　　sp. nov.
6917　　,,　　sp. nov.
7063　　,,　　sp.

| K.W. | Name |
| Number | |

8180 **Leycesteria** ('Goldon Leycesteria') **crocothyrsos**, Shaw.

5688 Lonicera setifera, Franch.

5753   „   litangensis, Batal.

5775   „   tricopoda, Franch.

5822   „   Webbiana, Wall. [Also No. 7113.]

5918   „   cyanocarpa, Franch.

5872   „   „   „ var. porphyrantha.

5988   „   hispida, Pall. [Also No. 7539?]

6106   „   ovalis, Batal.

7118   „   **tsarongensis**, Shaw.

7510   „   sp.

8574 Lysimachia ramosa.

7628 Magnolia rostrata, W. W. Sm.

7745 Manglietia insignis, Blume.

6862 Meconopsis betonicifolia, Franch. var. Baileyi. [Also No. 5784. A.M. 1926, F.C.C. 1927. Gold Medal, Ghent, 1928. 'Tibetan Blue Poppy.']

6974   „   **ruba**, Ward.

            „   **violacea**, Ward.

5809 Nomocharis nana, E. H. Wilson. [Also No. 6976.]

7006   „   sp. nov. ? [Also No. 8370.]

8399   „   aperta, W. W. Sm. et W. E. Evans.

6821 Omphalogramma Souliei, Franch. A.M. 1929. [Also No. 8234.]

8187 Piptanthus sp.

8096 Pittosporum floribundum, W. and A.

6975 Primula apoclita, Balf. f. et Forrest. [Also No. 8406.]

5664   „   atrodentata, W. W. Sm.

5985   „   **Baileyana**, Ward. A.M. 1926.

5741   „   **Cawdoriana**, Ward. A.M. 1926.

8235   „   **Clutterbuckii**, Ward.

6981   „   cyanantha, Balf. f. et Forrest.

8381   „   **deleiensis**, Ward.

6822   „   eucyclia, W. W. Sm. et Forrest. A.M. 1930.

5781   „   **Florindæ**, Ward. F.C.C. 1926. ('Giant Cowslip Primula.')

5819   „   **latisecta**, W. W. Sm.

5972   „   Maximowiczii, Regel.

6901   „   **melanodonta**, W. W. Sm.

6117   „   microdonta, Franch.

5746   „   „   „ var. alpicola. A.M. 1927. ('Moonlight Primula.')

K.W.	*Name*

Number

5818 Primula microdonta, Franch. var. alpicola purpurea. A.M. 1926.
5858   ,,   **Morsheadiana,** Ward. ('Golden Primula.')
8295   ,,   **Normaniana,** Ward.
5745   ,,   **ninguida,** W. W. Sm. A.M. 1927.
4911   ,,   nivalis, ? A.M. 1925.
8388   ,,   **polonensis,** Ward.
6430   ,,   prionotes, Balf. f. et Watt.
5096   ,,   pudibunda, W. W. Sm.
8380   ,,   **rubra,** Ward. ('Maroon Meadow Primula.')
8346   ,,   septemloba, Franch. (variety).
5739   ,,   tibetica, Watt.
6094   ,,   Waltoni, Watt. ('Ruby Primula.')
8319 Prunus sp.
5806   ,,   cinerascens, Franch.
6851 Pryus sp. nov.
8657   ,,   sp.
6851   ,,   Harrowianus, Balf. f. et W. W. Sm.

7101 Rheum sp. ('Giant Rhubarb.')
6818 Rhododendron arizelum, Balf. f. et Forrest. [Also Nos. 5877, 8163.]
7108   ,,   brevistylum, Franch.
6984   ,,   **calciphila,** Hutch. et Ward. ('Limestone Rose.')
6923   ,,   **cerasinum,** Tagg. ('Cherry Brandy.' Also Nos. 5830, 8258, 'Coals-of-Fire.')
7455   ,,   **chrysolepis,** Hutch. et Ward.
8289   ,,   coelicum, Balf. f. et Farrer. ('Glowbell.')
8227   ,,   **concinnoides,** Hutch. et Ward.
8337   ,,   **crebreflorum,** Hutch. et Ward.
8164   ,,   crinigerum, Franch. [Also No. 7123.]
5843   ,,   **curvistylum,** Hutch. et Ward.
8165   ,,   **deleiense,** Hutch. et Ward.
5863   ,,   **doshongense,** Tagg.
6900   ,,   eclecteum, Balf. f. et Forrest (variety). [Also Nos. 6920, 6921, 6922, 6936.]
8250   ,,   **exasperatum,** Tagg. [Also No. 6855.]
7327   ,,   **facetum,** Balf. f. et Ward.
6313   ,,   **flavantherum,** Hutch. et Ward.
5734   ,,   **fragariflorum,** Ward. ('Strawberry Saluenense.')
8300   ,,   fulvoides, Balf. f. et Forrest
5659   ,,   **hirtipes,** Tagg.
6991   ,,   horæum, Balf. f. et Forrest.
6884   ,,   **imperator,** Hutch. et Ward. ('Purple Emperor.')

K.W. Number		Name
6735	,,	**insculptum**, Hutch. et Ward.
8522	,,	**kasoense**, Hutch. et Ward. [Also No. 8700.]
8288	,,	lanatum, Hook. f. (variety).
8251	,,	**lanigerum**, Tagg.
6273	,,	**leucaspis**, Tagg. A.M. 1929.
7724	,,	Macabeanum, Watt.
6781	,,	**megacalyx**, Balf. f. et Ward. [Also Nos. 6286, 8205.]
8225	,,	megeratum, Balf. f. et Forrest. [Also No. 6819.]
7058	,,	microphyllum. [Also No. 7001.]
8113	,,	**mishmiense**, Hutch. et Ward.
6279	,,	oleifolium, Franch. A.M. 1927.
8260	,,	**patulum**, Hutch. et Ward. ('Rock Rose.')
6924	,,	**pruniflorum**, Hutch. et Ward. [Also Nos. 7188, 8257.]
6961	,,	pumilum, Hook. f. ('Pink Baby.') [Also No. 5856. New to cultivation.]
7189	,,	rhaibocarpum, Balf. f. et W. W. Sm. (variety).
6903	,,	**riparium**, Ward. A.M. 1930. [Also Nos. 5828, 7061, 7062, 8229.]
7048	,,	rupicola, W. W. Sm. (variety).
6934	,,	saluenense, Franch.
6793	,,	**seinghkuense**, Ward.
6325	,,	**scopulorum**, Hutch. [Also No. 6354.]
7642	,,	sidereum, Balf. f. [Also No. 6753.]
8255	,,	Smithii, Nutt. var. intonsum.
6960	,,	suaveolens.
6809	,,	Taggianum, Hutch.
8044	,,	**tanastylum**, Balf. f. et Ward.
6868	,,	telopeum, Balf. f. et Forrest.
5844	,,	**tsangpoense**, Ward.
5876	,,	**uniflorum**, Hutch. et Ward.
5656	,,	**vellereum**, Hutch.
6856	,,	**vesiculiferum**, Tagg.
6301	,,	sp. A.M. 1929.
6235		Ribes sp.
7740		Rosa longicuspis.
6101		,, Sweginzowii, Koehne, var. inermis.
8665		Schizandra sp.
5637		Sophora Moorcroftiana, Benth.
5899		**Thalictrum diffusiflorum**, Marquand et Shaw.

K.W.   *Name*
Number

7134   Vaccinium sp.
7008   Veronica sp.
8103   Viola serpens, Wall.

Index